Tree & Shrub Gardening for Ontario

Alison Beck
Kathy Renwald

Principal Photography by Tim Matheson

LONE PINE

Lone Pine Publishing

First printed in 2001 10 9 8 7 6 5 4 3
Printed in Canada

The Publisher: Lone Pine Publishing
10145 – 81 Avenue
Edmonton, AB T6E 1W9
Canada

1901 Raymond Ave. SW,
Suite C, Renton, WA 98055
USA

Website: http://www.lonepinepublishing.com

Canadian Cataloguing in Publication Data
Beck, Alison, 1971–
Tree and shrub gardening for Ontario

Includes bibliographical references and index.
ISBN 1-55105-273-3

1. Ornamental trees—Ontario. 2. Ornamental shrubs—Ontario. I. Renwald, Kathy, 1951–
SB435.6.C32O5 2001 635.9'77'09713 C2001-910201-1

Editorial Director: Nancy Foulds
Project Editors: Shelagh Kubish, Dawn Loewen
Editorial: Shelagh Kubish, Dawn Loewen
Photo Editor & Research: Don Williamson
Research Assistant: Allison Penko
Illustrations Coordinator: Carol Woo
Production Manager: Jody Reekie
Cover Design: Robert Weidemann
Book Design: Heather Markham
Layout & Production: Heather Markham
Image Editing: Elliot Engley, Arlana Anderson-Hale, Ian Dawe
Illustrations: Ian Sheldon
Scanning, Separations & Film: Elite Lithographers Company

Photography: All photographs by Tim Matheson (with field identification by Dawna Ehman) or Tamara Eder except Agriculture & Agri-Food Canada (Morden Research Centre) 163b, 253c; J.C. Bakker & Sons Ltd. 324a; Alison Beck 312b; Alan Bibby 164a; Janet Davis 85a; Don Doucette 16a, 16b, 23a, 54a, 77a, 77b, 79b, 131c, 133a, 174, 191b, 191c, 209a, 209c, 213b, 258b, 259d, 270, 271a, 306, 307a; Erich Haber 249d, 265a; Linda Kershaw 94, 95a, 95b, 247c, 249c, 253a, 297a, 297b, 320a, 324b, 324c; Dawn Loewen 162, 165, 236a; Heather Markham 14a, 30, 269a, 322a; David McDonald 84, 85b, 105a, 105b, 158, 159a; Allison Penko 17a, 17b, 29b, 73, 114, 116, 117a, 121b, 143a, 178, 179a, 179b, 194b, 226, 229d, 237a, 243c, 266, 267a, 275a, 275b, 280, 283, 298, 299b, 300, 301b, 307b, 308, 309a, 320b; Royal Botanical Gardens 131a, 131b, 132c, 133e, 159b, 210b, 212a, 213a, 213c, 213d, 241c, 242a, 258a, 258c, 259a, 259c; Robert Ritchie 240c, 242a, 269b, 289b, 289c.

Front cover photos by Tim Matheson and Tamara Eder: beech, viburnum, redbud, maple
Back cover author photos: Alison Beck by Alan Bibby, Kathy Renwald by Tim Leyes

Map: adapted from Agriculture & Agri-Food Canada publication 'Canadian Hardiness Zones Map.' Reproduced with the permission of the Minister of Public Works and Government Services Canada 2000.

We acknowledge the financial support of the Government of Canada through the Book Publishing Industry Development Program (BPIDP) for our publishing activities.

PC: P4

Contents

Acknowledgements

We express our appreciation to all who were involved in this project. Special thanks are extended to the following individuals and organizations: Mark Carfae, Elisabeth Eder, Lesley Knight, Todd Major and Pension Fund Realty Ltd. at Park and Tilford Gardens, Heather Markham, Tim Matheson and assistant Dawna Ehman, Nancy Matheson, Paul Montpellier and the Vancouver Board of Parks and Recreation, Bill Stephen, J.C. Bakker & Sons Ltd., the Devonian Botanical Gardens, Free Spirit Nursery, Gibbs Nurseryland and Florist, Niagara College Horticulture Program, Niagara Parks Botanical Gardens and School of Horticulture, Niagara Parks Commission, Riverview Arboretum, the Royal Botanical Gardens in Hamilton, UBC Arboretum, VanDusen Botanical Garden. Alison Beck extends thanks to her mother, Rosalind, who always wanted a good book on trees and shrubs, and her father, Norman, who first piqued her interest in woody plants.

The Trees & Shrubs at a Glance

A Pictorial Guide in Alphabetical Order, by Common Name

Aralia
p. 74

Arborvitae (Cedar)
p. 76

Ash
p. 80

Bearberry
p. 82

Beauty Bush
p. 84

Bog Rosemary
p. 94

Beech
p. 86

Birch
p. 90

Boxwood
p. 96

Butterfly Bush
p. 100

Caryopteris
p. 104

Cherry, Plum & Almond
p. 106

Clematis
p. 112

Cotoneaster
p. 114

Crabapple
p. 118

Daphne
p. 122

Dawn Redwood
p. 126

Deutzia
p. 128

Dogwood
p. 130

Elder
p. 134

English Ivy
p. 138

Euonymus
p. 140

Firethorn
p. 154

False Arborvitae
p. 144

False Cypress
p. 146

Fir
p. 150

Fiveleaf Akebia
p. 158

Flowering Quince
p. 160

Ginkgo
p. 170

Forsythia
p. 162

Fothergilla
p. 166

Fringe Tree
p. 168

Goldenchain Tree
p. 172

Grape
p. 174

Hazel (Filbert)
p. 180

Hawthorn
p. 176

Heather (Spring Heath, Winter Heath)
p. 184

Hemlock
p. 186

Holly
p. 190

Honeysuckle
p. 192

Hornbeam
p. 196

Horsechestnut (Buckeye)
p. 198

Hydrangea
p. 202

Japanese Pagoda-Tree
p. 206

Juniper
p. 208

Kalmia (Mountain Laurel), p. 214

Katsuratree
p. 216

Kerria (Japanese Kerria)
p. 218

Kiwi
p. 220

Larch
p. 222

Leucothoe (Rainbow Bush), p. 224

Lilac
p. 226

Linden
p. 230

London Planetree
p. 232

Magnolia
p. 234

Mock-Orange
p. 244

Maple
p. 238

Oak
p. 246

Oregon Grapeholly
p. 250

Peashrub
p. 252

Pieris
p. 254

Redbud
p. 264

Pine
p. 256

Potentilla (Shrubby Cinquefoil), p. 260

Rhododendron, Azalea
p. 266

Rose-of-Sharon (Hibiscus), p. 270

Russian Olive
p. 274

Serviceberry
p. 276

Smokebush (Smoketree)
p. 278

Spirea
p. 280

Spruce
p. 284

Summersweet Clethra
p. 290

Thornless Honeylocust
p. 294

Sumac
p. 288

Sweetgum
p. 292

Trumpetcreeper
p. 296

Tulip Tree
p. 298

Viburnum
p. 300

Wisteria
p. 308

Virginia Creeper
p. 304

Weigela
p. 306

Witch-Hazel
p. 310

Yew
p. 314

Yucca (Adam's Needle)
p. 318

Other Trees & Shrubs to Consider

Pages 320–327

Black Walnut

Douglas-Fir

Bald Cypress

Blueberry

Camperdown Elm

Cedar

Dove Tree

False Spirea

Kentucky Coffee Tree

Mountain Ash

Ninebark

Privet

Silverbell

Snowbell

Weeping Willow

INTRODUCTION

Trees and shrubs are woody perennials. Their life cycles take three or often many more years to complete, and they maintain a permanent live structure above ground all year. In cold climates, a few shrubs die back to the ground each winter. The root system, protected by the soil over winter, sends up new shoots in spring, and if the shrub forms flowers on new wood it will bloom that same year. Such shrubs act like herbaceous perennials, but because they are woody in their native climates they are still treated as shrubs. Some hydrangeas fall into this category.

A tree is generally defined as a woody plant having a single trunk and growing greater than 4.5 m (15') tall. A shrub is multi-stemmed and no taller than 4.5 m (15'). These definitions are not absolute because some tall trees are multi-stemmed and some short shrubs have single trunks. Even the height definitions are open to interpretation. For example, a Japanese Maple may be multi-stemmed and may grow about 3 m (10') tall, but it is often still referred to as a tree. To make matters more complicated, a given species may grow as a tree in favourable conditions and as a shrub in harsher sites. It is always best to simply look at the expected mature size of a tree or shrub and judge its suitability for your garden based on this. If you have a small garden, a large, tree-like shrub, such as Smokebush or Rose-of-Sharon, may be all you have room for.

Vines are also included in this guide. Like trees and shrubs, these plants maintain living woody stems above ground over winter. They generally require a supporting structure to grow upon, but many can also be grown as trailing groundcovers.

Juniper corkscrew topiary, Euonymus (foreground)

Again, the definition is not absolute, because some vines, such as wisteria, can be trained to grow as free-standing shrubs with proper pruning. Similarly, certain shrubs, such as Firethorn, can be trained to grow up and over walls and other structures.

Woody plants can be characterized by leaf type, whether deciduous or evergreen, needled or broad-leaved. Deciduous plants lose all their leaves each fall or winter. They can be needled, like Dawn Redwood and larches, or broad-leaved, like the maples and dogwoods. Evergreen trees and shrubs do not lose their leaves in the winter and can also be needled or broad-leaved, like pines and rhododendrons, respectively. Some plants are semi-evergreen;

Trailing cotoneaster

Variety of textures and colours

these are generally evergreens that in cold climates lose some or all of their leaves. Some viburnums fall into this category.

In most of Ontario the winters are cold and the summers are warm. This general pattern, along with the dependable rainfall, makes Ontario a great place to grow a wide variety of woody plants. The cold winters allow a good period of dormancy for plants that need cold in order to produce flowers. The summers are warm and long enough to give plants plenty of time to grow. Despite the overall similarities, conditions do vary within the province.

The northernmost reaches of Ontario are sparsely populated and for the

Purple Weeping Beech

White Spruce (above), Dogwood (below)

most part accessible only by air. Here gardeners are wisest to take their cues from the wilderness. Choose native woody plants that thrive in the forests and muskegs that dominate this region. A few exotic (non-native) plants will also do well here—select those that come from equally rugged climes. Siberian natives, low alpine groundcovers and very hardy plants from farther south and west may be grown successfully.

Moving south towards Lake Superior we find more people but little change in terrain. Rock, forests and lakes dominate, but the climate is much improved by the tempering effect of Lake Superior. A dependable cover of snow protects low plants and roots from the cold. Plants rated hardy to Zone 3 and some of those rated Zone 4 are the best choices for gardening here. Choose a majority of hardy plants to form the backbone of your garden, but don't be afraid to try a few of the more tender plants—there's a chance you will be delighted with the results. By protecting your trees and shrubs from the winter winds you may be able to expand the growing potential of your garden.

East of Lake Superior, the central parts of Ontario contain more urban centres and an increase in population. From Sault Ste. Marie east to Sudbury, North Bay and Pembroke, a climate change opens up more possibilities for gardeners. The Great Lakes moderate the cold arctic air, and there is consistent snowcover and a longer frost-free period. Zone 4 plants and some Zone 5 plants are easily hardy in this area. On the other hand, ice storms and heavy, wet snow can cause irreparable damage to trees and shrubs. If at all possible, try to brush or knock heavy snow and ice off branches before they are damaged. Evergreens such as dwarf arborvitae can be wrapped with a layer of burlap to prevent snow from damaging or bending their branches out of shape.

Euonymus (above), Magnolia (below)

South and southwest of Guelph, Barrie, Peterborough and Ottawa, winter temperatures are not as cold, but snowcover may not be as consistent. Zone 5 plants will thrive in this region, and closer to and south of Toronto, Zone 6 plants will do well. The temperature fluctuations cause a series of freeze and thaw cycles that are very stressful to woody plants. Plenty of winter mulch will protect low plants and shallow roots from the cycles of freeze and thaw.

Some of the warmest growing conditions in Canada occur in the Niagara Peninsula and at the very southern tip of Ontario in the Windsor region. Large parts of these areas are devoted to farming and fruit and wine production. Gardeners in these areas enjoy being able to grow many plants too tender to grow anywhere else in Ontario.

Soil conditions also vary greatly in the different areas of Ontario. From the rocky outcrops and sometimes thin soil of the Canadian Shield, to the limestone of the Niagara Escarpment and the variable soil of ancient seabeds, the diverse geological features have as great an influence on successful gardening as climate does. Plants are adapted to growing in different conditions, and gardens on rocky, windblown escarpments and in sheltered river valleys will each have woody plants well suited to those conditions.

A trip to a nearby park or botanical garden that has unusual specimens, and where trees are labelled, is invaluable in helping select outstanding trees, shrubs and vines that will do well in your area. Keep your eyes open when walking through your neighbourhood, and you may see a tree or shrub that you hadn't noticed before or that you were told wouldn't grow where you live. What is actually growing is a better guide. No matter what challenges you face in your garden, you will find a tree, shrub or vine that will thrive in your space and provide interest to your garden.

Many enthusiastic and creative people garden in Ontario. Across the province, individuals, growers, societies, schools, publications and public and private gardens provide information, encouragement and fruitful debate for the novice or experienced gardener. Many Ontario gardeners have a detailed knowledge of planting and propagation methods, skill in identifying specific plants and a plethora of passionate opinions on what is best for any little patch of ground.

Outstanding garden shows, public gardens, arboretums and show gardens in Ottawa, Toronto, Hamilton, Guelph and Niagara Falls attract gardeners and growers from all over the world and are sources of inspiration as well as information. Open yourself to the possibilities and you will be surprised by the diversity of woody plants that thrive in Ontario's varied climates. You may want to plant mostly tried and true, dependable varieties, but don't be afraid to try something different or new. Gardening with trees and shrubs is fun and can be a great adventure if you're willing to take up the challenge.

Hardiness Zones Map

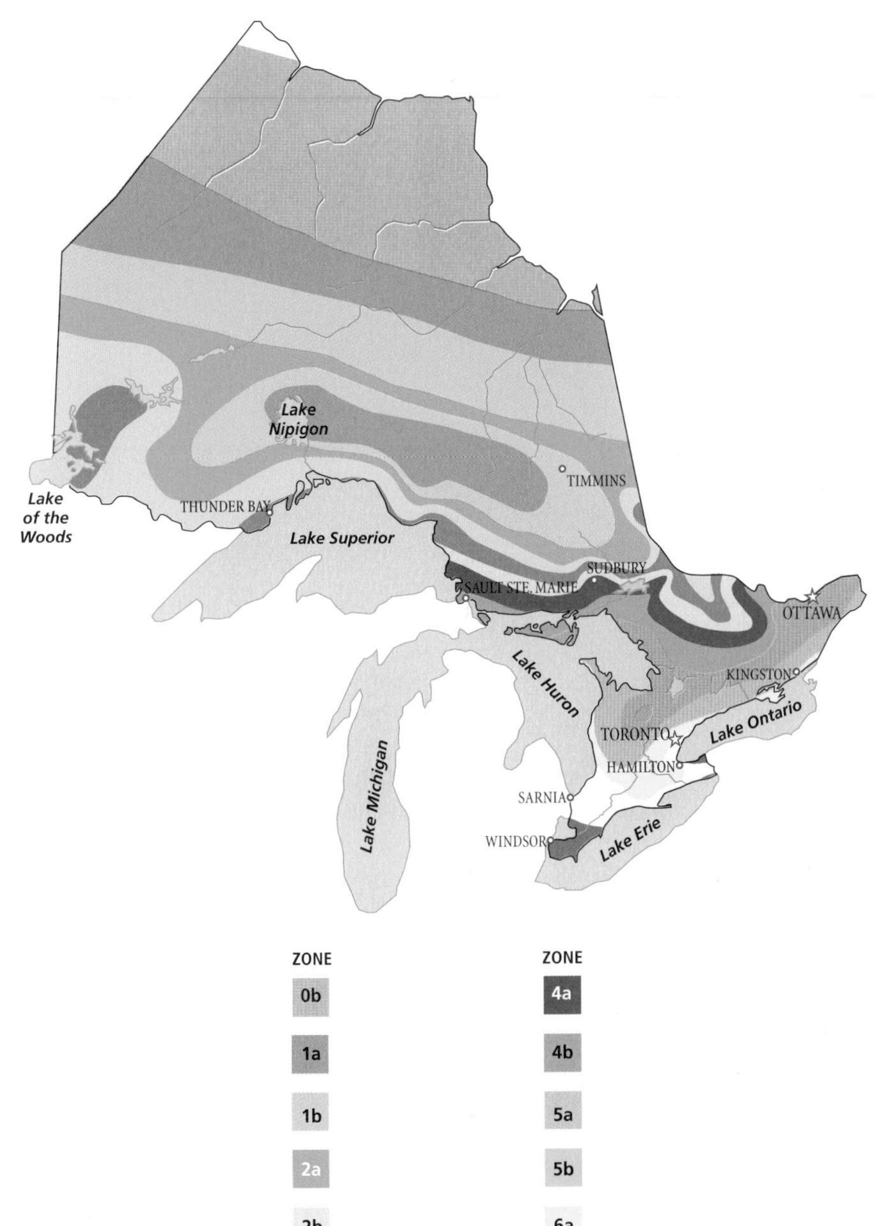

Woody Plants in the Garden

Trees and shrubs create a framework around which a garden is designed. These permanent features anchor the landscape, and in a well-designed garden they create interest all year round. In spring and summer, woody plants provide shade and beauty with flowers and foliage. In the fall, leaves of many tree and shrub species change colour, and brightly coloured fruits attract attention and birds. In winter, the bare bones of the garden are revealed; the branches of deciduous trees and shrubs are laid bare, perhaps dusted with snow or frost, and evergreens take precedence in keeping the garden colourful.

Carefully selected and placed, woody plants are a vital and vibrant element of any garden, from the smallest city lot to the largest country acreage. They can provide privacy and keep unattractive views hidden from sight. Conversely, they can frame an attractive view and draw attention to particular features or areas of the garden. Trees and shrubs soften hard lines in the landscape created by structures such as buildings, fences, walls and driveways. Well-positioned plants create an attractive background against which other plants will shine. Trees and shrubs can be used in groups for spectacular flower or fall colour shows, and a truly exceptional species, with year-round appeal, can stand alone as a specimen plant in a prime location.

Beech in fall colour (above)

Woody plants help moderate the climate in your home and garden. As a windbreak, trees provide shelter from the winter cold, reducing heating costs and protecting tender plants in the garden. A well-placed deciduous tree keeps the house cool and shaded in summer but allows the sun through in winter, when the warmth and light are appreciated. Woody plants also prevent soil erosion, retain soil moisture, reduce noise and filter the air.

Attracting wildlife is an often overlooked benefit of gardening. As cities expand, our living space encroaches on more and more wildlife habitat. By choosing plants, especially native plants, that are beneficial to the local wildlife, we provide food and shelter to birds and other animals and at the same time fulfill our obligation as stewards of the environment. We can bring nature closer to home. The unfortunate difficulty is that the local wildlife may so enjoy a garden that they consume it. It is possible, though, to find a balance and attract wildlife while protecting the garden from ruin.

When the time comes to select woody plants, give careful thought to the various physical constraints of

A large horsechestnut provides shade.

your garden and the purposes you wish the plants to serve. First and foremost, consider the size of your garden in relation to the mature size of the plants in question. Very large plants are always a bad idea in a small garden. Remember, too, that trees and shrubs not only grow up, they also grow out. Within a few years what started as a small plant may become a large, spreading tree. Spruces are often sold as very small trees, but they eventually grow too large for a small garden.

Another consideration that relates to size is placement. Don't plant trees and shrubs too close to houses, walkways, entryways or driveways. A tree planted right next to a house may hit the overhang of the roof, and trying to fix the problem by pruning will only spoil the natural appearance of the tree. Plants placed too close to paths, doors and driveways may eventually block access completely and will give an unkempt appearance.

Poor placement (above); flowering shrubs (Butterfly Bush) add height and form to the garden (below).

Consider, too, the various features of trees and shrub species. A feature is an outstanding element, such as flowers, bark or shape, that attracts you to the plant. Decide which of the following features are most important to you and which will best enhance your garden. It is possible, with careful selection, to choose woody plants that will add interest to your garden in all four seasons. Woody plants that flower, fruit and boast good fall colour and attractive bark will add beauty to the garden year-round. Whether you are looking for showy flowers, fall colour, fast growth or a beautiful fragrance, you can find trees or shrubs with features to suit your design; consult the individual accounts and the Quick Reference Chart (p. 328).

Form and colour in the winter landscape

Form is the general shape and growth habit of the plant. From tall and columnar to wide and gracefully weeping, trees come in a wide variety of shapes. Similarly, shrubs may be rounded and bushy or low and ground hugging. Form can also vary as the year progresses. Often an interesting winter habit makes a tree or shrub truly outstanding.

Hazel (above), Weeping Beech (below)

You should be familiar with some growth form terminology when considering a purchase. A 'shade tree' commonly refers to a large, deciduous tree but can be any tree that provides shade. An 'upright,' 'fastigiate' or 'columnar' plant has the main branches and stems pointing upward and is often quite narrow. 'Dwarf' properly refers to any variety, cultivar or hybrid that is smaller than the

species, but the term is sometimes mistakenly used to mean a small, slow-growing plant. The crucial statistic is the expected size at maturity; if a species grows to 30 m (100'), then a 15 m (50') variety would be a dwarf but might still be too big for your garden. 'Prostrate' and 'procumbent' plants are low growing, bearing branches and stems that spread horizontally across the ground. These forms are sometimes grafted onto upright stems to create interesting, weeping plant forms.

Foliage is one of the most enduring and important features of a plant. Leaves come in a variety of colours, shapes, sizes, textures and arrangements. You can find shades of green, blue, red, purple, yellow, white or silver; variegated types have two or more colours combined on a single leaf. The variety of shapes is even more astounding, from short, sharply pointed needles to broad, rounded leaves the size of dinner plates. Leaf margins can be smooth, like those of many rhododendrons, or so finely divided the foliage appears fern-like, as with some Japanese Maple cultivars. Foliage often varies seasonally, progressing from tiny, pale green spring buds to the vibrant colours of fall. Evergreen trees provide welcome greenery throughout the winter.

An entire garden can be designed based on varied foliage. Whether it forms a neutral backdrop or stands out in sharp contrast with the plants

Top to bottom: Norway Maple, Euonymus, English Ivy, Juniper

around it, foliage is a vital consideration in any garden.

Flowers are such an influential feature that their beauty may be enough reason to grow trees or shrubs that are dull or even unattractive the rest of the year, such as the Goldenchain Tree. Flowering generally takes place over a few weeks or occasionally a month; only a few woody plants flower for the entire summer. Keep this limitation in mind when selecting woody plants. If you choose species with staggered flowering periods, you will always have something in bloom. You can achieve different but equally striking effects by grouping plants that flower at the same time or by spreading them out around the garden.

Fruit comes in many forms, including winged maple samaras, dangling birch catkins, spiny horsechestnut capsules and the more obviously 'fruity' serviceberries and crabapples. This feature can be a double-edged sword. It is often very attractive and provides interest in the garden in late summer and fall, when most plants are past their prime. When the fruit drops, however, it can create quite a mess and even odour if allowed to rot on the ground. Choose the location of your fruiting tree carefully. If you know the fruit can be messy, don't plant near a patio or a sidewalk. Most fruit isn't all that troublesome, but keep in mind that there may be some clean-up required during fruiting season.

Top to bottom: Goldenchain Tree, Cherry, Amur Maple samaras, Crabapple

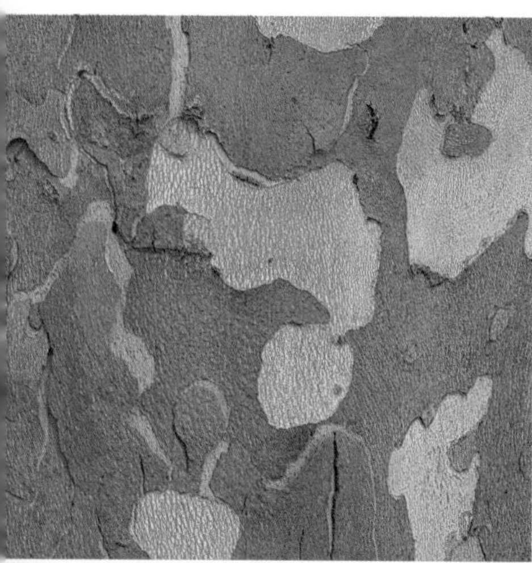
London Planetree (above)

Flowering Quince (centre)
Corkscrew Hazel (below)

Bark is an often overlooked feature of trees and shrubs. Species with interesting bark will greatly enhance your landscape, particularly in winter. Bark can be furrowed, smooth, ridged, papery, scaly, exfoliating or colourful. A few trees valued for their bark are birches, London Planetree, cherries and Paperbark Maple.

Fragrance, though usually associated with flowers, is also a potential feature of the leaves, fruit and even wood of trees and shrubs. The flowering quinces, witch-hazels, arborvitae, katsuratrees and of course lilacs are examples of plants with appealing scents. Try to plant a species whose fragrance you enjoy where the scent will waft into an open window.

Branches as a feature fall somewhere between form and bark, and, like those two features, they can be an important winter attribute for the garden. Branches may have an unusual gnarled or twisted shape, like those of the Corkscrew Hazel; they may bear protective spines or thorns, like those of Firethorn; or they may be brightly coloured, like those of the Red-twig Dogwood and Kerria.

Growth rate and **life span**, though not really aesthetic features of woody plants, are nonetheless important aspects to consider. A fast-growing tree or shrub that grows 60 cm (24") or more a year will mature quickly and can be used to fill in space in a new garden. A slow-growing species that grows less than 30 cm (12") a year may be more suitable in a space-limited garden. A short-lived plant appeals to some people because they enjoy changing their garden design or aren't sure exactly what they want in their garden. Short-lived plants, such as Sumac, usually mature quickly and therefore reach flowering age quickly as well. A long-lived tree, such as Sugar Maple, on the other hand, is an investment in time. Some trees can take a human lifetime to reach their mature size, and some may not flower for ten years after you plant them. You can enjoy a long-lived tree as it develops, and you will also leave a legacy for future generations, because the tree may very well outlive you.

Katsuratree 'Pendula' (above)

Yew hedges are slow to develop.

FAST-GROWING TREES & SHRUBS

Birch
Butterfly Bush
Elder
Forsythia
Hydrangea (except *H. quercifolia*)
Katsuratree
Kiwi
Lilac
Staghorn Sumac
Thornless Honeylocust
Virginia Creeper
Wisteria

SLOW-GROWING TREES & SHRUBS

Bearberry
Bog Rosemary
Boxwood
Euonymus
Fir
Fothergilla
Fringe Tree
Ginkgo
Holly
Kalmia
Pieris
Rhododendron
Yew

GETTING STARTED

Before you fall in love with the idea of having a certain tree or shrub in your garden, it's important to consider the type of environment the species needs and whether any areas of your garden are appropriate for it. Your plant will need to not only survive, but thrive, in order for its flowers or other features to reach their full potential.

All plants are adapted to certain growing conditions in which they do best. Choosing plants to match your garden conditions is far more practical than trying to alter your garden to match the plants. Yet it is through the very use of trees and shrubs that we can best alter the conditions in a garden. Over time a tree can change a sunny, exposed garden into a shaded one, and a hedge can turn a windswept area into a sheltered one. The woody plants you choose must be able to thrive in the garden as it exists now or they may not live long enough to produce these changes.

Light, soil conditions and exposure are all factors that will guide your selection. As you plan, look at your garden as it exists now, but keep in mind the changes trees and shrubs will bring.

Light

Buildings, trees, fences, the time of day and the time of year influence the amount of light that gets into your garden. There are four basic levels of light in the garden: full sun, partial shade (partial sun), light shade and full shade. Some plants are adapted to a variety of light levels, but most have a preference for a narrower range.

Full sun locations receive direct sunlight most of the day. An example would be a location along a south-facing wall. *Partial shade* locations receive direct sun for part of the day and shade for the rest. An east- or west-facing wall gets only partial shade. *Light shade* locations receive shade most or all of the day, but with some sun getting through to ground level. The ground under a small-leaved tree is often lightly shaded, with dappled light visible on the ground beneath the tree. *Full shade* locations receive no direct sunlight. The north wall of a house is considered to be in full shade.

Ginkgo likes full sun.

It is important to remember that heat from the sun may be more intense in some locations than others. A light-coloured, south- or west-facing wall will reflect the sunlight and intensify the heat, particularly if air circulation is poor. Full sun in an open area with

Crabapple provides light shade.

Azaleas like acidic soil.

air always moving through it will not be as hot. The shady side of a building may shelter plants in the heat of summer but can cause a longer, harder freeze in winter than some plants can tolerate. If you wish to grow plants that are borderline hardy, you may find they do better planted on the warmer side of the house.

Soil

Plants have a unique relationship with the soil they grow in. Many important plant functions take place underground. Soil holds air, water, nutrients and organic matter. Plant roots depend upon these resources for growth, while using the soil to hold the plant body upright.

Soil is made up of particles of different sizes. Sand particles are the largest. Water drains quickly from a sandy soil and nutrients can be quickly washed away. Sand has lots of air spaces and doesn't compact easily. Clay particles are the smallest, visible only through a microscope. Water penetrates clay very slowly and drains away even more slowly. Clay holds the most nutrients, but there is very little room for air and a clay soil compacts quite easily. Most soils are made up of a combination of different particle sizes and are called loams.

Particle size is one influence on the drainage and moisture-holding properties of your soil; slope is another. Knowing how quickly the water drains out of your soil will help you decide whether you should plant moisture-loving or drought-tolerant plants. Rocky soil on a hillside will probably drain very quickly and should be reserved for those plants that prefer a very well-drained soil. Low-lying areas tend to retain water longer, and some areas may rarely drain at all. Moist areas suit plants that require a consistent water supply; constantly wet areas suit plants that are adapted to boggy conditions. Drainage can be improved in very wet areas by adding sand or gravel to the soil or by building raised beds. (If the soil is a heavy clay, add gravel rather than sand or you may end up with concrete.) Water retention in sandy or rocky soil can be improved by adding organic matter.

Another aspect of soil that is important to consider is the pH, a measure of acidity or alkalinity. Soil pH influences the availability of nutrients for plants. A pH of 7 is neutral, values lower than 7 are acidic and values higher than 7 are alkaline. Most plants prefer a neutral soil pH, between 6.5 and 7.5. You can test your soil if you plan to amend it. Soil can be made more alkaline with the addition of horticultural lime. It is more difficult to acidify soil, but you can try adding composted bark, leaves or needles. It is much easier to amend soil in a small area rather than in an entire garden. The soil in a raised bed or planter can easily be adjusted to suit a few plants whose soil requirements vary greatly from the conditions in your garden.

Full sun exposure on south-facing slope

Exposure

Exposure is a very important consideration in all gardens that include woody plants. Wind, heat, cold, rain and snow are the elements to which your garden may be exposed, and some plants are more tolerant than others of the potential damage these forces can cause. Buildings, walls, fences, hills and existing hedges or other shrubs and trees can all influence your garden's exposure.

Sheltering Firethorn hedge

Wind can cause extensive damage to woody plants, particularly to evergreens in winter. Plants can become too dehydrated in windy locations because they may not be able to draw water out of the soil fast enough to replace that lost through the leaves. Evergreens in areas where the ground freezes often face this problem because they are unable to draw any water out of the frozen ground; therefore, it is important to keep them well watered in the fall until the ground freezes. Broad-leaved evergreens, such as rhododendrons and Oregon Grapeholly, are most at risk from winter dehydration, so a sheltered site is often suggested for them.

Strong winds can cause even bigger problems if large trees may be blown over by them. However, woody plants often make excellent windbreaks that will shelter other plants in the garden. Hedges and trees temper the effect of the wind without the turbulence that is created on the leeward side of a more solid structure like a wall or fence. Windbreak trees should be flexible in the wind or planted far enough from any buildings to avoid extensive damage should they blow over.

Hardiness zones (see map, p. 19, and Quick Reference Chart, p. 328) indicate whether species will tolerate minimum winter temperatures in your area, but they are only guidelines. Daphnes are generally listed as Zone 4 plants but can thrive in a sheltered spot in Zone 3. Don't be afraid to try species that are not listed as hardy for your area. Plants are incredibly adaptable and just might surprise you. Every garden is composed of microclimates that will shelter a more tender plant or one that prefers a cooler garden. Buildings, windbreaks, low spots, hills, drainage and prevailing winds all influence your garden and the microclimates that occur in it.

Oregon Grapeholly

Here are some tips for growing out-of-zone plants.

- Before planting, observe your garden on a frosty morning. Are there areas that escape frost? These are potential sites for tender plants.
- Shelter tender plants from the prevailing wind.
- Plant in groups to create windbreaks and favourable microclimates. Rhododendrons, for instance, grow better when planted in small groupings.
- Mulch young plants in fall with a thick layer of clean organic mulch, such as bark chips, bark dust, composted leaves or compost mixed with peat moss, or with special insulating blankets you can find at garden centres. Organic mulches should have a minimum depth of 30 cm (12") for good winter protection. Mulch for at least the first two winters.
- Water thoroughly before the ground freezes for the winter.
- In regions with plenty of snow, cover an entire frost-tender shrub with salt-free snow for the winter. You can also cover or wrap it with a layer of burlap or horticultural cloth, or, if the plant is in a container or planter, place it under shelter or against a house for protection.

Purchasing Woody Plants

Now that you have thought about what sorts of features you like and what range of growing conditions your garden offers, you can select the plants. Any reputable garden centre should have a good selection of popular woody plants. Finding a more unusual specimen may require a few phone calls and a trip to a specialized nursery.

Many garden centres and nurseries offer a one-year warranty on trees and shrubs, but because trees take a long time to mature, it is always in your best interest to choose the healthiest plants. Never purchase weak, damaged or diseased plants, even if they cost less. Examine the bark and avoid plants with visible damage. Observe the leaf and flower buds. If they are dry and fall off easily, the plant has been deprived of moisture. The stem or stems should be strong, supple and unbroken. The rootball should be soft and moist when touched. Do not buy a plant with a dry rootball. The growth should be even and appropriate for the species. Shrubs should be bushy and branched to the ground. Trees should have a strong leader. Selecting a healthy tree or shrub will give it the best chance in your garden.

Woody plants are available for purchase in three forms. There are benefits and detriments to each.

Bare-root stock has roots surrounded by nothing but moist sawdust or peat moss within a plastic wrapping. The roots must be kept moist and cool, and planting should take place as soon as possible in spring. You should avoid stock that has been frozen during shipping, but unfortunately it is hard to tell if a plant has been frozen. Bare-root stock is the least expensive of the three forms. Trees and shrubs from mail-order companies usually come this way.

Balled-and-burlapped (B & B) stock comes with the roots surrounded by soil and wrapped in burlap, often secured with a wire cage for larger plants. The plants are usually field grown and then balled and burlapped the year they are sold. It is essential that the rootball remain moist. Large trees are available in this form; be aware that the soil and rootball are often very heavy and there may be an extra expense for delivery and planting. Balled-and-burlapped stock is usually less expensive to purchase than container-grown stock. Be aware that some field-grown stock may be placed in plastic pots or other containers instead of burlap; ask if you are not sure. Such plants must be treated like balled-and-burlapped stock rather than like container-grown plants.

Container plants are grown in pots filled with potting soil and have established root systems. This form is the most common at garden centres and nurseries. It is the most expensive way to buy plants because the plants have been cared for over months or years in the container. Container stock establishes very quickly after planting and can be planted almost any time during the growing season. It is also easy to transplant. When choosing a plant, make sure it hasn't been in the container too long. If the roots are densely encircling the inside of the pot, then the plant has become root-bound. A root-bound tree or shrub will not establish well, and as the roots mature and thicken, they can choke and kill the plant.

Bigger is not always better when it comes to choosing woody plants. Research and observation have shown that smaller stock often ends up healthier and more robust than larger stock, particularly for field-grown (as opposed to container-grown) plants. When a plant is dug up out of the field, the roots are severely cut back. The smaller the plant, the more quickly it can recover from the shock of being uprooted.

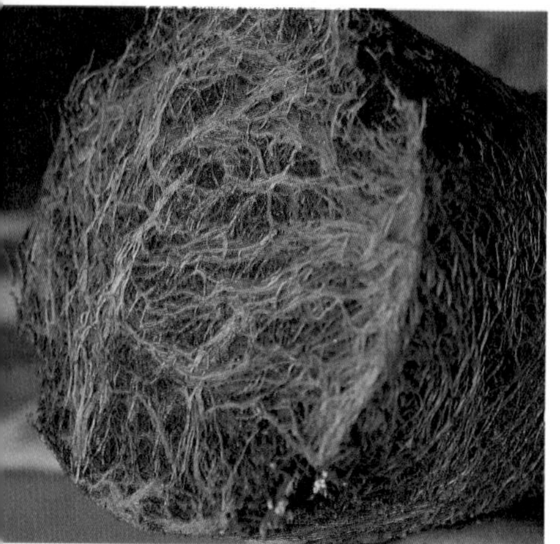

Root-bound specimen

Plants can be damaged by improper transportation and handling. You can lift bare-root stock by the stem, but do not lift any other trees or shrubs by the trunk or branches. Rather, lift by the rootball or container, or if the plant is too large to lift, place it on a tarp or mat and drag it. Remember, too, that the heat produced inside a car can quickly dehydrate a plant. If you are using a truck for transport, lay the plant down or cover it to shield it from the wind. Even a short trip home from the nursery can be traumatic for a plant. Avoid mechanical damage such as rubbing or breakage of the plant during transport.

At home, water the plant if it is dry and keep it in a sheltered location until you plant it. Remove damaged growth and broken branches, but do no other pruning. Plant your tree or shrub as soon as possible. A bare-root tree or shrub should be planted in a large container of potting soil if it will not be planted outdoors immediately. If you must store container plants over a cold winter before planting, bury the entire container until spring.

Fall selection is often limited (above); temporary winter storage (below)

Planting Trees & Shrubs

Before you pick up a shovel and start digging, step back for a moment and make sure the site you're considering is appropriate. The most important thing to check is the location of any underground wires or pipes. Even if you don't damage anything by digging, the tree roots may in the future cause trouble, or if there is a problem with the pipes or wires you may have to cut down the tree in order to service them. Most utility companies will, at no charge, come to your house and locate any underground lines. Prevent injury and save time and money by locating utilities before you dig.

Check also the mature plant size. The plant you have in front of you is most likely pretty small. Once it reaches its mature height and spread, will it still fit in the space you have chosen? Is it far enough away from the house, the driveway and the sidewalk? Will it hit the overhang of the house? Are there any overhead power lines? If you are planting several shrubs, make sure they won't grow too close together once they are mature. The rule of thumb for spacing: add the mature spreads together and divide by two. For example, when planting a shrub with an expected spread of 1.2 m (4') and another shrub with an expected spread of 1.8 m (6'), you would plant them 1.5 m (5') apart. For hedges and windbreaks, the spacing should be one-half to two-thirds the spread of the mature plant to ensure there is no observable space between plants when they are fully grown.

Finally, double-check the conditions. Will the soil drainage be adequate? Will the plant get the right amount of light? Is the site very windy? Remember, it's easier to start with the plant in the right spot and in the best conditions you can give it. Planning ahead saves time and money in the long run.

When to Plant

For the most part, trees and shrubs can be planted at any time of year, though some seasons are better for the plants and more convenient than others. Spring is the best time to plant because it gives the tree or shrub an entire growing season to become established. Bare-root stock must be planted in spring because it is generally available only at that time, and it must be planted as soon as possible to avoid moisture loss. Balled-and-burlapped and container stock can be planted at any time, as long as you can get a shovel into the ground. They can even be planted in frozen ground if you had the foresight to dig the hole before the ground froze. Keep the backfill (the dirt that came out of the hole) in a warm place so it won't be frozen when you need to use it. Most plants will benefit, especially in cold winter regions, from having some time to become established before winter sets in. Many gardeners also avoid planting during the hottest and driest part of summer, mainly because of the extra work that may be involved in terms of supplemental watering.

The time of day to plant is also a consideration. Avoid planting during the heat of the day. Planting in the mornings, in the evenings or on cloudy, calm days will be easier on both you and the plant. It is a good idea to plant as soon as possible after you bring your specimen home. If you have to store the tree or shrub for a short time before planting, keep it out of the direct sun and ensure the rootball remains moist.

Plan your landscape for best results.

Preparing the Hole

Trees and shrubs should always be planted at the depth at which they were growing, or just above the roots if you are unsure where this was for bare-root stock. The depth in the centre of the hole should be equal to the depth of the rootball or container, whereas the depth around the edges should be one and one-half times the depth of the rootball or container. Making the centre higher will prevent the plant from sinking as the soil settles and will encourage excess water to drain away from the new plant.

Be sure that the plants are not set too deep because problems are possible if plants are even 5–10 cm (2–4") too deep. Most potted field-grown trees are planted deeply in the pot in order to help keep the freshly dug tree from tipping over, and there may be mulch on top of the soil as well. Planting such a tree to the same depth as the

Sizing up the hole

Digging the hole

Adding organic matter to backfill

level in the pot may not be a good idea. Scrape off the soil until you find the root mass, and then plant to just above it.

The diameter of the hole for balled-and-burlapped and container stock should be about twice the width of the rootball or container. The hole for bare-root stock should be big enough to completely contain the expanded roots with a little extra room on the sides.

The soil around the rootball or in the container is not likely to be the same as the soil you just removed from the hole. The extra size of the hole allows the new roots an easier medium (backfill) to grow into than undisturbed soil, providing a transition zone from the rootball soil to the existing on-site soil. It is a good practice to rough up the sides and bottom of the hole to aid in root transition.

A couple of handfuls or so of organic matter can be mixed into the backfill. This small amount will encourage the plant to become established, but too much will create a pocket of rich soil that the roots are reluctant to move beyond. If the roots do not venture beyond the immediate area of the hole, the tree or shrub will be weaker and much more susceptible to problems, and the encircling roots could eventually choke the plant. Such a tree will also be more vulnerable to blowdown in a strong wind.

Planting Balled-and-Burlapped Stock

Burlap was originally made of natural fibres. It could be left wrapped around the rootball and would eventually decompose. Modern burlap may or may not be made of natural fibres, and it can be very difficult to tell the difference. Synthetic fibres will not decompose and will eventually choke the roots. To be sure your new plant has a healthy future, it is always best to remove the burlap from around the rootball. If there is a wire basket holding the burlap in place, it should be removed as well. Strong wire cutters may be needed to get the basket off.

With the basket removed, sit the still-burlapped plant on the centre mound in the hole. Lean the plant to one side and roll the burlap down to the ground. When you lean the plant in the opposite direction, you should be able to pull the burlap out from under the roots. If you know the burlap is natural and decide to leave it in place, be sure to cut it back so that none shows above ground level. Exposed burlap can wick moisture out of the soil, robbing your new plant of essential water.

If possible, plants should be oriented so that they face the same direction that they have always grown in. Don't worry if you aren't sure—the plant will just take a little longer to get established. As a general rule, the most leafy side was probably facing south.

Past horticultural wisdom suggested removing some of the top branches when planting to make up for the roots lost when the plant was dug out of the field. The theory was that the roots could not provide enough water to the leaves, so top growth should be removed to achieve 'balance.' We now know that the top growth—where photosynthesis occurs and thus where energy is produced—is necessary for root development. The new tree or shrub might drop some leaves but don't be alarmed; the plant is doing its own balancing. A very light pruning will not adversely affect the plant, but remove only those branches that have been damaged during transportation and planting. Leave the new plant to settle in for a year before you start any formative pruning.

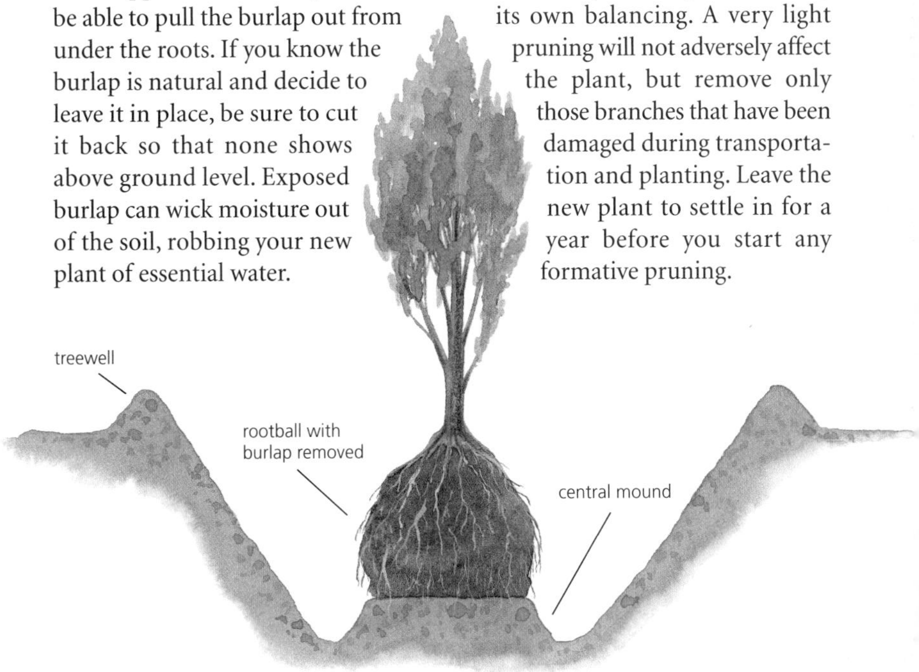

Planting Container Stock

Containers are usually made of plastic or pressed fibre. All should be removed before planting. Although some containers appear to be made of peat moss, they do not decompose well. The roots will be unable to penetrate the pot sides and the fibre will wick moisture away from the roots.

Container stock is very easy to plant. Gently remove or cut off the container and observe the root mass to see if the plant is root-bound. If roots are circling around the inside of the container, they should be loosened or sliced. Any large roots encircling the soil or growing into the centre of the root mass instead of outward should be removed before planting. A sharp pair of hand pruners (secateurs) or a pocket knife will work well.

Place the plant on the central mound. Orientation is less important with container-grown stock than with balled-and-burlapped stock because container plants may have been moved around during their development.

Planting Bare-root Stock

Remove the plastic and sawdust from the roots. Fan out the roots and centre the plant over the central mound in the hole. The central mound for bare-root stock is often made cone-shaped and larger than the mound for other types of plants. Use the cone to help spread out and support the roots. Make sure the hole is big enough so the roots can be fully extended.

Backfill

With the plant in the hole and standing straight up, it is time to replace the soil. Backfill should reach the same depth the plant was grown at previously, or just above the rootball. If planting into a heavier soil, raise the plant about 2.5 cm (1") to help improve surface drainage away from the crown and roots. Graft unions of grafted stock are generally kept above ground to make it easy to spot and remove suckers coming up from the rootstock. If you have amended the soil, ensure it is well mixed before putting it into the hole.

When backfilling, it is important to have good root-to-soil contact for initial stability and good establishment. Large air pockets remaining after backfilling could result in unwanted settling. The old method was to tamp or step down the backfilled soil, but the risk of soil compaction and root damage made this practice fall out of favour. Use water to settle the soil gently around the roots and in the hole, taking care not to drown the plant. It is a good idea to backfill in small amounts rather than all at once. Add some soil, then water it down, repeating until the hole is full. Stockpile any remaining soil after backfilling and use it to top up the soil level around the plant after the backfill settles.

Ensure good surface drainage away from the new transplant. Do not allow the plant to sit in a puddle, but do not allow it to dry out, either.

1. Gently remove container.

2. Ensure proper planting depth.

3. Backfill with amended soil.

4. Settle backfilled soil with water.

5. Ensure newly planted shrub is well watered.

6. Add mulch.

Russian Olive in its new home

STAKING

Staking provides support to a plant while the roots establish. It is no longer recommended, unless it is absolutely necessary, because unstaked trees develop more roots and stronger trunks. Generally, newly planted trees will be able to stand on their own without staking. Do not stake to keep a weak-stemmed tree upright. In windy locations, trees over 1.5 m (5') tall will need some support, until the roots establish, to prevent them from blowing over.

There are two common methods for staking newly planted trees. For both methods you can use either wood or metal stakes.

The **two-stake** method is used for small trees, about 1.5–2 m (5–6') tall, and for trees in low-wind areas. Drive stakes into the undisturbed soil just outside the planting hole on opposite sides of the tree, 180° apart. Driving stakes in right beside the

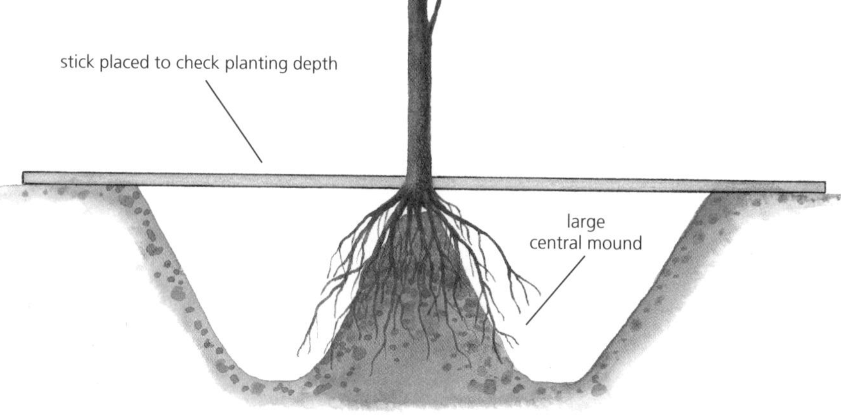

Planting bare-root stock

newly planted tree can damage the roots and will not provide adequate support. Tie string, rope, cable or wire to the stakes and attach to the tree about 1 m (3–4') above the ground.

The **three-stake** method is used for larger trees and trees in areas subject to strong or shifting winds. The technique is much the same as the two-stake method, but with three stakes evenly spaced around the tree.

Here are a few points to keep in mind, regardless of the staking method used:

- Never wrap a tie or cable directly around a tree trunk. Thread it through an old piece of garden hose or use some other buffer to protect the trunk from being cut or worn.
- Never tie trees so firmly that they can't move. Young trees need to be able to move in the wind to produce strong trunks and so that roots develop more thickly in appropriate places to compensate for the prevailing wind.
- Don't leave the stakes in place too long. One year is sufficient for almost all trees. The stake should be there only long enough to allow the roots some time to fill in. The tree will actually be weaker if the stake is left for too long, and over time the ties can damage the trunk and weaken or kill the tree.

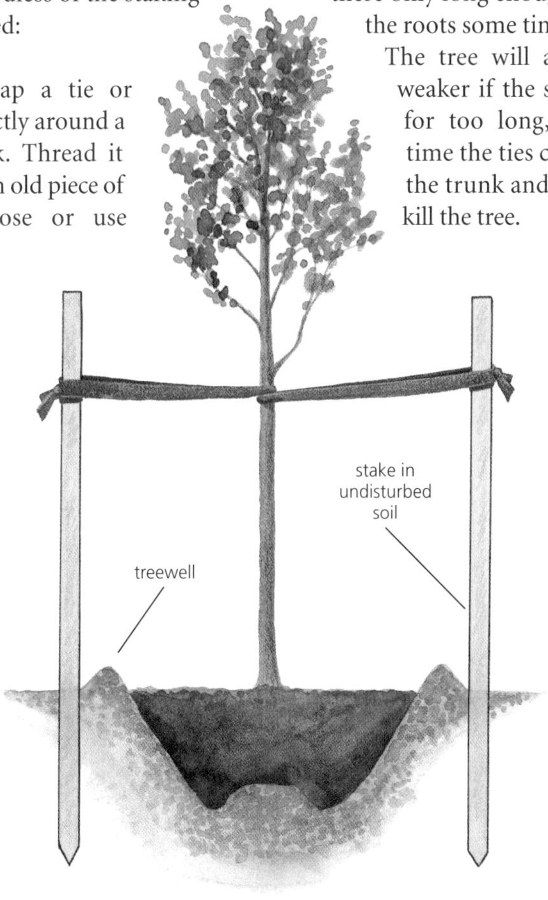

Two-stake method

Treewells

A treewell is a low mound of soil built up in a ring around the outer edge of the filled-in planting hole. When you water your tree, this ring will keep the water from running away before it soaks down to the roots. Though a treewell is not necessary, it can help keep your new plant well watered until it becomes established. The treewell will be most useful during dry periods and should be removed during very rainy periods to prevent the roots from becoming waterlogged. Once the tree has become established, after a year or two, the treewell will no longer be needed and should be permanently removed.

Transplanting

If you plan your garden carefully, you should only rarely need to move trees or shrubs. Some woody plants (indicated as such in the individual species entries) resent being moved once established, and for these species transplanting should be avoided wherever possible. For all species, the younger the tree or shrub, the more likely it is to re-establish successfully when moved to a new location.

Woody plants inevitably lose most of their root mass when they are transplanted. The size of the tree or shrub will determine the minimum size of the rootball that must be dug out in order for the plant to survive. As a general guideline, for every 2.5 cm (1") of main stem width, which is measured 15–30 cm (6–12") above the ground, you need to excavate a rootball a *minimum* of 30 cm (12") wide, and preferably larger. Trees with stems more than 5 cm (2") wide should be moved by professionals with heavy equipment.

Follow these steps to transplant a shrub or small tree:

1) Calculate the width of the rootball to be removed (see above).

2) Water the proposed rootball area to a depth of 30 cm (12") and allow excess water to drain away. The moist soil will help hold the rootball together.

3) Wrap or tie the branches together to minimize branch damage and to ease transport from the old to the new site.

4) Slice down vertically with a shovel or long spade into the soil, cutting a circle around the plant; the circle should be as wide as the calculated rootball width. Cut down to about 30 cm (12"). (This depth should contain most of the roots for the size of tree or shrub that can be transplanted without heavy equipment.)

5) Cut another circle one shovel-width outside the first circle, to the same depth.

6) Excavate the soil between the two cut circles.

7) When the appropriate rootball depth is reached, cut horizontally through the bottom of the rootball to free it from the surrounding soil.

8) Lift the rootball out of the hole *by the rootball*, not by the stem or branches. Place the freed plant on a tarp.

9) Lift or drag the tarp to the new location and plant immediately. See planting instructions given in preceding sections for information on when to plant, how to plant, staking, etc. Transplanted trees and shrubs can be treated as balled-and-burlapped stock.

Some older sources may recommend pruning the roots of a tree or shrub a year or so before transplanting. We strongly discourage this practice. It adds additional, unnecessary stress to the major trauma of transplanting, making the plant more vulnerable to pests and diseases and reducing the likelihood that it will re-establish successfully.

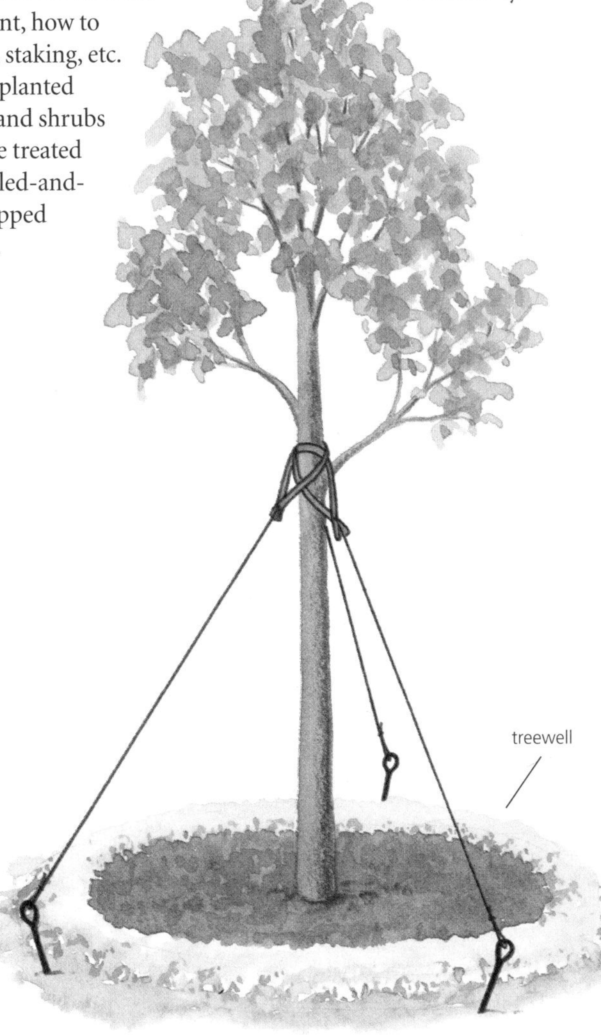

Three-stake method

Caring for Woody Plants

The care you give your new tree or shrub in the first year or two after planting is the most important. During this period of establishment, it is critical to keep the plant well watered and fed (but not overfed), to remove competing weeds and to avoid all mechanical damage. Be careful with lawn mowers and string trimmers, which can quickly girdle the base of the tree and cut off the flow of food and water between roots and branches. Remember that whatever you do to the top of the plant affects the roots, and vice versa.

Once trees and shrubs are established, they generally require minimal care. A few basic maintenance tasks, performed on a regular basis, will save time and trouble in the long run.

Weeding

Weeding is a consideration for trees and shrubs in a garden bed. Weeds compete with plants for space, light and nutrients, so keep them under control and give your garden ornamentals the upper hand. When pulling weeds or scuffing the soil with a hoe, avoid damaging the delicate feeder roots of shallow-rooted shrubs and trees. Weed killers may not kill your woody plants but will weaken them, leaving them susceptible to attack by pests and diseases. A layer of mulch is a good way to suppress weeds.

Mulching

Mulch is an important gardening tool. It helps soil retain moisture, it buffers soil temperatures and it prevents soil erosion during heavy rain or strong winds. Mulch prevents weed seeds from germinating by blocking out the light, and it can deter pests and help prevent diseases. It keeps lawn mowers and line trimmers away from plants, reducing the chance of damage. Mulch can also add aesthetic value to a planting.

Organic mulches can consist of compost, bark chips, shredded leaves and grass clippings. These mulches are desirable because they add nutrients to the soil as they break down. Because they break down, however, they must be replenished on a regular basis. Inorganic mulches consist of materials such as stones, gravel or plastic, which do not break down and therefore do not have to be topped up regularly.

For good weed suppression, the mulch layer should be 8 cm (3") or more thick and be placed on top of a layer of newspaper. Avoid piling mulch up around the trunk or stems at the base of the plant because this can encourage fungal decay and rot. Try to maintain a mulch-free zone immediately around the trunk or stem bases.

Watering

The weather, type of plant, type of soil and time of year all influence the amount of watering that will be required. If your region is naturally dry or if there has been a stretch of hot, dry weather, you will need to water more often than if you live in a naturally wet region or if your area has received a lot of rain. Pay attention to the wind, because it can dry out soil and plants quickly. Different plants require different amounts of water; some, such as birches, will grow in waterlogged soil while others, such as pines, prefer a dry, gravelly soil. Heavy, clay soils retain water for a longer period than light, sandy soils. Plants will need more water when they are on slopes, when they are flowering and when they are producing fruit.

Plants are good at letting us know when they are thirsty. Look for wilted, flagging leaves and twigs as a sign of water deprivation. Make sure your trees and shrubs are well watered in fall, especially before the ground freezes. You should continue to water as needed until the ground does freeze. This is very important for evergreen plants because once the ground has frozen the roots can no longer draw moisture from it, leaving the foliage exposed and susceptible to desiccation.

Once trees and shrubs are established, they will likely need watering only during periods of excessive drought. To keep water use to a minimum, avoid watering in the heat of the day because much will be lost to evaporation. Also, add organic matter to the soil to help the soil absorb and retain water. Mulch also helps prevent water loss. Collect and use rainwater—a barrel set up to catch roof runoff is ideal.

Fertilizing

Most garden soils provide all the nutrients plants need, particularly if you mix compost or other organic fertilizers into the soil each year. Not all plants have the same nutritional requirements, however. Some plants are heavy feeders while others thrive in poor soils. Be sure to use only the recommended quantity of fertilizer (if any), because too much does more harm than good. Roots can easily be burned by fertilizer applied in too high a concentration. Chemical fertilizers are more concentrated and therefore may cause more problems than organic fertilizers.

Granular fertilizers consist of small, dry particles that can be spread with a fertilizer spreader or by hand. Slow-release types are available. These reduce the risk of overapplication because the nutrients are released gradually over the growing season. One application per year is normally sufficient; applying the fertilizer in early spring will provide nutrients for spring growth. In garden beds the fertilizer can be mixed into the soil.

Tree spikes are slow-release fertilizers that are quick and easy to use. Pound the spikes into the ground around the dripline of the tree or shrub, avoiding any roots. These spikes work very well for fertilizing trees in lawns, because the grass tends to consume most of the nutrients released from surface applications.

If you do not wish to encourage fast growth, do not fertilize. Remember that most trees and shrubs do not need fertilizer. In particular, fall fertilizing is not recommended because it may encourage tender growth that is easily damaged in winter.

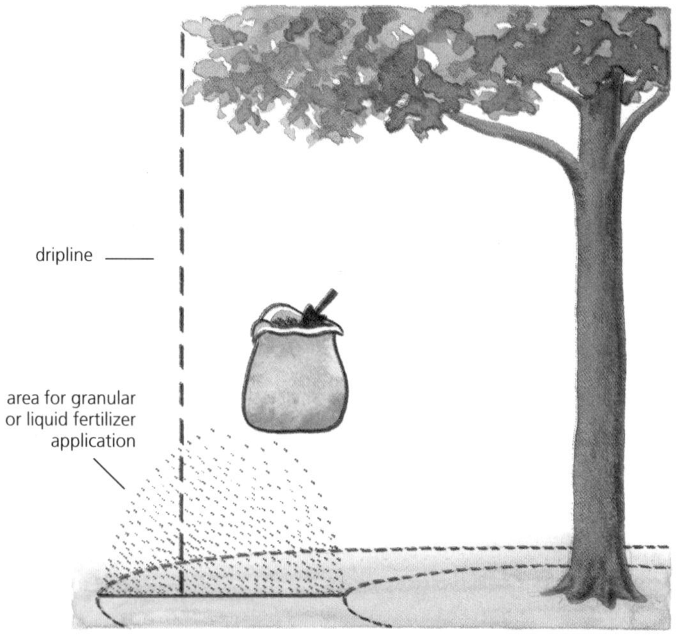

PRUNING

Pruning helps maintain the health of a plant and its attractive shape; increases the quality and yield of fruit; controls and directs growth; and creates interesting plant forms and shapes such as espalier, topiary and bonsai. Pruning is possibly the most important maintenance task when growing trees and shrubs—and the easiest to mess up. Fortunately, it is not difficult to learn and is quite enjoyable if done correctly from the beginning and continued on a regular basis.

Proper pruning combines knowledge and skill. General knowledge about how woody plants grow and specific knowledge about the growth habits of your particular plant can help you avoid pruning mistakes that can ruin a plant's shape or make it susceptible to disease and insect damage.

If you are unsure about pruning, take a pruning course or hire a professional, such as a certified member of the International Society of Arborists (ISA). Pruning courses may be offered by a local garden centre, botanical garden, post-secondary institution or master gardener. Certified professionals understand the plants and have all the specialty pruning equipment to do a proper job. They might even be willing to show you some pruning basics. You should **always** call a professional to

Professional tree service

prune a tree growing near a power line or other hazardous area, or to prune a large branch that could damage a building, fence, car or pedestrian when it falls.

Plants are genetically programmed to grow to a certain size, and they will always try to reach that potential. If you are spending a lot of time pruning to keep a tree or shrub in check, the plant is probably wrong for that location. It cannot be emphasized enough how important it is to consider the mature size of a plant before you put it into the ground.

When to Prune

Aside from removing damaged growth, do not prune for the first year after planting a tree or shrub. After that time, the first pruning should develop the structure of the plant. For a strong framework, leave branches with a wide angle at the crotch (where the branch meets the trunk or another branch), because these branches are the strongest. Prune out branches with narrower crotches, while ensuring an even distribution of the main (scaffold) branches. These branches will support all future top growth.

Trees and shrubs vary greatly in their pruning needs. Some plants, such as boxwoods, can handle heavy pruning and shearing, while other plants, such as cherries, may be killed if given the same treatment. The amount of pruning also depends on your reasons for doing it; much less work is involved in simply tidying the growth, for example, than in creating an elaborate bonsai specimen. Inspect trees and shrubs annually for any dead, damaged, diseased or awkwardly growing branches and to determine what pruning, if any, is needed.

Many gardeners are unsure about what time of year they should prune. Knowing when a plant flowers is the easiest way to know when to prune. Trees and shrubs that flower in the early part of the year, before about July, such as rhododendrons and forsythias, should be pruned after they are finished flowering. These plants form flower buds for the following year over summer and fall. Pruning just after the current year's flowers fade allows plenty of time for the next year's flowers to develop, without removing any of the current year's blooms. Trees and shrubs that flower in about July or later, such as Pee Gee Hydrangea and Rose-of-Sharon, can be pruned early in the year. These plants form flower buds as the season progresses, and pruning in spring just before the new growth begins developing will encourage the best growth and flowering.

Plants with a heavy flow of sap in spring, such as maples, should not be pruned in spring. To avoid excessive bleeding of the sap, wait until these species have started their summer growth before pruning.

Pruning trees in fall is not recommended because a number of wood-rotting fungal species release spores at that time.

Always remove dead, diseased, damaged, rubbing and crossing branches as soon as you discover them, at any time of year.

The Kindest Cut

Trees and shrubs have a remarkable ability to heal themselves. Making pruning cuts properly allows the tree or shrub to heal as quickly as possible, preventing disease and insect attacks.

Using the right tools makes pruning easier and more effective. The size of the branch being cut determines the type of tool to use. *Secateurs*, or hand pruners, should be used for cutting branches up to 2 cm (3/4") in diameter. Using secateurs for cutting larger stems increases the risk of damage, and it can be physically strenuous. *Loppers* are long-handled pruners used for branches up to 4 cm (1 1/2") in diameter. Loppers are good for removing old stems. Secateurs and loppers must be properly oriented when making a cut. The blade of the secateurs or loppers should be to the plant side of the cut and the hook to the side being removed. If the cut is made with the hook toward the plant, the cut will be ragged and slow to heal.

Pruning saws have teeth specially designed to cut through green wood. They can be used to cut branches up to 15 cm (6") in diameter and sometimes larger. Pruning saws are easier to use and much safer than chainsaws. *Hedge clippers* or *shears* are good for shearing and shaping hedges.

Make sure your tools are sharp and clean before you begin any pruning task. If the branch you are cutting is diseased, you will need to sterilize the tool before using it again. A solution of bleach and water (1 part bleach to 10 parts water) is effective for cleaning and sterilizing.

Proper secateur orientation

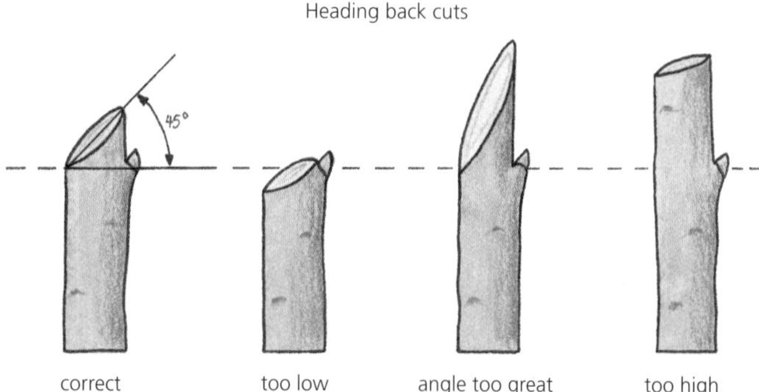

You should have a basic familiarity with the following types of pruning cuts.

Heading back cuts are used for shortening a branch, redirecting growth or maintaining the size of a tree or shrub. The cut should be made slightly less than 0.5 cm (1/4") above a bud. If the cut is too far away from or too close to the bud, the wound will not heal properly. Make sure to cut back to buds that are pointing in the direction you want the new growth to grow in.

Cutting to a lateral branch is used to shorten limbs and redirect growth. This cut is similar to the heading back cut. The diameter of the branch to which you are cutting back must be at least one-third of the diameter of the branch you are cutting. The cut should be made slightly less than 0.5 cm (1/4") above the lateral branch and should line up with the angle of the branch. Make cuts at an angle whenever possible so that rain won't sit on the open wound.

Removing limbs can be a complicated operation for large branches. Because of the large size of the wound, it is critical to cut in the correct place—at the branch collar—to ensure quick healing. The cut must be done in steps to avoid damaging the bark. The first cut is on the bottom

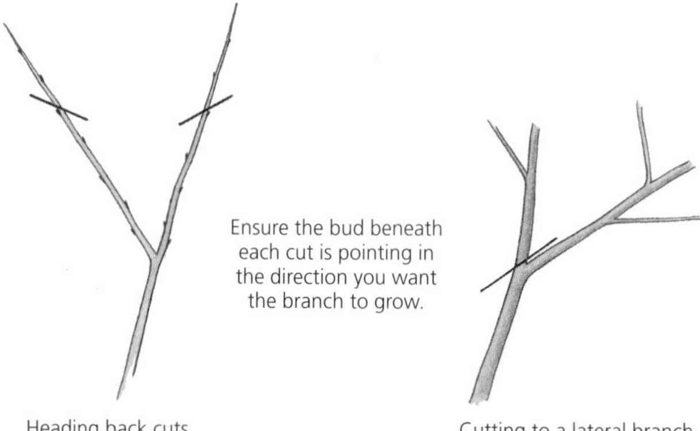

of the branch a short distance from the trunk of the tree. The purpose of this cut is to prevent bark from peeling down the tree when the second cut causes the main part of the branch to fall. The first cut should be 30–45 cm (12–18") up from the crotch and should extend one-third of the way through the branch. The second cut is made a bit farther along the branch from the first cut and is made from the top of the branch. This cut removes most of the branch. The final cut should be made just above the branch collar. The plant tissues at the branch collar quickly create a barrier against insects and diseases. Some sources suggest that using a sharp knife to bevel the edges of the cut promotes quicker healing.

Heading back cuts

The use of pruning paint or paste has been much debated. The current consensus is that these substances do more harm than good. Trees and shrubs have a natural ability to create a barrier between living wood and dead and decaying sections. An unpainted cut will eventually heal over, but a cut that has been treated with paint or paste may never heal properly.

To prune or cut down large trees, it is best to hire a certified arborist. These professionals are trained for the task and have the necessary equipment. Many fences, cars and even houses have been damaged by people who simply didn't have the equipment or the know-how when they tried to remove a large branch or tree.

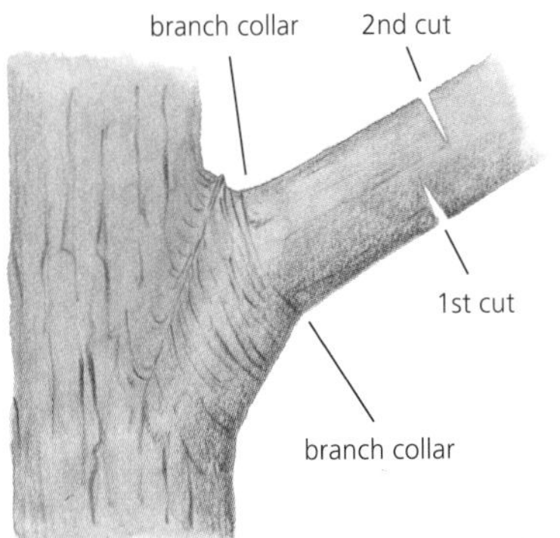

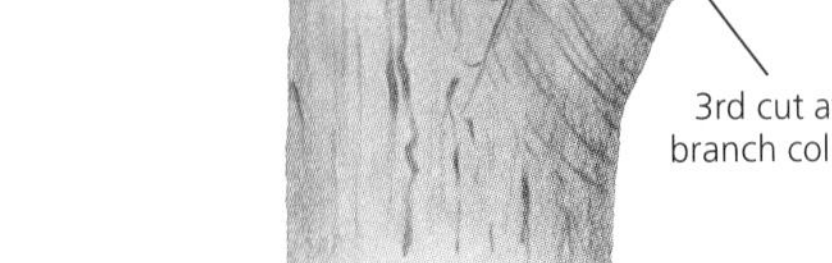

Limb removal steps

Good pruning is especially evident in winter.

Shearing is used to trim and shape hedges. Only plants that can handle heavy pruning should be sheared because some of the normal pruning rules (such as being careful where you cut in relation to buds) are disregarded here. Informal hedges take advantage of the natural shape of the plant and require only minimal trimming. These hedges generally take up more room than formal hedges, which are trimmed more severely to assume a neat, even appearance. Formal hedges are generally sheared a minimum of twice per growing season. Make sure all sides of the hedge are trimmed to encourage even growth. The base of the hedge should always be wider than the top to allow light to reach the entire hedge and to prevent it from thinning out at the base. Remember that a hedge will gradually increase in size despite shearing, so allow room for this expansion when planting your hedge.

Thinning is a rejuvenation process that maintains the shape, health and productivity of trees and shrubs. It opens up space for air and light to penetrate and provides room for younger, healthier branches and selected suckers to grow. Thinning often combines the first three cuts discussed above, and it is the most frequently performed pruning practice. Plants that produce new growth (suckers) from ground level should be pruned this way.

A plant that is thinned annually should have one-quarter to one-third of the growth removed. Cutting the oldest stems encourages new growth without causing excess stress from loss of top growth. Although some plants can be cut back completely to the ground and seem to suffer no ill effects, it is generally better to remove only up to one-third of the growth.

incorrect

correct

Hedge shape

The following steps can be followed to thin most multi-stemmed shrubs.

1) Remove all dead, diseased, damaged, rubbing and crossing branches to branch junctions, buds or ground level.

2) Remove about one-third of the growth each year, leaving a mix of old and new growth, and cutting unwanted stems at or close to the ground. Avoid cutting stems below ground level because many disease organisms are present in soil.

3) Thin the top of the shrub to allow air and light penetration and to balance the growth. This step is not always necessary because removing one-third of the stems generally thins out the top as well.

4) Repeat the process each year on established, mature shrubs. Regular pruning of shrubs will keep them healthy and productive for many years.

Thinning cuts

Topping disfigures and stresses trees.

Pom-pom topiary

Tree Topping

One pruning practice that should **never** be used is tree topping. Trees are topped to control height or size, to prevent trees from growing into overhead power lines, to allow more light onto a property or to prevent a tall tree from potentially toppling onto a building.

Topped trees are weak and can create a hazard. A tree may be killed by the stress of losing half its live growth, or by the gaping, slow-to-heal wounds that make the tree vulnerable to insects and wood-rotting fungi. The heartwood of topped trees rots out quickly, resulting in a weak trunk. The crotches on new growth also tend to be weak. Topped trees, therefore, are susceptible to storm damage and blowdown. Hazards aside, topping trees spoils the aesthetic value of a landscape.

It is better to completely remove a tree, and start again with one that will grow to a more appropriate size, than to attempt to reduce the size of a large, mature specimen.

Specialty Pruning

Custom pruning methods such as topiary, espalier and bonsai are used to create interesting plant shapes.

Topiary is the shaping of plants into animal, abstract or geometric forms. True topiary uses species of hedge plants sheared into their desired shape. Species that can handle heavy pruning, such as boxwoods, are chosen. A simpler form of topiary involves growing vines or other trailing plants over a wire frame to achieve the desired form. Small-leaved ivies and other flexible, climbing or trailing plants work well for this kind of topiary.

Espalier involves training a tree or shrub to grow in two dimensions instead of three, with the aid of a solid wire framework. The plant is often trained against a wall or fence, but it can also be free standing. This method is popularly applied to fruit trees, such as apples, when space is at a premium. Many gardeners consider the forms attractive and unusual, and you may wish to try your hand at it even if you have lots of space.

Bonsai is the art of creating miniature versions of large trees and landscapes. A gardener prunes the top growth and roots and uses wire to train the plant to the desired form. The severe pruning creates a dwarfed form of the species.

Topiary (above), espalier (centre)

Bonsai (below)

PROPAGATION

Some gardeners are daunted by the often hefty expense of purchasing trees and shrubs. These plants cost more than perennials and annuals because nurseries must spend much more time and effort raising woody plants to a marketable size. Though many gardeners are willing to try starting annuals from seeds and perennials from seeds, cuttings or divisions, they may be unsure how to go about propagating their own trees and shrubs. Yet many woody plants can be propagated with ease, allowing the gardener to buy a single specimen and then clone it, rather than buying several expensive plants.

Do-it-yourself propagating is more than a way to cut costs. It can become an enjoyable part of gardening and an interesting hobby in itself. As well, it allows gardeners to add species to their gardens that may be hard to find at nurseries.

A number of methods can be used to propagate trees and shrubs. Many species can be started from seed; this can be a long, slow process, but some gardeners enjoy the variable and sometimes unusual results. Simpler techniques include cuttings, ground layering and mound layering.

CUTTINGS

Cut segments of stems can be encouraged to develop their own roots and form new plants. Taking cuttings is a more difficult method for starting your own plants than layering, but the basic principles are useful to know nonetheless.

Cuttings are treated differently depending on the maturity of the growth. Those taken in spring or early summer from new growth are called *greenwood* or *softwood* cuttings. These can actually be the most difficult cuttings to start because they require warm, humid conditions that are as likely to cause the cuttings to rot as to root.

Cuttings taken in fall from mature, woody growth are called *hardwood* or *ripe* cuttings. In order to root, these cuttings require a coarse, gritty, moist soil mix and cold, but not freezing, temperatures. They may take all winter to root. These special conditions make it difficult to start hardwood cuttings unless you have a cold frame, heated greenhouse or propagator.

The easiest cuttings to start are taken in late summer or early fall from new, but mature, growth that has not become completely woody yet. These cuttings are called *semi-ripe, semi-mature* or *semi-hardwood* cuttings.

Follow these basic steps when taking and planting semi-ripe cuttings.

- Make cuttings about 5–10 cm (2–4") long from the tip of a stem, cutting just below a leaf node (the node is the place where the leaf meets the stem). There should be at least four nodes on the cutting. Each cutting's tip will be soft, but the base will be starting to harden.

- Remove the leaves from the lower half of the cutting. Moisten the stripped end and dust it lightly with rooting hormone powder. Consult your local garden centre to find an appropriate rooting hormone for your cutting.

- Plant cuttings directly in the garden, in a cold frame or in pots. The soil mix should be well drained but moist. Firm the cuttings into the soil to ensure there are no air spaces that will dry out roots as they emerge.

- Keep the cuttings out of direct sunlight and keep the soil moist.

- Plants should root by the time winter begins. Make sure roots are well established before transplanting.

- Protect the new plants from extreme cold for the first winter. Plants in pots should be kept in a cold but frost-free location.

PLANTS FOR SEMI-RIPE CUTTINGS

Butterfly Bush
Cotoneaster
Dawn Redwood
Euonymus
False Cypress
Firethorn
Forsythia
Hornbeam
Hydrangea
Katsuratree
Potentilla
Russian Olive

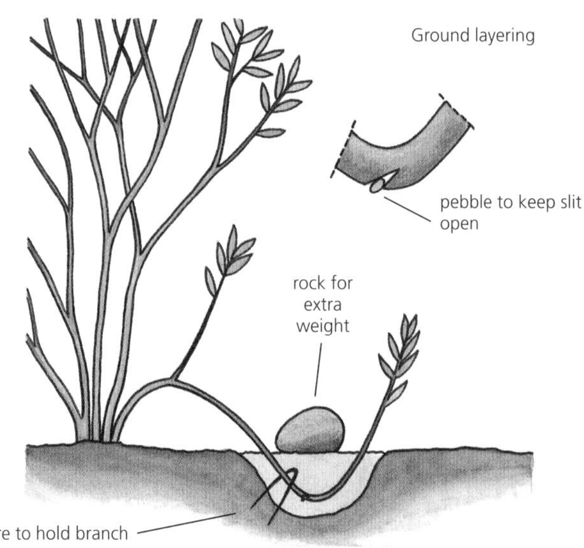

Ground Layering

Layering, and particularly ground layering, is the easiest method of propagation and the one most likely to produce successful results. Layering allows future cuttings to form their own roots before they are removed from the parent plant. In ground layering, a section of a flexible branch is buried until it produces roots, at which time it is removed from the parent plant. The method is quite simple.

- Choose a branch or shoot growing low enough on the plant to reach the ground. Remove the leaves from the section that will be underground. At least four nodes should be buried, and at least another four should protrude above ground.
- Twist this section of the branch or make a small cut on the underside near a leaf node. This damage will stimulate root growth. A toothpick or small pebble can be used to hold the cut open.
- Bend the branch down to see where it will touch the ground, and dig a shallow trench about 10 cm (4") deep in this position. The end of the trench nearest the shrub can slope gradually upwards, but the end where the branch tip will be should be vertical to force the tip upwards.
- Use a peg or bent wire to hold the branch in place. Fill the soil back into the trench, and water well. A rock or brick on top of the soil will help keep the branch in place.
- Keep the soil moist, but not soggy. Roots may take a year or more to develop. Once roots are well established, the new plant can be severed from the parent and planted in a permanent location.

The best shrubs for layering have low, flexible branches. The time of year that you start the layer is also important. Spring and fall are the best times to start, and many species respond better in one season or the other. Some plants, such as rhododendrons, respond equally well in spring and fall.

PLANTS TO LAYER IN SPRING

Daphne	Russian Olive
Dogwood	Smoketree
English Ivy	Virginia Creeper
Grape	Wisteria
Lilac	Witch-hazel
Magnolia	

PLANTS TO LAYER IN FALL

Arborvitae	Kalmia
Euonymus	Katsuratree
Forsythia	Kiwi
Fothergilla	Pieris
Hazel	Viburnum

PLANTS TO MOUND LAYER

Cotoneaster	Forsythia
Daphne	Heather
Dogwood	Lilac
Euonymus	Potentilla

Mound Layering

Mound layering is a simple way to propagate low, shrubby plants. With this technique, the shrub is partially buried in a mound of well-drained soil mix. The buried stems will then sprout roots along their lengths. This method can provide quite a few new plants with little effort.

Mound layering should be initiated in spring, once new shoots begin to grow. Make a mound from a mixture of sand, peat moss and soil over half or more of the plant. Leave the tips of the branches exposed. More soil can be mounded up over the course of the summer. Keep the mound moist, but not soggy. At the end of summer, gently wash the mound away and detach the rooted branches. Plant them directly where you want them or in a protected, temporary spot to shelter them for the first winter.

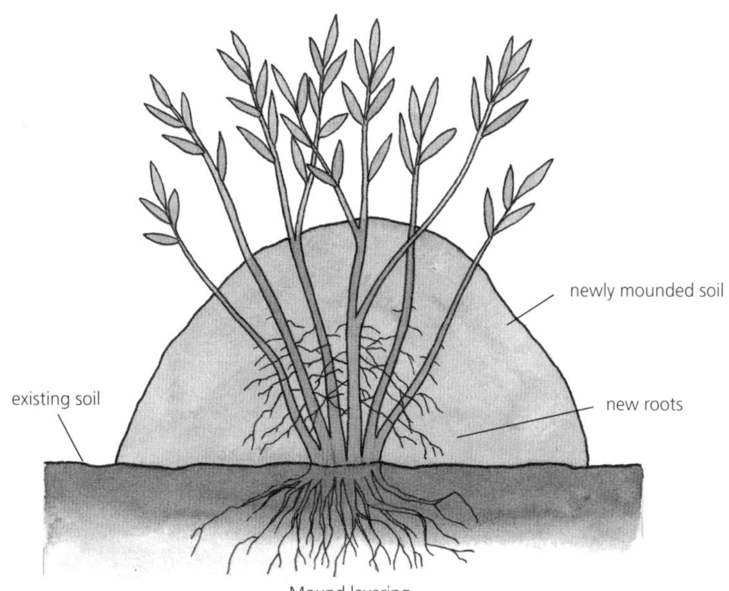

Mound layering

PESTS & DISEASES

Tree and shrub plantings can be both assets and liabilities when it comes to pests and diseases. Many insects and diseases attack only one plant species. Mixed plantings can make it difficult for pests and diseases to find their preferred hosts and establish a population. At the same time, because woody plants are in the same spot for many years, the problems can become permanent. The advantage is that beneficial insects, birds and other pest-devouring organisms can also develop permanent populations.

For many years pest control meant spraying or dusting, with the goal to eliminate every pest in the landscape. A more moderate approach advocated by many authorities today is known as IPM (Integrated Pest Management or Integrated Plant Management). The goal of IPM is to reduce pest problems to levels at which only negligible damage is done. Of course, you, the gardener, must determine what degree of damage is acceptable to you. Consider whether a pest's damage is localized or covers the entire plant. Will the damage being done kill the plant or is it affecting only the outward appearance? Are there methods of controlling the pest without chemicals?

Chemicals are the last resort, because they may do more harm than good. They can endanger the gardener and his or her family and pets, and they kill as many good as bad organisms, leaving the whole garden vulnerable to even worse attacks. A good IPM program includes learning about your plants and the conditions they need for healthy growth; what pests might affect your plants; where and when to look for those pests; and how to control them. Keep records of pest damage because your observations can reveal patterns useful in spotting recurring problems and in planning your maintenance regime.

There are four steps in effective and responsible pest management. Cultural controls are the most important. Physical controls should be attempted next, followed by biological controls. Resort to chemical controls only when the first three possibilities have been exhausted.

Cultural controls are the gardening techniques you use in the day-to-day care of your garden. Keeping your plants as healthy as possible is the best defence against pests. Growing trees and shrubs in the conditions they prefer and keeping your soil healthy, with plenty of organic matter, are just two of the cultural controls you can use to keep pests manageable. Choose resistant varieties of trees and shrubs that are not prone to problems. Space the plants so that they have good air circulation around them and are not stressed from competing for light, nutrients and space. Remove diseased foliage and branches and either burn the material or take it to a permitted dump site. Prevent the spread of disease by keeping your gardening tools clean and by tidying up fallen leaves and dead plant matter at the end of every growing season. Remove plants from the landscape if they are decimated by the same pests every year.

Sticky trap

Leaf galls

Physical controls are generally used to combat problems with insects. An example of such a control is picking insects off shrubs by hand, which is not as daunting as it may seem if you catch the problem when it is just beginning. Other physical controls include barriers that stop insects

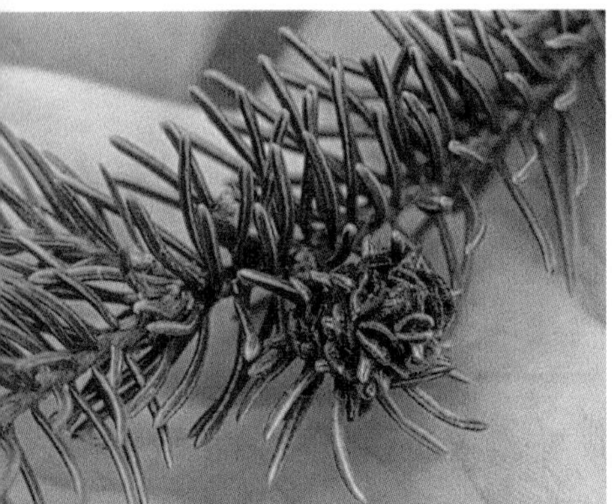

Adelgid gall (above), ladybird beetle (below)

from getting to the plant, and traps that catch or confuse insects. Physical control of diseases often necessitates removing the infected plant part or parts to prevent the spread of the problem.

Biological controls make use of populations of predators that prey on pests. Animals such as birds, snakes, frogs, spiders, ladybird beetles and certain bacteria can play an important role in keeping pest populations at a manageable level. Encourage these creatures to take up permanent residence in your garden. A birdbath and birdfeeder will encourage birds to enjoy your yard and feed on a wide variety of insect pests. Beneficial insects are probably already living in your landscape, and you can encourage them to stay by planting appropriate food sources. Many beneficial insects eat nectar from flowers such as the perennial yarrow.

Chemical controls should rarely be necessary, but if you must use them there are some 'organic' options available. Organic sprays are no less dangerous than chemical ones, but they will break down into harmless compounds. The main drawback to using any chemicals is that they may also kill the beneficial insects you have been trying to attract to your garden. Organic chemicals are available at most garden centres and you should follow the manufacturer's instructions very carefully. A large amount of insecticide is not going to be any more effective in controlling insect pests than the recommended amount. Note that if a particular pest is not listed on the package, it will not be controlled by that product. Proper and early identification of pests is vital to finding a quick solution.

Whereas cultural, physical, biological and chemical controls are all possible defences against insects, diseases can only be controlled culturally. It is most often weakened plants that succumb to diseases. Healthy plants can often fight off illness, although some diseases can infect plants regardless of their level of health. Prevention is often the only hope; once a plant has been infected, it should probably be destroyed in order to prevent the disease from spreading.

Glossary of Pests & Diseases

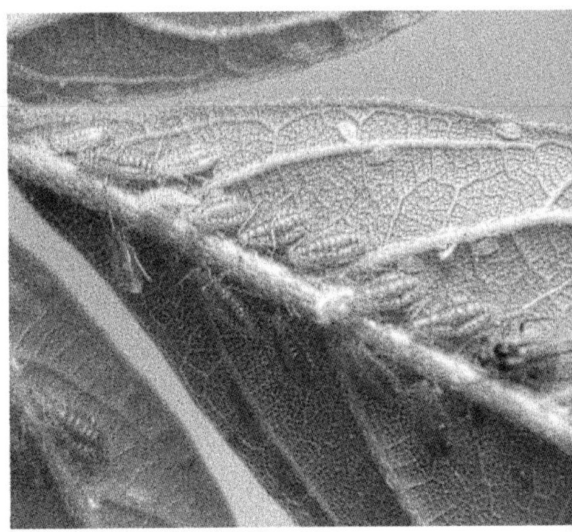
Aphids on leaf underside

ANTHRACNOSE

Fungus. Yellow or brown spots on leaves; sunken lesions and blisters on stems; can kill plant.

What to Do. Choose resistant varieties and cultivars; keep soil well drained; thin out stems to improve air circulation; avoid handling wet foliage. Remove and destroy infected plant parts; clean up and destroy debris from infected plants at end of growing season.

APHIDS

Tiny, pear-shaped insects, winged or wingless; green, black, brown, red or grey. Cluster along stems, on buds and on leaves. Example: woolly adelgids. Suck sap from plants; cause distorted or stunted growth. Sticky honeydew forms on surfaces and encourages sooty mould growth.

What to Do. Squish small colonies by hand; brisk water spray dislodges them; many predatory insects and birds feed on them; spray serious infestations with insecticidal soap.

BEETLES

Many types and sizes; usually rounded in shape with hard, shell-like outer wings covering membranous inner wings. Some types are beneficial, e.g., ladybird beetles ('ladybugs'); others are not, e.g., June beetles, leaf skeletonizers and weevils. Larvae: see Borers, Grubs. Leave wide range of chewing damage: make small or large holes in or around margins of leaves; consume entire leaves or areas between leaf veins ('skeletonize'); may also chew holes in flowers. Some bark beetle species carry deadly plant diseases.

What to Do. On shrubs, pick beetles off at night and drop them into an old coffee can half filled with soapy water (soap prevents them from floating); spread an old sheet under small trees and shrubs and shake off beetles to collect and dispose of them; use a broom to reach tall branches.

BLIGHT

Fungal diseases, many types; e.g., leaf blight, needle blight, snow blight. Leaves, stems and flowers blacken, rot and die.

What to Do. Thin stems to improve air circulation; keep mulch away from base of plant; remove debris from garden at end of growing season. Remove and destroy infected plant parts.

Leaf skeletonizer damage

BORERS

Larvae of some moths, wasps, and beetles; among the most damaging plant pests. Burrow into plant stems, leaves and/or roots; destroy vascular tissue (plant veins and arteries) and structural strength. Worm-like; vary in size and get bigger as they bore under bark and sometimes into heartwood. Tunnels left by borers create sites for infection and decomposition to begin.

What to Do. Keeping tree or shrub as healthy as possible with proper fertilizing and watering prevents some borer damage; may be able to squish borers within leaves. Remove and destroy bored parts; may need to remove entire plant.

BUGS (TRUE BUGS)

Small insects, up to 1 cm (1/2") long; green, brown, black or brightly coloured and patterned. Many beneficial; a few pests, such as lace bugs, pierce plants to suck out sap. Toxins may be injected that deform plants; sunken areas left where tissue pierced; leaves rip as they grow; leaves, buds and new growth may be dwarfed and deformed.

What to Do. Remove debris and weeds from around plants in fall to destroy overwintering sites. Spray plants with insecticidal soap.

CANKER

Swollen or sunken lesion on stem or branch, surrounded by living tissue. Caused by many different bacterial and fungal diseases. Most canker-causing diseases enter through wounded wood. Woodpeckers may unwittingly infect plants when they drill for insects.

What to Do. Maintain plant vigour; avoid wounds on trees; control borers and other bark-dwelling insects. Prune out and destroy infected material. Sterilize pruning tools before and after use on infected plants.

CASE BEARERS

see Caterpillars

CATERPILLARS

Larvae of butterflies, moths, sawflies. Include bagworms, budworms, case bearers, cutworms, leaf rollers, leaf tiers, loopers. Chew foliage and buds. Can completely defoliate a plant if infestation severe.

What to Do. Removal from plant is best control. Use high-pressure water and soap or pick caterpillars off by hand if plant is small enough. Cut off and burn large tents or webs of larvae. Control biologically using the naturally occurring soil bacterium *Bacillus thuringiensis* var. *kurstaki*, or *B.t.* for short (commercially available), which breaks down gut lining of caterpillars. Dormant oil can be applied in spring. Tree trunks can be wrapped or banded to prevent caterpillars from climbing tree to access leaves.

FIRE BLIGHT

Highly destructive bacterial disease of the rose family, whose members include the apples, cotoneasters, hawthorns, cherries and Firethorn. Infected areas appear to have been burned. Look for bent-over twigs, branches that retain leaves over winter and cankers forming on lower parts of plant.

What to Do. Choose resistant plant varieties. Remove and burn infected material, making cuts a minimum of 60 cm (24") below infected area. Sterilize tools after each cut on infected plant. Reinfection is possible because fire blight is often carried by pollinating birds and insects and enters plant through flowers. If whole plant is infected it must be removed and burned.

GALLS

Unusual swellings of plant tissues. Can affect leaves, buds, stems, flowers, fruit or trunks. May be caused by insects or diseases. Often a specific gall affects a single genus or species.

Caterpillar on fir

What to Do. Cut galls out of plant and destroy them. Galls caused by insects usually contain the insect's eggs and juvenile forms. Prevent these galls by controlling insect before it lays eggs; otherwise try to remove and destroy infected tissue before young insects emerge. Generally insect galls more unsightly than damaging to plant. Galls caused by diseases often require destruction of plant. Avoid placing other plants susceptible to same disease in that location.

GRUBS

Larvae of different beetles, commonly found below soil level; usually curled in C-shape. Body white or grey; head may be white, grey, brown or reddish. Problematic in lawns; may feed on roots of shallow-rooted trees and shrubs. Plant wilts despite regular watering; may pull easily out of ground in severe cases.

What to Do. Toss any grubs found while digging onto a stone path or patio for birds to devour; apply parasitic nematodes or milky disease spore to infested soil (ask at your local garden centre).

Fuzzy oak galls

LEAFHOPPERS & TREEHOPPERS

Small, wedge-shaped insects; can be green, brown, grey or multicoloured. Jump around frantically when disturbed. Suck juice from plant leaves. Cause distorted growth. Carry diseases such as aster yellows. Treehoppers also damage tree bark when they slit it to lay eggs.

What to Do. Encourage predators by planting nectar-producing plants. Wash insects off with strong spray of water; spray with insecticidal soap.

LEAF MINERS

Tiny, stubby larvae of some butterflies and moths; may be yellow or green. Tunnel within leaves leaving winding trails; tunnelled areas lighter in colour than rest of leaf. Unsightly rather than health risk to plant.

What to Do. Remove debris from area in fall to destroy overwintering sites; attract parasitic wasps with nectar plants such as yarrow. Remove and destroy infected foliage; can sometimes squish by hand within leaf.

LEAF ROLLERS

see Caterpillars

LEAF SKELETONIZERS

see Beetles

LEAF SPOT

Two common types. *Bacterial:* small speckled spots grow to encompass entire leaves; brown or purple in colour; leaves may drop. *Fungal:* black, brown or yellow spots; leaves wither; e.g., scab, tar spot.

What to Do. Bacterial infection more severe; must remove entire plant. For fungal infection, remove and destroy infected plant parts. Sterilize removal tools; avoid wetting foliage or touching wet foliage; remove and destroy debris at end of growing season.

MEALYBUGS

Tiny crawling insects related to aphids; appear to be covered with white fuzz or flour. Sucking damage stunts and stresses plant. Mealybugs excrete honeydew that promotes growth of sooty mould.

What to Do. Remove by hand on smaller plants; wash plant off with soap and water; wipe off with alcohol-soaked swabs; remove leaves with heavy infestations; encourage or introduce natural predators such as mealybug destroyer beetle and parasitic wasps; spray with insecticidal soap. Keep in mind larvae of mealybug destroyer beetles look like very large mealybugs.

MILDEW

Two types, both caused by fungus, but with slightly different symptoms. *Downy mildew:* yellow spots on the upper sides of leaves and downy fuzz on undersides; fuzz may be yellow, white or grey. *Powdery mildew:* white or grey powdery coating on leaf surfaces, doesn't brush off.

What to Do. Choose resistant cultivars; space plants well; thin stems to encourage air circulation; tidy any debris in fall. Remove and destroy infected leaves or other parts.

MITES

Tiny, eight-legged relatives of spiders; do not eat insects, but may spin webs. Almost invisible to naked eye; red, yellow or green; usually found on undersides of plant leaves. Examples: bud mites, spider mites, spruce mites. Suck juice out of leaves. May see fine webbing on leaves and stems; may see mites moving on leaf undersides. Leaves become discoloured, speckled; then turn brown and shrivel up.

What to Do. Wash off with strong spray of water daily until all signs of infestation are gone; predatory mites available through garden centres; spray plants with insecticidal soap.

MOSAIC

see Viruses

NEMATODES

Tiny worms that give plants disease symptoms. One type infects foliage and stems; the other infects roots. *Foliar:* yellow spots that turn brown on leaves; leaves shrivel and wither; problem starts on lowest leaves and works up plant. *Root-knot:* plant is stunted; may wilt; yellow spots on leaves; roots have tiny bumps or knots.

Leaf miner damage on Honeysuckle

What to Do. Mulch soil, add organic matter, clean up debris in fall. Don't touch wet foliage of infected plants. Can add parasitic nematodes to soil. Remove infected plants in extreme cases.

ROT

Several different fungi that affect different parts of the plant and can kill plant. *Crown rot:* affects base of plant, causing stems to blacken and fall over and leaves to yellow and wilt. *Root rot:* leaves yellow and plant wilts; digging up plant will show roots rotted away.

What to Do. Keep soil well drained; don't damage plant if you are digging around it; keep mulches away from plant base. Destroy infected plant if whole plant affected.

Snail eating leaf

RUST

Fungi. Pale spots on upper leaf surfaces; orange, fuzzy or dusty spots on leaf undersides. Examples: blister rust, cedar-apple rust.

What to Do. Choose varieties and cultivars resistant to rust; avoid handling wet leaves; provide plant with good air circulation; clear up garden debris at end of season. Remove and destroy infected plant parts.

SAWFLIES

see Caterpillars

SCAB

see Leaf Spot

SCALE INSECTS

Tiny, shelled insects that suck sap, weakening and possibly killing plant or making it vulnerable to other problems. Once female scale insect has pierced plant with mouthpart it is there for life. Juvenile scale insects are called crawlers.
What to Do. Wipe off with alcohol-soaked swabs; spray with water to dislodge crawlers; prune out heavily infested branches; encourage natural predators and parasites; spray dormant oil in spring before bud break.

SLUGS & SNAILS

Both are molluscs; slugs lack shells whereas snails have spiral shells. Slimy, smooth skin; can be up to 20 cm (8") long, many are smaller; grey, green, black, beige, yellow or spotted. Leave large, ragged holes in leaves and silvery slime trails on and around plants.

What to Do. Attach strips of copper to wood around raised beds or to smaller boards inserted around susceptible groups of plants; slugs and snails will get shocked if they touch copper surfaces. Pick off by hand in the evening and squish with boot or drop in can of soapy water. Spread wood ash or diatomaceous earth (available in garden centres) on the ground around plants; it will pierce their soft bodies and cause them to dehydrate.

SOOTY MOULD

Fungus. Thin black film forms on leaf surfaces and reduces amount of light getting to leaf surfaces.

What to Do. Wipe mould off leaf surfaces; control insects like aphids, mealybugs, whiteflies (honeydew left on leaves encourages sooty mould).

TAR SPOT

see Leaf Spot

THRIPS

Difficult to see; may be visible if you disturb them by blowing gently on an infested flower. Yellow, black or brown;

tiny, slender; narrow, fringed wings. Suck juice out of plant cells, particularly in flowers and buds, resulting in mottled petals and leaves, dying buds and distorted and stunted growth.

What to Do. Remove and destroy infected plant parts; encourage native predatory insects with nectar plants like yarrow; spray severe infestations with insecticidal soap.

VIRUSES

Plant may be stunted and leaves and flowers distorted, streaked or discoloured. Viral diseases in plants cannot be treated. Examples: mosaic virus, ringspot virus.

What to Do. Control insects like aphids, leafhoppers and whiteflies that spread disease. Destroy infected plants.

WEEVILS

see Beetles

WHITEFLIES

Tiny flying insects that flutter up into the air when plant is disturbed. Tiny, moth-like, white; live on undersides of plant leaves. Suck juice out of leaves, causing yellowed leaves and weakened plants; leave behind sticky honeydew on leaves, encouraging sooty mould growth.

What to Do. Destroy weeds where insects may live. Attract native predatory beetles and parasitic wasps with nectar plants like yarrow; spray severe cases with insecticidal soap. Can make a sticky flypaper-like trap by mounting tin can on stake; wrap can with yellow paper and cover with clear plastic bag smeared with petroleum jelly; replace bag when full of flies.

Wood-rotting fungi and other decay organisms

WILT

If watering hasn't helped a wilted plant, one of two wilt fungi may be at fault. *Fusarium wilt:* plant wilts, leaves turn yellow then die; symptoms generally appear first on one part of plant before spreading elsewhere on plant. *Verticillium wilt:* plant wilts; leaves curl up at edges; leaves turn yellow then drop off; plant may die.

What to Do. Both wilts difficult to control. Choose resistant plant varieties and cultivars; clean up debris at end of growing season. Destroy infected plants; solarize (sterilize) soil before replanting (this may help if you've lost an entire bed of plants to these fungi)—contact local garden centre for assistance.

WOOLLY ADELGIDS

see Aphids

WORMS

see Caterpillars, Nematodes

About This Guide

The trees and shrubs in this book are organized alphabetically by common name. Alternative common names and scientific names are given beneath the main headings and in the index. The illustrated **Trees & Shrubs at a Glance** (p. 5) will help you find a plant if you aren't sure what it's called.

Clearly displayed at the beginning of each entry are the special features of the plant or group of plants; height and spread ranges; preferred planting forms (container, B & B or bare-root) and planting seasons; and hardiness zones (see map, p. 19).

The **Quick Reference Chart** at the back of the book is a handy guide to planning a diversity of features, forms, foliage types and blooming times in your garden.

Our favourite species, hybrids and cultivars are listed in each entry's 'Recommended' section. Sizes and zones are given only if these differ from the information at the beginning of the entry. Keep in mind there are often many more types available; check with your local garden centre.

Common pests and problems, if any, are noted for each entry. Consult the 'Pests & Diseases' section of the Introduction for information on how to solve these problems.

Because our region is climatically diverse, we can refer to seasons only in a general sense. Keep in mind the timing and duration of seasons in your area when planning your garden. Hardiness zones, too, can vary within a region; consult a local horticulturalist or garden centre.

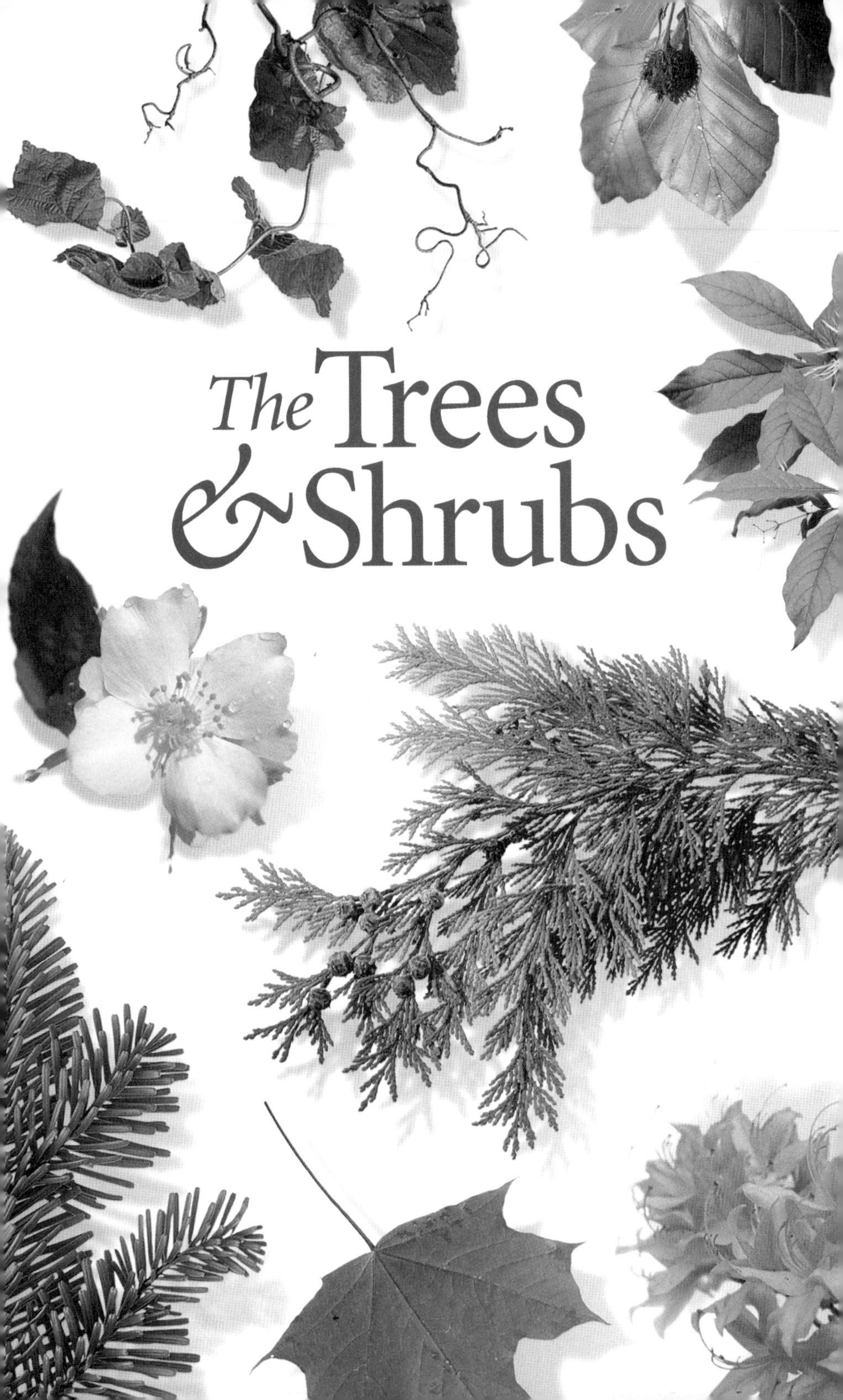

The Trees & Shrubs

Aralia

Devil's Walking Stick, Hercules' Club

Aralia

Features: foliage, flowers, fruit, stems **Habit:** deciduous small trees or large shrubs
Height: 3–9 m (10–30') **Spread:** 3–6 m (10–20')
Planting: early spring to early winter **Zones:** 4–8

Aralias are as tough as the thorns on their trunks. Look closely and you'll see them being used by urban foresters in median plantings and in box planters on rooftops. I had one given to me in a large plastic pot, and it has survived unprotected for four years. I've left it in the pot because I'm afraid to let it loose in the garden. *A. spinosa* will snake through the garden with fearsome vigour. *A. alata* is more restrained. Both species add the lush look of a palm without demanding a winter in Florida.

GROWING

Aralias prefer **full sun** or **light shade.** They grow best in **fertile, moist, well-drained** soil, but will tolerate dry soils, clay soils and rocky soils. Provide **shelter** from strong winds, which can dry out the foliage.

These shrubs rarely require pruning, which is fortunate, considering their plentiful prickles. You will, however, have to spend some time controlling these suckering plants. Barriers such as buildings and driveways can help prevent spread, but you may still want to pull some or all of the suckers. If you get the suckers while they are small, they are easier to remove and the prickles are a bit softer.

Tough gloves are an absolute requirement when handling aralias. I have found thick rubber gloves useful for pulling up suckers. They allow a good grip and will stretch rather than puncture when prickles are encountered.

TIPS

These shrubs are best suited to an informal garden. They can be included in a border at the edge of a wooded area and should be used where their spread can be controlled and where you won't inadvertently brush against the thorny stems.

The berries should not be eaten; they are thought to be **poisonous.** The berries rarely last long because they are quickly eaten by birds.

A. elata (this page)

Aralias make an excellent burglar deterrent along the foundation of a house, though they can grow tall enough to block windows.

RECOMMENDED

A. elata (Japanese Angelica Tree) is the larger of the two recommended species, potentially growing to 9 m (30'). It bears clusters of creamy flowers in late summer, followed by berries that ripen to dark purple. The foliage turns purple, orange or yellow in fall. This species doesn't sucker quite as vigorously and is not quite as spiny as *A. spinosa.* The cultivar **'Variegata'** has creamy margins on the leaves, but its suckers may produce solid green foliage.

A. spinosa (Hercules' Club, Devil's Walking Stick) usually grows 3–6 m (10–20') tall. What it lacks in height, compared to *A. elata,* it makes up for by spreading vigorously. Unless you can provide this plant with lots of room to grow, be prepared to wade in with thick gloves at least once a year to pull up suckers. This species bears large clusters of white flowers in late summer, followed by black berries.

PESTS & PROBLEMS

Problems are rare, limited to occasional trouble with fungal leaf spot, aphids or mealybugs.

Arborvitae
Cedar
Thuja

Features: foliage, bark, form **Habit:** small to large, evergreen shrubs and trees
Height: 1–9 m (3–30') **Spread:** 1–4 m (3–13')
Planting: B & B, container; spring, fall **Zones:** 2–9

Planted as a hedge in the garden, an arborvitae shrub makes a gorgeous backdrop for a perennial border. The scaly, aromatic foliage, on close inspection, appears to have been hammered flat with a rock. Arborvitae are rot resistant, durable and long lived, earning quiet admiration from gardeners everywhere. Individual specimens can be truly commanding—an American Arborvitae in Michigan has made the record books with a height of 34 m (113') and spread of 13 m (43'). Diminutive cultivars also exist. You can enjoy these trees and shrubs for a long time—*Thuja occidentalis* has a potential lifespan of over 200 years.

GROWING

Arborvitae prefer **full sun**. The soil should be of **average fertility, moist** and **well drained**. These plants enjoy humidity and in the wild are often found growing near marshy areas. Arborvitae will perform best in a location with some **shelter** from the wind, especially in winter, when the foliage can easily dry out and give the entire plant a rather brown, drab appearance.

These plants take very well to pruning and are often grown as hedges. Though they may be kept formally shaped, they are also attractive if just clipped to maintain a loose but compact shape and size.

TIPS

Large varieties of arborvitae make excellent specimen trees, and smaller cultivars can be used in foundation plantings, shrub borders and formal or informal hedges.

T. occidentalis 'Emerald'

T. occidentalis *was grown in Europe as early as 1536. It was named 'arborvitae' (Latin for 'tree of life') because a Vitamin C–rich tea made from its foliage and bark saved Jacques Cartier's crew from scurvy.*

T. occidentalis dwarf cultivar

T. occidentalis

Deer enjoy eating arborvitae foliage. If deer or other ungulates are a problem in your area, you may wish to avoid using this plant. Alternatively, mechanical protection, such as a fence or chicken wire, may help reduce damage caused by deer.

RECOMMENDED

T. occidentalis (American Arborvitae, Eastern Arborvitae) is native in Ontario and much of eastern and central North America. In the wild this tree can grow to about 18 m (60') in height. In cultivation it grows about half this size or smaller. **'Emerald'** ('Smaragd') can grow 3–4.5 m (10–15') tall, spreading about 1.2 m (4'). This cultivar is small and very cold hardy; the foliage does not lose colour in winter. **'Hetz Midget'** is a dwarf, rounded cultivar. It grows to 1.2 m (4') tall and wide, but can be kept smaller with pruning. **'Little Gem'** is a globe-shaped dwarf cultivar with dark green foliage. It grows 1 m (3') tall and 1.2–1.8 m (4–6') wide. **'Rheingold'** has bright golden yellow foliage that turns coppery gold in winter. It grows to about 1.8 m (6') tall and is popular for hedges. (Zones 2–7; cultivars may be less cold hardy.)

Crush some foliage between your fingers to enjoy the wonderful aroma. Be cautious, though, if you have sensitive skin; the pungent oils may irritate.

T. occidentalis 'Little Gem'

T. orientalis (*Platycladus orientalis*) (Oriental Arborvitae) can grow as high as 15 m (50'), but usually grows 4.5–7.5 m (15–25') high in the garden. Many cultivars are available, including **'Aurea Nana'** (Berkman's Golden Arborvitae), a popular dwarf cultivar. It grows up to 1.5 m (5') tall. New foliage is a golden colour that fades to yellow-green as it matures. (Zones 5–9.)

PESTS & PROBLEMS

Bagworm, heart rot, leaf miners, scale insects, blight, canker and red spider mites are possible, though not frequent, problems. The most likely problem is winter browning, which usually occurs in cold, windy areas where foliage easily loses moisture. Leaf miner damage may resemble winter browning—hold branch tips up to the light and look for tiny caterpillars feeding inside. Trim and destroy infested foliage before June.

T. orientalis

T. occidentalis 'Emerald'

Ash

Fraxinus

Features: fall colour, adaptability, fast growth
Habit: upright or spreading, deciduous trees
Height: 15–24 m (50–80') **Spread:** 7.5–24 m (25–80')
Planting: B & B, container, bare-root; any time **Zones:** 3–9

Ashes are full-steam-ahead trees. A friend with a small backyard in the middle of the city wanted privacy from his many nosy neighbours. He planted a White Ash and several Silver Lace Vines. Within two years he was sitting in a tent of green, sipping merlot. Ashes are not flashy, but they have many solid qualities. They survive in traffic medians and parking lots and provide shade by the poolside. Planted in a line with their perfectly straight trunks, they look like a well-trained honour guard. They add to the garden a fall colour that is gently glowing and luminous, a harmonious complement to the usual vivid orange and red of other autumn showoffs. Seek out the cultivars rather than the species. Look at a photo of 'Autumn Purple' in a nursery catalogue and prepare to be smitten.

The prized wood of ash has been shaped into tool handles, spears and bows. Baseball enthusiasts will recall the deeply satisfying sound made when Babe Ruth cracked his electrifying home-run hits with ash baseball bats.

GROWING

Ashes grow best in **full sun**. Young plants tolerate partial shade. The soil should be **fertile** and **moist** with lots of room for root growth. These trees will adapt to a wide range of conditions, tolerating drought, poor soil, salt and pollution, but are least susceptible to problems when grown in ideal conditions. White Ash is more ornamental but less adaptable than Green Ash. Little pruning is required. Remove dead, damaged, diseased and wayward branches as needed.

TIPS

Ashes are quick-growing shade trees. They grow well in the moist soil alongside streams and ponds.

F. pennsylvanica (this page)

RECOMMENDED

F. americana (White Ash) is a wide-spreading tree. It grows 15–24 m (50–80') tall, with an equal spread. Fall colour ranges from yellow to purple. **'Autumn Purple'** has deep purple fall colour.

F. pennsylvanica (Green Ash, Red Ash) is an irregular, spreading tree. It grows 15–21 m (50–70') tall, with an equal spread. Its foliage turns yellow, sometimes with orange or red, in fall. **'Summit'** is a neat, upright tree growing up to 15 m (50') tall and spreading about 7.5 m (25'). In fall it is bright yellow.

PESTS & PROBLEMS

Rust, leaf spot, canker, dieback, borers, leaf miners, sawflies, webworm, flower galls, scale insects and powdery mildew are possible problems. Healthy plants grown in good conditions are resistant.

Bearberry
Kinnikinnick
Arctostaphylos

Features: late-spring flowers, fruit, foliage
Habit: low-growing, mat-forming, evergreen shrub
Height: 10–15 cm (4–6") **Spread:** 45–120 cm (18–48")
Planting: container; spring, fall **Zones:** 2–7

When Bearberry appears in a nursery catalogue, it is often followed by the phrase 'limited quantities.' This species can be difficult to transplant but responds well to a properly prepared bed. It is one of the prettiest groundcovers with its lustrous, dark green foliage and red fruit in summer.

GROWING

Bearberry grows well in **full sun** or **partial shade**. The soil should be of **poor to average fertility, acidic** and **moist**. Bearberry will adapt to alkaline soils. Generally no pruning is required.

TIPS

Bearberry can be used as a groundcover or can be included in a rock garden. Once established, Bearberry is a vigorous, wide-spreading grower, but it can be slow to get started. Use mulch to keep the weeds down while the plant is becoming established.

RECOMMENDED

A. uva-ursi is a native shrub with white flowers that appear in late spring, followed by berries that ripen to bright red. It grows 10–15 cm (4–6") tall and spreads 45–50 cm (18–20"). The cultivars share the white flowers and red fruit but also have leaves that turn bright red in winter. **'Vancouver Jade'** is a low-growing plant with arching stems. It grows 15 cm (6") high and spreads 45 cm (18"). This cultivar is resistant to the leaf spot that can afflict Bearberry. **'Wood's Compact'** (Wood's Red) is a compact shrub that spreads about 90–120 cm (36–48"). It bears pink flowers and showy red fruit.

PESTS & PROBLEMS

Possible problems include bud and leaf galls as well as fungal diseases of the leaves, stems and fruit.

This plant's alternative common name, 'Kinnikinnick,' is said to be an Algonquian term meaning 'smoking mixture,' reflecting that traditional use for the leaves.

A. uva-ursi 'Vancouver Jade'

A. uva-ursi

Beauty Bush

Kolkwitzia

Features: late-spring flowers
Habit: suckering, deciduous shrub with arching branches
Height: 2–4.5 m (6–15') **Spread:** 1.5–3.5 m (5–11')
Planting: B & B; spring or fall **Zones:** 4–8

Beauty Bush was a darling of the Victorian age, but now its popularity is on the decline as gardeners look for plants with year-round interest. This shrub puts on an impressive display of pink flowers in June, but once the shell pink blossoms have fluttered to the ground, the bush fades into the background. Prune it once flowering is complete and let it provide a green background for showy summer flowers. Beauty Bush will be most appreciated by nostalgic gardeners with acres of land to plant and a love of all shrubs.

GROWING

Beauty Bush flowers most profusely in **full sun**. The soil should be **fertile** and **well drained**. This shrub is pH adaptable. Prune out one-third of the old wood each year. Old, overgrown plants can be cut right back to the ground if they need rejuvenation. Start new plants by removing rooted suckers from the base of the plant in spring.

TIPS

Beauty Bush can be included in a shrub border. It can also be grown as a specimen shrub, but it isn't exceptionally attractive when not in flower.

RECOMMENDED

K. amabilis is a large shrub with arching canes. Clusters of bell-shaped flowers in many shades of pink are borne in late spring or early summer. **'Pink Cloud'** is a popular cultivar with deep pink flowers. It is not quite as cold hardy as the species.

The name Kolkwitzia *honours Richard Kolkwitz, a German professor of botany;* amabilis, *appropriately, is Latin for 'lovely.'*

Beauty Bush is resistant to most pests and diseases.

Beech

Fagus

Features: foliage, bark, habit, fall colour, fruit **Habit:** large, oval, deciduous shade trees **Height:** 15–25 m (50–80') **Spread:** 10–20 m (35–66') **Planting:** B & B, container; spring **Zones:** 4–9

The majestic beeches are the aristocrats of the large shade trees, and in winter their muscular beauty continues to make a strong impact. The gorgeous smooth bark is endearing. The leaves of the American Beech are a fresh shimmery green in spring, turning a rich gold and then brown in fall and persisting long into winter. The European Beech produces trees of towering stature, but also of slender grace and magnetic beauty in the cultivar 'Tricolor.' With careful placement the copper, pink and white leaves appear to pulsate when backlit by the sun.

GROWING

Beeches grow equally well in **full sun** or **partial shade**. The soil should be of **average fertility, acidic, loamy** and **well drained**, although almost all well-drained soils will be tolerated.

Very little pruning is required. Remove dead or damaged branches in spring or any time after the damage occurs. European Beech is a popular plant for hedges because it responds well to severe pruning.

TIPS

Beeches make excellent specimen trees. They are also used as street trees and shade trees, or in woodland gardens. These trees need a lot of space. The European Beech's adaptability to pruning makes it a better choice in a small garden.

The nuts are edible when roasted.

RECOMMENDED

F. grandifolia (American Beech) is a broad-canopied tree. It can grow 15–25 m (50–80') tall and often grows almost as wide. This species is native to most of eastern North America. It doesn't like having its roots disturbed and should be transplanted only when very young.

F. sylvatica (European Beech) is a spectacular tree that can grow 18 m (60') tall and wide or even larger. Too massive for most settings, the

F. sylvatica 'Tricolor'

Beeches retain their very smooth and elastic bark long into maturity.

F. grandifolia

species is best used for hedges in smaller gardens. It transplants easily and is more tolerant of varied soil conditions than American Beech. You can find a number of interesting cultivars of this tree, and several are small enough to use in the home garden. **'Fastigiata'** ('Dawyck') is a narrow, upright tree. It can grow to 25 m (80'), but spreads only about 3 m (10'). Yellow- or purple-leaved forms are available. **'Pendula'** (Weeping Beech) is a dramatic tree whose pendulous branches reach down to the ground. It varies in form; some spread widely, resulting in a cascade effect, while other specimens may be rather upright with branches drooping from the central trunk. This cultivar can grow as tall as the species, but a specimen with the branches drooping from the central trunk may be narrow enough for a home garden. **'Purpurea'** is a cultivar with purple leaves and the same habit as the species. Purple-leaved weeping forms are also available. **'Tricolor'** ('Roseo-Marginata') has striking foliage with pink-and-white variegation that develops best in partial shade. This slow-growing tree matures to about 9 m (30'). It can be grown as a smaller tree in a large planter.

F. sylvatica 'Purpurea'

PESTS & PROBLEMS

Canker, powdery mildew, leaf spot, bark disease, borers, scale insects and aphids can afflict beech trees. None of these pests cause serious problems.

Beech nuts provide food for a wide variety of animals, including squirrels and birds, and they were a favourite food of the passenger pigeon, now extinct.

F. sylvatica 'Purpurea' (above), 'Pendula' (below)

Birch

Betula

Features: foliage, fall colour, habit, bark, winter and early-spring catkins
Habit: open, deciduous trees
Height: 8–27 m (26–90') **Spread:** 6–9 m (20–30')
Planting: B & B, container; spring, fall **Zones:** 2–9

The common European White Birch, *Betula pendula,* is a good plant gone wrong. It has been seriously overplanted and is now beset by bugs and disease. Turn away from that risky species with its 'no guarantee it will live' tag at the nursery, and explore other fine birch possibilities.

The Paper Birch has exquisite white bark, and it is heat tolerant and resistant to the fatal Bronze Birch borer. More forgiving still is the handsome River Birch. This big tree may be the most heat tolerant of all the North American birches. The bark peels in attractive curls of cinnamon brown. More difficult to find, but worth the search, is the Cherry Birch. It has the best golden fall colour of all the birches. Though it likes a deep, moist soil, it grows quite well in the dry, thin soil of my garden. Best of all, the twigs taste of wintergreen.

GROWING

Birches grow well in **full sun, partial shade** or **light shade**. The soil should be of **average to rich fertility, moist** and **fairly well drained**. Many birch species naturally grow in wet areas, such as along streams. They don't, however, like to grow in permanently soggy conditions.

Minimal pruning is required. Remove any dead, damaged, diseased or awkward branches as needed.

Any pruning of live wood should be done in late summer or fall to prevent the bleeding of sap that occurs if branches are cut in spring.

TIPS

Birch trees are generally grown for their attractive, often white and horizontally striped bark that contrasts nicely with the glossy red or chestnut younger branches and twigs. Often used as specimen trees, birches' small leaves and open canopy provide light shade that allows perennials, annuals or lawns to flourish beneath. Birch trees are also attractive when grown in groups near natural or artificial water features. They do need room to grow and are not the best choice in gardens with limited space.

The common and popular European White Birch *(B. pendula)* and its weeping cultivars are poor choices for gardens because of their susceptibility to pests and diseases, particularly the fatal Bronze Birch borer. If you plan to grow or already have one of these trees, consult a local gardening centre or tree specialist to begin a preventive program.

RECOMMENDED

B. jacquemontii *(B. utilis* var. *jacquemontii)* (Whitebarked Himalayan Birch) has striking, pure white bark. It grows 12–18 m (40–60') tall and spreads about half as wide. This tree is very effective in winter against a dark green background. (Zones 5–7.)

Some people make birch syrup from the heavy flow of sap in spring, in the same way maple syrup is made.

B. papyrifera (this page)

B. lenta (Cherry Birch) has glossy, serrated leaves and brown-black bark. The fall colour is a delicate gold. This birch is a good choice for naturalizing. It will grow 8–16 m (26–52') tall. (Zones 3-7.)

B. nigra (River Birch, Black Birch) has shaggy, cinnamon brown bark that flakes off in sheets when it is young, but thickens and becomes ridged as it matures. This fast-growing tree attains a height of 18–27 m (60–90'). The bright green leaves are silvery white on the undersides. River Birch is one of the most disease-resistant species. (Zones 4–9.)

B. papyrifera (Paper Birch, Canoe Birch) has creamy white bark that peels off in layers, exposing cinnamon-coloured bark beneath. It grows about 21 m (70') tall and spreads about 9 m (30'). Yellowish catkins dangle from the branches in early spring. This tree prefers moist soil. Native to most cool climates in North America, the Paper Birch dislikes hot summer weather. (Zones 2–7.)

The bark of B. papyrifera *has been used to make canoes, shelters, utensils and—as both the Latin and common names imply—paper.*

B. nigra

PESTS & PROBLEMS

Aphids are fond of birch trees, and the sticky honeydew these insects secrete may drip off the leaves. Avoid planting birch where drips can fall onto parked cars, patios or decks. Other potential problems include leaf miners, birch skeletonizer and tent caterpillars. The Bronze Birch borer can be fatal. River Birch and Paper Birch are resistant to this borer.

B. papyrifera (above), *B. jacquemontii* (below)

Bog Rosemary

Marsh Rosemary

Andromeda

Features: foliage, flowers **Habit:** low-growing, evergreen shrub
Height: 15–60 cm (6–24") **Spread:** 20–90 cm (8–36")
Planting: container; spring, fall **Zones:** 2–6

Living in southern Ontario with its soupy summer heat, I have never seen Bog Rosemary growing. It dislikes heat and humidity, and it needs constant moisture and acidic soil. In cooler gardens with the right conditions, this pretty evergreen groundcover is perfect for edging or naturalizing. Northern gardeners rejoice—Bog Rosemary is a plant you can grow that your southern neighbours can't.

GROWING

Bog Rosemary can grow well in **light shade** or **full sun.** The soil should be **moist, well drained** and **acidic** with lots of **organic** matter worked in.

It is not the cold of winter but the heat and humidity of summer that bear the greatest influence on how well this plant will do. In southern Ontario plant Bog Rosemary in a cool part of the garden in light shade to protect it from the summer heat. This is one plant that will grow better for northern gardeners than for southern gardeners.

TIPS

Include this pink- or white-flowered plant in a rock garden or woodland garden, by a water feature or as a groundcover underneath other acid-loving shrubs.

Do not make a tea with or otherwise ingest Bog Rosemary—it contains **andromedotoxin**, which can lower blood pressure, disrupt breathing and cause cramps and vomiting.

RECOMMENDED

A. polifolia is an attractive plant that bears light pink flowers in late spring and early summer. It grows 30–60 cm (12–24") tall and spreads up to 90 cm (36"). There are also several cultivars. **'Alba'** is a dwarf cultivar with white flowers. It grows about 15 cm (6") tall and spreads about 20 cm (8"). **'Compacta'** is a dwarf cultivar with pink flowers. It grows about 30 cm (12") tall and spreads about 20 cm (8").

In Greek mythology, Andromeda was the daughter of Cassiopeia. She angered Poseidon and was chained to a rock in the ocean—as isolated as wild Bog Rosemary, which grows on moss hummocks surrounded by swamp.

Boxwood

Box

Buxus

Features: foliage **Habit:** dense, rounded, evergreen shrubs
Height: 0.6–6 m (2–20') **Spread:** equal to height
Planting: B & B, container; spring **Zones:** 4–9

How indispensable boxwoods have become. At our home, one covers up an atrociously patched foundation. In other gardens I see them used more and more in the European way—to enclose herb gardens or encircle a collection of roses. As hedging, these shrubs are beyond criticism; as single specimens, they have impact without excess. Trimming one is not a chore but a Zen-like joy. If only they would overwinter in containers—then we would have the perfect plant.

GROWING

Boxwoods prefer **partial shade**, but they tolerate full sun if kept well watered. The soil should be **fertile, moist** and **well drained**.

Many formal gardens include boxwoods because they can be pruned to form neat hedges, geometric shapes or fanciful creatures. The dense growth and small leaves form an even green surface, which, along with the slow rate of growth, makes this plant one of the most popular for creating topiary. When left unpruned, a boxwood shrub forms an attractive, rounded mound.

Boxwoods will sprout new growth from old wood. A plant that has been neglected or is growing in a lopsided manner can be cut back hard in spring. By the end of summer the exposed areas will have filled in with new green growth.

A good mulch will benefit these shrubs because their roots grow very close to the surface. For this same reason it is best not to disturb the earth around a boxwood once it is established.

TIPS

These shrubs make excellent background plants in a mixed border.

B. microphylla var. *koreana*

Boxwoods are steeped in legend and lore. The foliage was a main ingredient in an old mad-dog bite remedy, and boxwood hedges were traditionally planted around graves to keep the spirits from wandering.

B. sempervirens

Brightly coloured flowers show up well against the even, dark green surface of boxwood. Dwarf cultivars can be trimmed into small hedges for edging garden beds or walkways. An interesting topiary piece can create a formal or whimsical focal point in any garden. Larger species and cultivars are often used to form dense evergreen hedges.

Boxwood foliage contains **toxic** compounds that, when ingested, can cause severe digestive upset and possibly even death.

RECOMMENDED

B. microphylla (Littleleaf Boxwood) grows about 1.2 m (4') in height and spread. This species is quite pest resistant. It is hardy in Zones 6–9. The foliage tends to lose its green in winter, turning shades of bronze, yellow or brown. **Var. *koreana*** is far more cold resistant than the species; it is hardy to Zone 4.

B. sempervirens (Common Boxwood) is a much larger species. If left unpruned it can grow to 6 m (20') in height and width. It has a low tolerance to extremes of heat and cold and should be grown in a sheltered spot in southern gardens. The foliage stays green in winter. Many cultivars are available with interesting features such as compact or dwarf growth, variegated foliage and pendulous branches. (Zones 5–8.)

Several cultivars have been developed from crosses between *B. m.* var. *koreana* and *B. sempervirens.* Some of these have inherited the best

B. sempervirens

attributes of each parent—with hardiness and pest resistance on the one hand and attractive foliage year-round on the other. **'Green Gem'** forms a rounded 60 cm (24") mound. The deep green foliage stays green all winter. **'Green Mountain'** forms a large upright shrub 1.5 m (5') tall with dark green foliage. (Zones 4–8.)

PESTS & PROBLEMS

Leaf miners, psyllids, scale insects, mites, powdery mildew, root rot and leaf spot are all possible problems affecting boxwoods.

The wood of Buxus, *particularly the wood of the root, is very dense and fine-grained, making it valuable for carving. It has been used to make ornate boxes, hence the common name.*

B. microphylla (this page)

Butterfly Bush

Summer Lilac

Buddleia (Buddleja)

Features: flowers, habit, foliage
Habit: deciduous large shrubs with arching branches
Height: 1.2–6 m (4–20') **Spread:** 1.2–6 m (4–20')
Planting: container; spring, fall **Zones:** 4–9

For great value in a shrub, choose a butterfly bush. You'll pay no more than you would for a showy perennial, and you'll have a plant that will sprout from a dead-looking twig to a fountain of purple blossoms in your garden. These shrubs bloom in late summer when other shrubs are just bulking up for the winter. The varieties with purple flowers will remind you of lilacs, and you can pretend it's spring again. The fragrance is complex and subtle, as if the flowers have stored up all the warmth of summer. Best of all, pull up a chair, forget about your obligations and watch the Monarch butterflies flit around the flowers on their last stop before migrating to California and Mexico. Does gardening get any better?

GROWING

Butterfly bushes prefer to grow in **full sun.** Plants grown in shady conditions will produce few, if any, flowers. The soil should be **fertile** and **well drained**. These shrubs adapt to most average to fertile, well-drained soils.

Pruning is different for the two species mentioned below. *B. alternifolia* forms flowers on the previous year's growth. Each year, once the flowers have faded, cut the flowering shoots back to within a couple of buds of the main plant framework. This species will also benefit from some formative pruning. It can be trained as a shrub or into a tree form.

B. davidii forms flowers on the current year's growth. Early each spring cut the shrub back to within about 15–30 cm (6–12") of the ground to encourage new growth and plenty of flowers. Removing spent flowerheads will encourage new shoots and extend the blooming period.

Butterfly bushes have a habit of self-seeding, and you may find tiny bushes popping up in unlikely places in the garden.

B. davidii 'Black Knight' (above), *B. davidii* (below)

TIPS

These species make beautiful additions to shrub and mixed borders. The graceful, arching branches make a butterfly bush an excellent specimen plant. *B. alternifolia* is a particularly beautiful specimen when trained to form a small weeping tree. The dwarf forms under 1.5 m (5') are suitable for small gardens.

RECOMMENDED

B. alternifolia (Alternate-Leaved Butterfly Bush) grows 3–6 m (10–20') tall, with a spread that is equal to or slightly narrower than the height. It can be trained to form a tree, leaving the branches lots of room to arch down around the trunk. In late spring or early summer, panicles of light purple flowers form at the ends of the branches, flopping around in a wonderful state of disarray. The cultivar **'Argentea'** has silvery grey leaves.

B. davidii (Orange-Eye Butterfly Bush, Summer Lilac) is the most commonly grown species. It grows 1.2–3 m (4–10') tall, with an equal spread. This plant has a long blooming period, bearing flowers in bright and pastel shades of purple, white, pink or blue from mid-summer to

Butterfly bushes are among the best shrubs for attracting butterflies and bees to your garden. Don't spray your bush for pests—you will harm the beautiful and beneficial insects that make their homes there.

fall. Many cultivars are available. A few are **'Black Knight,'** with dark purple flowers; **'Dubonnet,'** with large spikes of pinky-purple flowers; **'Pink Delight,'** with pink flowers; and **'White Bouquet,'** with white flowers. (Zones 5–9.)

PESTS & PROBLEMS

Many insects are attracted to butterfly bushes, but most just come for the pollen and any others aren't likely to be a big problem. Good air circulation will help prevent fungal problems that might otherwise afflict these plants.

B. davidii (both pages)

Caryopteris

Bluebird, Blue Spirea, Bluebeard

Caryopteris x *clandonensis*

Features: flowers, foliage, scent **Habit:** rounded, spreading, deciduous shrub
Height: 60–90 cm (24–36") **Spread:** 0.5–1.8 m (2–6')
Planting: spring, fall **Zones:** 5–9

When you see Caryopteris in bloom in the summer garden, it's like being splashed by a cool wave. Other plants may be parched or scorched, orange flowers are pulsing with dramatic colour, and there, icy and aloof, is the beautiful Caryopteris with its soothing blue flowers and grey foliage. I remember a lovely flowering specimen at the Royal Botanical Gardens in Hamilton. I thought the branches were waving in the breeze, but they were actually bending with the weight of many bees dropping in for a drink at their local botanical watering hole.

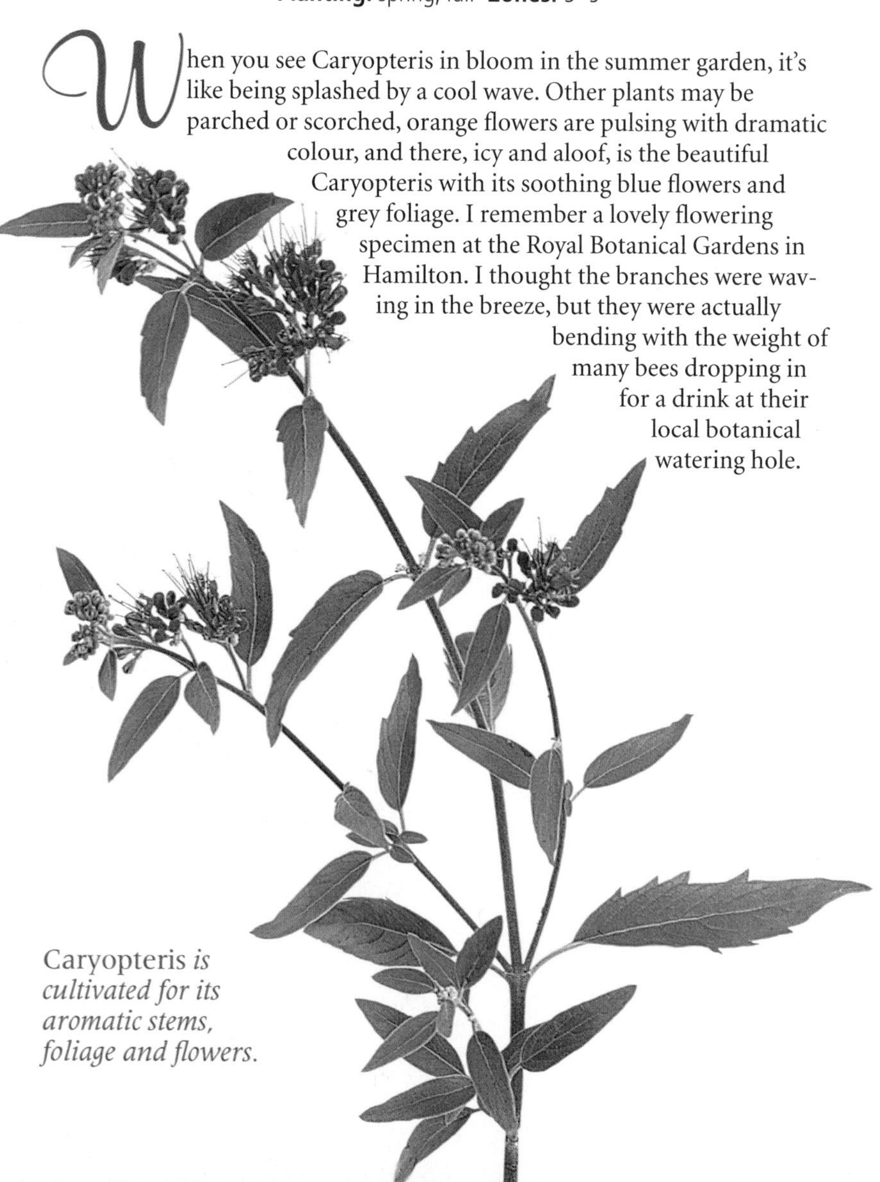

Caryopteris *is cultivated for its aromatic stems, foliage and flowers.*

GROWING

Caryopteris prefers **full sun** but tolerates light shade. It does best in soil of **average fertility** that is **light** and **well drained**.

Pruning this shrub is easy. It flowers in late summer, so each spring cut the plant back to within 5–15 cm (2–6") of the ground. Flowers will form on the new growth that emerges. Deadheading or lightly shearing once the flowers begin to fade may encourage more flowering. This plant can be treated as a herbaceous perennial in areas where it is killed back each winter.

TIPS

Include Caryopteris in your shrub or mixed border. The bright blue, late-season flowers are welcome when many other plants are looking past their flowering best.

RECOMMENDED

'Blue Mist' has fragrant, light blue flowers. It is a low-growing, mounding plant, rarely exceeding 60 cm (24") in height.

'Worcester Gold' has bright yellow-green foliage that contrasts vividly with the violet-blue flowers. It grows about 90 cm (36") tall, with an equal spread. This cultivar is often treated like a herbaceous perennial because the growth may be killed back in winter. New growth will sprout from the base in the spring if this occurs.

The name Caryopteris *is derived from the Greek* karyon *(nut) and* pteron *(wing), referring to the winged fruit.*

'Worcester Gold' (below)

Pissard Plum was one of the first purple-leaved cultivars, introduced into cultivation in 1880.

Cherry, Plum & Almond

Prunus

Features: spring to early-summer flowers, fruit, bark, fall foliage
Habit: upright, rounded, spreading or weeping, deciduous trees or shrubs
Height: 1.2–23 m (4–75')
Spread: 1.2–15 m (4–50')
Planting: bare-root, B & B, container; spring
Zones: 2–9

Cherries are so beautiful and uplifting after the grey days of winter that few gardeners can resist them, despite their troubled natures. There is a feminine mystique to their pink, many-petalled flowers. If you intend to fall in love with your cherry tree, plant one with some longevity or be prepared to replace it when it is inevitably overcome by the many possible pest problems. Higan Cherry has strong survival instincts. It is disease, heat and cold resistant, and its light pink flowers are a welcome spring sight. The new hybrid 'Snow Fountain' is a superb, hardy cherry with double white flowers on cascading branches.

GROWING

These flowering fruit trees prefer **full sun**. The soil should be of **average fertility, moist** and **well drained.**

Pruning should be done after flowering. See below for specific pruning requirements for each species.

Plant on mounds when possible to encourage drainage. Shallow roots will emerge up from the lawn if the tree is not getting sufficient water.

TIPS

Prunus species are beautiful as specimen plants and many are small enough to be included in almost any garden. Small species and cultivars can also be included in borders or grouped to form informal hedges or barriers. Pissard Plum and Purpleleaf Sand Cherry can be trained to form formal hedges.

Because of the pest problems that afflict many of the cherries, they can be rather short-lived. Choose resistant species like Sargent Cherry or Higan Cherry. If you plant a more susceptible species, like the Japanese Flowering Cherry, enjoy it while it thrives but be prepared to replace it.

The fruits, but not the pits, of *Prunus* species are edible. Too much of the often sour fruit can cause stomach aches.

RECOMMENDED

***P. cerasifera* 'Atropurpurea'** (Pissard Plum) is a shrubby, often multi-stemmed tree that grows 6–9 m (20–30') tall, with an equal spread. Light pink flowers that fade to white emerge before the deep purple foliage. The leaves turn dark green as they mature. Pissard Plum can be pruned to form a hedge, but plants grown as shrubs or trees need very little pruning. After flowering is finished, remove damaged growth and awkward branches as required. (Zones 4–8.)

P. serrulata (above)

P. x cistena (Purpleleaf Sand Cherry, Purpleleaf Dwarf Plum) is a dainty, upright shrub that grows 1.5–3 m (5–10') high, with an equal or lesser spread. The deep purple leaves keep their colour all season. The fragrant white or slightly pink flowers open in mid- to late spring after the leaves have developed. The fruits ripen to purple-black in July. This hybrid needs very little pruning if grown as a shrub. It can be trained to form a small tree in space-restricted gardens. Hedges can be trimmed back after flowering is complete. (Zones 3–8.)

P. glandulosa (Dwarf Flowering Almond) is a scruffy-looking shrub that grows 1.2–1.8 m (4–6') in height and width. The beautiful pink double flowers completely cover the stems in early spring, before the leaves emerge. Though very attractive when in flower, this species loses much of its appeal once flowering is done. Companion planting with other trees and shrubs will allow it to fade gracefully into the background as the season wears on. This shrub may spread by suckers; keep an eye open for plants that may turn up in unexpected and unwanted places. Prune one-third of the old wood to the ground each year, after flowering is complete. (Zones 4–8.)

P. maackii (Amur Chokecherry) is a rounded tree that grows 9–14 m (30–45') tall and spreads 7.5–14 m (25–45'). It tolerates cold winter weather and does better in the central and northern regions of Ontario. Fragrant, white mid-spring flowers are followed by red fruits that ripen to black. The glossy, peeling bark is a reddish or golden brown and provides interest in the garden all year. Amur Chokecherry

P. serrulata 'Shirofugan'

needs little or no pruning. Remove damaged growth and wayward branches as required. (Zones 2–6.)

P. sargentii (Sargent Cherry) is a rounded or spreading tree that grows 6–21 m (20–70') tall, with a spread of 6–15 m (20–50'). Fragrant light pink or white flowers appear in mid- to late spring, and the fruits ripen to a deep red by midsummer. The orange fall colour and glossy, red-brown bark are very attractive. This tree needs little pruning; remove damaged growth and wayward branches as needed. **'Columnaris'** is a narrow, upright cultivar that is suitable for tight spots and small gardens. (Zones 4–9.)

P. serrulata (Japanese Flowering Cherry) is a large tree that grows up to 23 m (75') tall, with a spread of up to 15 m (50'). It bears white or pink flowers in mid- to late spring. The species is rarely grown in favour of the cultivars. **'Kwanzan'** (Kwanzan Cherry) is a popular cultivar with drooping clusters of pink double flowers. It is sometimes grafted onto a single trunk, creating a

P. serrulata 'Kwanzan' (above)
P. subhirtella 'Pendula' (below)

small, vase-shaped tree. Grown on its own roots it becomes a large spreading tree 9–12 m (30–40') tall, with an equal spread. Because this cultivar has been planted in such large numbers, it has become susceptible to many problems. These problems may shorten the life of the tree, but for 20 to 25 years it can be a beautiful addition to the garden. **'Mount Fuji'** ('Shirotae') bears pink buds that open to fragrant white flowers in early spring. It has a spreading habit and grows 4.5–9 m (15–30') tall, with an equal spread. **'Shirofugan'** is a spreading, vigorous tree that grows 7.5 m (25') tall and 9 m (30') wide. The leaves are bronze when young and mature to dark green, turning orange-red in fall. Pink flower buds appear in mid-spring and open to fragrant white flowers. These cultivars need little pruning; remove damaged and wayward branches as needed. (Zones 5–8.)

***P.* x 'Snow Fountain'** is hardier than most flowering cherries, with graceful cascading branches covered in double white flowers. It grows about 7.5 m (25') tall. Little pruning is necessary; remove damaged and wayward branches as needed. (Zones 3–8.)

P. subhirtella (Higan Cherry) is a rounded or spreading tree that grows 6–12 m (20–40') tall and spreads 4.5–7.5 m (15–25'). The light pink or white flowers appear in early to mid-spring. The cultivars are grown more frequently than the species. **'Autumnalis'** (Autumn Flowering Cherry) bears light pink flowers sporadically in fall and prolifically in mid-spring. It grows up to 7.5 m (25') tall, with an equal spread. **'Pendula'** (Weeping Higan Cherry) has flowers in many shades of pink, appearing in mid-spring, before the leaves. The weeping branches make this tree a cascade of pink when in flower. It rarely needs pruning; remove damaged and way-

P. tomentosa (this page)

ward branches as needed. It is sometimes grafted onto a standard trunk, creating a small weeping tree under 2 m (7'). (Zones 4–8.)

P. tomentosa (Nanking Cherry, Manchu Cherry) is a hardy shrub cherry, popular for its tart, edible fruit. Fragrant, white flowers, borne in mid-spring, are followed by fruit that ripens by mid-summer. The shiny, exfoliating reddish bark is an attractive winter feature. This species grows 1.8–3 m (6–10') tall and spreads up to 4.5 m (15'). Little pruning is required. Remove awkward or damaged branches as needed to keep plant tidy. Pruning out some of the lower branches will make the interesting bark easier to see.

PESTS & PROBLEMS

The many possible problems include aphids, borers, caterpillars, leafhoppers, mites, nematodes, scale insects, canker, crown gall, fire blight, powdery mildew and viruses. Root rot can occur in poorly drained soils.

Clematis
Old Man's Beard
Clematis

Features: habit, flowers, seedheads
Habit: twining, woody or semi-woody, deciduous vine
Height: 3–5 m (10–16') or more **Spread:** 1.5 m (5') or more
Planting: bare-root, container; spring **Zones:** 3–9

These woody, semi-woody and woody-herbaceous vines are sometimes grouped with perennials and sometimes with woody plants. Even in cold regions where they are herbaceous, clematis plants are excellent companions for shrubs that put on a gorgeous display in spring but don't look very interesting for the rest of the season. Plant a clematis at the foot of the shrub. The foliage of the shrub will shade the clematis's tender roots, the branches will give the vine somewhere to climb and the clematis flowers will provide blooms and interest after the shrub flowers.

GROWING

Clematis plants prefer **full sun** and tolerate partial shade. The soil should be **fertile, humus rich, moist** and **well drained**. These vines will tolerate hot weather, but the roots must be kept cool. A thick layer of mulch or a planting of low, shade-providing perennials will protect the tender roots. These plants are quite cold hardy, but only when they are well protected from the winter wind.

Pruning differs for early- and late-blooming vines. For earlier bloomers such as Jackman Clematis, remove dead growth in spring and trim the plant back to strong buds on the main stems. For later-season bloomers, such as Virgin's Bower, trim back to leave just three or four strong buds on each stem above ground level. The bigger job is cleaning up all the growth that occurred the previous season once you've cut the vines back.

TIPS

Clematis plants can be used in a variety of ways. Let them climb up structures such as trellises, railings, fences and arbours. They can also be allowed to grow over shrubs and up trees and can be used as groundcovers.

RECOMMENDED

***C.* 'Gravetye Beauty'** (photo on facing page) is a late-season bloomer with small, bright red flowers that bloom on new growth. It grows about 2.5 m (8') tall. (Zones 4–9).

C.* x *jackmanii (Jackman Clematis) is a common early-summer bloomer. The twining vines of this hybrid grow about 3 m (10') tall each year and bear large purple flowers on side shoots from the previous season and on new growth for most of the summer.

C. tangutica (Virgin's Bower) is a late-season bloomer that grows 5 m (16') tall or more. Its great capacity for spreading makes it a good choice on a chain-link fence, where it will fill in, creating a privacy screen. The nodding yellow flowers of this species are followed by fuzzy seedheads that persist into winter.

PESTS & PROBLEMS

Scale insects, whiteflies, aphids, wilt, powdery mildew, rust, fungal spots and stem cankers can occur. Avoid damaging the stems because diseases can enter through these sites.

C. tangutica

The fuzzy seedheads of some species give these plants the alternative common name Old Man's Beard.

C. x *jackmanii*

Cotoneaster

Cotoneaster

Features: foliage, early-summer flowers, persistent fruit, variety of forms
Habit: evergreen groundcovers, shrubs or small trees
Height: 0.5–1 m (1–3')
Spread: 1–2.5 m (3–8')
Planting: container; spring, fall
Zones: 4–9

The various branching patterns of cotoneasters are geometrically fascinating. Rockspray Cotoneaster displays a perfect herringbone pattern, complemented by tiny, dark green, shiny leaves, good fall colour and red berries that add winter interest. This fine evergreen groundcover adds shape and pattern to the garden. The branches build up layer after layer, creating an almost impenetrable cover and lots of visual interest.

The name is pronounced cuh-tone-ee-aster *rather than* coton-easter.

GROWING

Cotoneasters grow well in **full sun** or **partial shade**. The soil should be of **average fertility** and **well drained.**

Though pruning is rarely required, these plants tolerate even a hard pruning. Pruning cotoneaster hedges in mid- to late summer will let you see how much you can trim off while still leaving some of the ornamental fruit in place. Hard pruning will encourage new growth and can rejuvenate plants that are looking worn out.

TIPS

Cotoneasters can be included in shrub or mixed borders. Low spreaders work well as groundcovers and shrubby species can be used to form hedges. Larger species are grown as small specimen trees and some low growers are grafted onto standards and grown as small, weeping trees.

Although cotoneaster berries are not poisonous, they can cause stomach upset if eaten in large quantities. The **foliage** may be **toxic**.

C. horizontalis (above), *C. dammeri* (below)

RECOMMENDED

C. adpressus (Creeping Cotoneaster) is a low-growing species that is used as a groundcover plant. It grows 30 cm (12") high, but spreads up to 2 m (7'). The foliage turns reddish purple in fall. **'Praecox'** (*C. a.* var. *praecox*) is a slightly larger plant with larger, showier fruit and foliage that turns bright red in fall. (Zones 4–6.)

C. apiculatus (Cranberry Cotoneaster) forms a mound of arching, tangled branches. It grows to about 90 cm (36") high and spreads up to 2 m (7'). The bright red fruits persist into winter. This species is sometimes available in a tree form. (Zones 4–7.)

C. dammeri (Bearberry Cotoneaster) has low-growing, arching stems that gradually stack up on top of one another as the plant matures. It grows to 45 cm (18") high and spreads to 2 m (7'). Small white flowers blanket the stems in early summer and are followed by bright red fruit in fall. One attractive cultivar is **'Coral Beauty,'** a groundcover that grows up to 90 cm (36") in height and spreads 2 m (7'). The abundant fruits are bright orange to red. (Zones 4-8.)

C. horizontalis (Rockspray Cotoneaster) is a low-growing species that has a distinct, attractive herringbone branching pattern. It grows 60–90 cm (24–36") tall and spreads 1.5–2.5 m (5–8'). The leaves turn bright red in fall. Light pink, early-summer flowers are followed by red fall fruit. (Zones 5–9.)

C. dammeri (above), *C. horizontalis* (right)

PESTS & PROBLEMS

These plants are generally problem free, but occasional attacks of rust, canker, powdery mildew, fire blight, scale insects, lace bugs, slugs, snails and spider mites are possible.

Try a mix of low-growing cotoneasters as a bank planting or use a shrubby type as a foundation plant.

C. apiculatus (above)

Crabapple

Malus

Features: spring flowers, late-summer and fall fruit, fall foliage, habit, bark
Habit: rounded, mounded or spreading, small to medium, deciduous trees
Height: 1.5–9 m (5–30') **Spread:** 2.5–9 m (8–30')
Planting: B & B, container; spring, fall **Zones:** 4–8

Thankfully, experts are diligent in their study and development of crabapples. They continue with success to search for specimens feisty enough to ward off the plague of pests and diseases that crabapples seem to attract. Many nurseries are offering stronger selections, including crabapples that can be grown in containers on decks and patios.

GROWING

Crabapples prefer **full sun** but tolerate partial shade. The soil should be of **average to rich fertility, moist** and **well drained.** These trees tolerate damp soil.

One of the best ways to prevent the spread of crabapple pests and diseases is to clean up all the leaves and fruit that fall off the tree. Many pests overwinter in the fruit, leaves or soil at the base of the tree. Clearing away their winter shelter helps keeps populations under control.

Crabapples require very little pruning but tolerate even hard pruning. Remove damaged or wayward branches and suckers when necessary. The next year's flower buds form in early summer, so any pruning done to form the shape of the tree should be done by late spring.

TIPS

Crabapples make excellent specimen plants. Many varieties are quite small, so there is one to suit almost any size of garden. Some forms are even small enough to grow in large containers. Crabapples' flexible young branches make them a good choice for creating espalier specimens along a wall or fence.

RECOMMENDED

The following are just a few suggestions among the hundreds of crabapples available. When choosing a species, variety or cultivar, one of the most important attributes to look for is disease resistance. Even the most beautiful flowers, fruit or habit will never look good if the plant is ravaged

Though crabapples are usually grown as trees, their excellent response to training makes them good candidates for use as bonsai and espalier.

An espalier specimen

by any of the numerous possible crabapple diseases and pests. Many new cultivars have been developed that have increased resistance. Ask for information at your local nursery or garden centre.

***M.* 'Centurion'** is highly resistant to all diseases. It is an upright tree that becomes rounded as it matures. It grows to 7.5 m (25') in height, with a spread of 6 m (20'). Dark pink flowers appear in late spring. The bright red fruits persist for a long time on the tree. (Zones 5–8.)

***M.* 'Donald Wyman'** is resistant to all diseases except powdery mildew, which can be prevented by pruning out enough growth to allow good air circulation. This cultivar has an open, rounded habit and grows to 6 m (20') tall and 7.5 m (25') in spread. Dark pink buds open to white flowers in mid-spring; flowering tends to be heavier in alternating years. The persistent fruits are bright red. (Zones 5–8.)

M. floribunda (Japanese Flowering Crabapple, Showy Crabapple) is a medium-sized, densely crowned, spreading tree. It grows up to 9 m (30') in both height and width. This species is fairly resistant to crabapple problems. Pink buds open to pale pink flowers in mid- to late spring. The fruits are small and yellow.

M. sargentii (Sargent Crabapple) is a small, mounding tree that is also fairly resistant to disease. It grows 1.8–3 m (6–10') tall and spreads 2.5–4.5 m (8–15'). In late spring, red buds open to white flowers. The dark red fruits are long lasting. **'Tina'** is almost identical to the species, except that it grows only 1.5 m (5') tall and spreads up to 3 m (10'). With a bit of pruning to control the spread, this

cultivar makes an interesting specimen for a large container on a balcony or patio.

***M.* 'Snowdrift'** is a dense, quick-growing, rounded tree that is somewhat susceptible to diseases. It grows 4.5–6 m (15–20') tall, with an equal spread. Red buds open to white flowers in late spring or early summer. The foliage is dark green and the fruits are bright orange. (Zones 5–8.)

PESTS & PROBLEMS

Aphids, beetles, borers, tent caterpillars, fruit worms, leaf rollers, leaf skeletonizers and scale insects are pests to watch for. Though the damage insect pests cause is largely cosmetic, the tree becomes weakened and more susceptible to diseases such as apple scab, cedar-apple rust, fire blight, heart rot, leaf spot, powdery mildew and root rot.

M. floribunda

Some gardeners use crabapple fruit to make preserves, cider or even wine.

Daphne

Daphne

Features: foliage, fragrant spring flowers
Habit: upright, rounded or low-growing, evergreen or semi-evergreen shrubs
Height: 0.2–1.5 m (0.5–5') **Spread:** 1–1.5 m (3–5')
Planting: container; early spring, early fall **Zones:** 4–7

I took a course many years ago at the Royal Botanical Gardens on delightful shrubs to select for the garden. The month was February, when our snow is a grimy grey and when candy wrappers and flyers cling to bare, windblown hedges. We needed botanical inspiration and found it in the cut branch of Burkwood Daphne. It was in delicate pink bloom and very fragrant. I planted a hedge of it that summer and enjoyed it for many years before it died of natural (or unnatural) causes. Burkwood Daphne is lovely, and prettier still is 'Carol Mackie' with its creamy margins on dark green leaves.

GROWING

Daphnes prefer **full sun** or **partial shade.** The soil should be **moist, well drained** and of **average to high fertility.** A layer of mulch will keep the shallow roots cool.

These plants have neat, dense growth that needs very little pruning. Remove damaged or diseased branches. Flowerheads can be removed if desired once flowering is finished. Cut flowering stems back to where they join main branches in order to preserve the natural growth habit of the shrub.

TIPS

Rose Daphne makes an attractive groundcover in a rock garden or woodland garden. Burkwood Daphne can be included in shrub or mixed borders. Plant daphnes near paths, doors, windows or other places where the wonderful scent can be enjoyed.

Though most sources claim daphnes are hardy to Zone 4, they will often thrive as smaller plants in colder climates. These plants do, however, have a strange habit of dying suddenly. Experts have various theories about why this happens and how to avoid it, but the best advice seems to be to plant daphnes in good, well-drained conditions and then leave them alone. Any disturbance that could stress the plants should be avoided. Don't move daphnes after they are planted.

All parts of daphne plants are **toxic** if eaten, and the sap may cause skin irritations. Avoid planting these species where children may be tempted to sample the berries.

D. x *burkwoodii* 'Somerset'

RECOMMENDED

D.* x *burkwoodii (Burkwood Daphne) is an upright, semi-evergreen shrub. It bears fragrant white or light pink flowers in late spring and sometimes again in fall. It grows 1–1.5 m (3–5') in height and spread. **'Carol Mackie'** is a common cultivar; its dark green leaves have creamy margins. **'Somerset'** has darker pink flowers than the hybrid species.

D. cneorum (Rose Daphne, Garland Flower) is a low-growing evergreen shrub. It grows 15–30 cm (6–12") tall and can spread to 1.2 m (4'). The fragrant pale to deep pink or white flowers are borne in late spring. **'Alba'** has white flowers, and **'Ruby Glow'** (sometimes attributed to *D. mezereum*) has reddish-pink flowers. **'Variegata'** has leaves edged with creamy yellow; its flowers are like those of the species.

In late winter cut a few stems and arrange them in a vase indoors—they should come into bloom in a warm, bright room. Enjoy both the sweet scent and the delicate flowers.

D. cneorum 'Variegata' (below & right)

PESTS & PROBLEMS

Viruses, leaf spot, crown or root rot, aphids, scale insects and twig blight affect daphnes. Poor growing conditions can result in greater susceptibility to these problems. A plant may wilt and die suddenly if diseased.

Daphnes have fragrant flowers and attractive, often evergreen, foliage, making these shrubs appealing all year round.

D. burkwoodii 'Somerset' (above)

Dawn Redwood

Metasequoia glyptostroboides

Features: foliage, bark, cones, buttressed trunk
Habit: narrow, conical, deciduous conifer
Height: 21–38 m (70–125') **Spread:** 4.5–7.5 m (15–25')
Planting: spring, fall **Zones:** 4–8

Though this tree grows to be an imposing giant, it's easy to feel tender-hearted toward the Dawn Redwood. This deciduous conifer has needles so soft you'll be tempted to stroke them as you pass by. The branches emerge in a curious way from within deep folds in the trunk, bringing to mind those eerie trees in *The Legend of Sleepy Hollow.* If my own garden were wider than 7 metres, I would plant this beautiful tree, which has a venerable history reaching back to the time of the dinosaurs.

This tree is often called a 'living fossil' because it was found in fossil form before it was observed growing in China in the 1940s.

GROWING

Dawn Redwood grows well in **full sun** or **light shade.** The soil should be **humus rich,** slightly **acidic, moist** and **well drained.** Wet or dry soils are tolerated, though the rate of growth will be reduced in dry conditions. This tree likes humid conditions and should be mulched and watered regularly until it becomes established.

Pruning is not necessary. The lower branches must be left in place in order for the buttressing to develop. Buttressed trunks are flared and grooved, and the branches appear to be growing from deep inside the grooves.

Don't worry when this tree drops its needles each fall; it's a deciduous conifer.

TIPS

These large trees need plenty of room to grow. Larger gardens and parks can best accommodate them. As single specimens or in group plantings, these trees are attractive and impressive. The cones may not develop in many Ontario gardens because the tree matures very slowly in cold winter climates.

RECOMMENDED

The cultivars do not differ significantly from *M. glyptostroboides.* Both **'National'** and **'Sheridan Spire'** are narrower than the species. They have not been in cultivation long enough to have reached their mature heights, but they are expected to be as tall as the species.

PESTS & PROBLEMS

Dawn Redwood is not generally prone to pest problems, although it can be killed by canker infections.

Deutzia

Deutzia

Features: early-summer flowers **Habit:** bushy, deciduous shrubs
Height: 0.5–2 m (2–7') **Spread:** 0.5–2 m (2–7')
Planting: preferably spring **Zones:** 4–9

Deutzia's resume could read 'self-starter, highly motivated, self-sufficient.' Full sun and occasional pruning will keep these low-maintenance shrubs perfectly happy in the garden. The Slender Deutzia billows forth in spring with white flowers on slim, cascading branches, a fine choice for a rock garden or as part of a perennial border.

GROWING

Deutzias grow best in **full sun.** They will tolerate light shade, but will not bear as many flowers. The soil should be of **average to high fertility, moist** and **well drained.** These shrubs bloom on the previous year's growth. After flowering, cut flowering stems back to strong buds, main stems or basal growth as required to shape the plant. Remove one-third of the old growth on established plants at ground level to encourage new growth.

TIPS

Include deutzias in shrub or mixed borders or in rock gardens; you can also use them as specimen plants.

Deutzias are quite frost hardy. If you live in a colder area than is generally recommended for these plants, try growing them in a sheltered spot where they will be protected from the worst extremes of weather.

RECOMMENDED

D. gracilis (Slender Deutzia) is a low-growing, mounding species hardy in Zones 5–8. It grows about 0.5–1.2 m (2–4') high, with a spread of 1–2 m (3–7'). In late spring the plant is completely covered with white flowers. **'Nikko'** has double white flowers and its foliage turns purple in fall. It is hardier than the species, to Zone 4.

D.* x *lemoinei is a dense, rounded, upright hybrid. It grows 1.5–2 m (5–7') high, with an equal spread. The early-summer blooms are white. **'Avalanche'** grows 1.2 m (4') tall and wide and bears white flowers on arching branches. **'Compacta'** ('Boule de Neige') has denser, more compact growth than the hybrid species. It has large clusters of white flowers. (Zones 5–9.)

The name Deutzia *comes from Dutchman Johan van der Deutz, an 18th-century patron of botany who supported expeditions of the famous botanist Carl Peter Thunberg.*

PESTS & PROBLEMS

Problems are rare, though these plants can have trouble with fungal leaf spot, aphids or leaf miners.

Dogwood

Cornus

Features: late-spring to early-summer flowers, fall foliage, fruit, habit
Habit: deciduous large shrubs or small trees
Height: 1.5–9 m (5–30') **Spread:** 1.5–9 m (5–30')
Planting: B & B, container; spring **Zones:** 2–9

All gardens should have one of these winning trees or shrubs. Whether your garden is wet, dry, sunny or shaded, there is a dogwood for almost every condition. I love the Flowering Dogwood, even though it can be challenging to grow in Ontario. If you want to save yourself possible heartache, try Kousa Dogwood or Pagoda Dogwood instead. I have a Pagoda Dogwood in my garden, in inhospitable full sun, poor soil and wicked winds. It just gets better every year, showing off a graceful horizontal branching pattern, beautiful creased leaves and white spring flowers. It casts dappled shade, perfect for an underplanting of perennial geraniums, sweet woodruff and corydalis.

C. kousa *is more dependable and disease resistant than many other dogwood species.*

GROWING

Dogwoods grow equally well in **full sun, light shade** or **partial shade,** with a slight preference for light shade. The soil should be of **average to high fertility,** high in **organic** matter, **neutral** or **slightly acidic** and **well drained.**

C. sericea (above & centre)

C. alba 'Sibirica' (below)

Most dogwoods require very little pruning. Simply removing damaged, dead or awkward branches in early spring is sufficient for most species. *C. alba* and *C. sericea,* which are grown for the colourful stems that are so striking in winter, require a little more effort because the colour is best on young growth.

There are two ways to encourage new growth for *C. alba* and *C. sericea.* One method is to cut back all stems to within a couple of buds of the ground, in early spring. Fertilize the plant once growth starts to make up for the loss of top growth. The second, less drastic, method is to cut back about one-third of the old growth to within a couple of buds of the ground, in early spring. This leaves most of the growth in place, and branches can be removed as they age and lose their colour.

TIPS

Shrub dogwoods can be included in a shrub or mixed border. They look best in groups rather than as single specimens. The tree species make wonderful specimen plants and are small enough to include in most gardens. Use them along the edge of a woodland, in a shrub or mixed border, alongside a house, or near a pond, water feature or patio.

C. kousa

Use the strong horizontal branching of C. alternifolia *for contrast with vertical lines in the landscape.*

RECOMMENDED

C. alba (Red-twig Dogwood, Tartarian Dogwood) is grown for the bright red stems that provide winter interest. The stems are green all summer, turning red as winter approaches. This species can grow 1.5–3 m (5–10') tall, with an equal spread. It prefers cool climates and can develop leaf scorch and canker problems if the weather gets very hot. **'Aureo-marginata'** ('Elegantissima') has grey-green leaves with creamy margins. **'Sibirica'** has bright red winter stems. (Zones 2–7.)

C. alternifolia (Pagoda Dogwood) is a native dogwood that can be grown as a large, multi-stemmed shrub or a small, single-stemmed tree. It grows 4.5–7.5 m (15–25') tall and spreads 3–7.5 m (10–25'). The branches have an attractive layered appearance. Clusters of small white flowers appear in early summer. This species prefers light shade. (Zones 3–8.)

C. florida (Flowering Dogwood) is native to southern Ontario. It is usually grown as a small tree 6–9 m (20–30') tall, with an equal or greater spread. It has horizontally layered branches. The inconspicuous flowers with showy pink or white bracts appear in late spring. **'Apple Blossom'** has light pink bracts that are white at the bases.

C. kousa var. chinensis

C. alternifolia

'Cherokee Chief' has dark pink bracts. **'Cloud Nine'** has large white bracts. **'Spring Song'** has rose pink bracts. This species and its cultivars are susceptible to blight. (Zones 5–9.)

C. kousa (Kousa Dogwood) is grown for its flowers, fruit, fall colour and interesting bark. It grows 6–9 m (20–30') tall and spreads 4.5–9 m (15–30'). This species is more resistant to leaf blight and the other problems that plague *C. florida.* The white-bracted, early-summer flowers are followed by bright red fruit. The foliage turns red and purple in fall. **Var. *chinensis*** (Chinese Dogwood) grows more vigorously and has larger flowers. (Zones 5–9.)

C. sericea *(C. stolonifera)* (Red-osier Dogwood) is a widespread, vigorous native shrub with red stems. It grows about 1.8 m (6') tall, spreads up to 3.5 m (12') and bears clusters of white flowers in early summer. The fall colour is red or orange. This species tolerates wet soil. **'Flaviramea'** has bright yellow-green stems. (Zones 2–8.)

PESTS & PROBLEMS

The many possible problems include blight, canker, leaf spot, powdery mildew, root rot, borers, aphids, leafhoppers, scale insects, weevils, nematodes and thrips.

C. sericea

C. florida (above)

C. kousa (centre photos)

C. alternifolia (below)

Elder
Elderberry
Sambucus

Features: early-summer flowers, fruit, foliage
Habit: large, bushy, deciduous shrubs
Height: 2.5–6 m (8–20') Spread: 2.5–6 m (8–20')
Planting: spring, fall **Zones:** 3–9

Elders work well in a naturalized garden. The berries attract birds, and the light shade provides good conditions for native woodland plants. The best choice for many parts of Ontario seems to be the American Elder, with its superior tolerance for heat. The cultivars 'Aurea' and 'Goldfinch' offer yellow foliage, and 'Goldfinch' also has deeply divided leaves. In a garden I once visited I saw a golden elder glowing next to a redbud in full bloom—an unusual, arresting combination.

GROWING

Elders grow well in **full sun** or **partial shade.** Cultivars and varieties grown for interesting leaf colour develop the best colour in light or partial shade. The soil should be of **average fertility, moist** and **well drained.** These plants tolerate dry soil once established.

Elders do not require pruning but can become straggly and untidy if ignored. They will tolerate even severe pruning. Plants can be cut back to within a couple of buds of the ground in early spring. This treatment controls the spread of these vigorous growers and encourages the best foliage colour on specimens grown for this purpose.

Plants cut right back to the ground will not flower or produce fruit. If you desire flowers and fruit as well as good foliage colour, remove only one-third to one-half of the growth in early spring. Fertilize or apply a layer of compost after pruning to encourage strong new growth.

S. nigra cultivar (above)
S. racemosa (below)

S. racemosa (above), *S. nigra* cultivar (below)

TIPS

Elders can be used in a shrub or mixed border, in a natural woodland garden or next to a pond or other water feature. Types with interesting or colourful foliage can be used as specimen plants or focal points in the garden.

Both the flowers and the fruit can be used to make wine. The berries are popular for pies and jelly. The raw berries are marginally edible but not palatable and can cause stomach upset, particularly in children. All other parts of elders are **toxic.**

RECOMMENDED

S. canadensis (American Elder/Elderberry) is a shrub about 3.5 m (12') tall, with an equal spread. White flowers in mid-summer are followed by dark purple berries. Native to eastern North America, this species is generally found growing in damp ditches and alongside rivers and streams. **'Aurea'** has yellow foliage and red fruit. **'Goldfinch'** grows to 3 m (10') tall and has deeply divided, bright yellow leaflets. (Zones 4–9.)

S. nigra (European Elder/Elderberry, Black Elder/Elderberry) is a large shrub that can grow 6 m (20') tall, with an equal spread. The early-summer flowers are followed by purple-black fruit. **'Guinicho Purple'** has dark bronze-green leaves that darken to purple over the summer and turn red in fall. The flowers are pinkish white. **'Laciniata'** has deeply dissected leaflets that give the shrub a feathery appearance. (Zones 6–8.)

S. racemosa (European Red Elder/Elderberry) grows 2.5–3.5 m (8–12') tall, with an equal spread. It bears pyramidal clusters of white flowers in spring, followed by bright red fruit. **'Plumosa Aurea'** has deeply divided foliage that emerges a bright golden colour and fades to green over the summer. (Zones 3–7.)

PESTS & PROBLEMS

Powdery mildew, borers, dieback, canker and leaf spot may occasionally affect elders.

The Italian liqueur sambuca is made from elder berries and flavoured with licorice.

S. racemosa (this page)

English Ivy

Hedera

Features: foliage, habit
Habit: evergreen or semi-evergreen, climbing or trailing vine
Height: indefinite **Spread:** indefinite
Planting: spring, fall **Zones:** 5–9

One of the loveliest things about English Ivy is the variation in green and blue tones it adds to groundcover plantings. The reflective, strikingly veined leaves add a pleasing texture to the garden. The cultivars 'Thorndale' and 'Baltica' have set the standard for cold hardiness, but, increasingly, nurseries are offering variegated varieties. Will they withstand Ontario winters? Only time will tell. But we certainly have room for experimenting in our gardens. Far better to test cold tolerance with a few small vines than with an expensive tree.

Some tender ivy cultivars have variegated, curly or other unusual foliage and are often grown as houseplants.

GROWING

English Ivy prefers **light or partial shade** but will adapt to any light conditions from full shade to full sun. The foliage can become damaged or dried out in winter if the plant is growing in a sunny, exposed site. The soil should be of **average to rich fertility, moist** and **well drained.** The richer the soil, the better this vine will grow.

Once established, English Ivy can be pruned as much as necessary, at any time of the year, to keep this strong grower where you want it.

TIPS

English Ivy is grown as a trailing groundcover or as a climbing vine. It clings tenaciously to house walls, tree trunks and many other rough-textured surfaces. Ivy rootlets can damage walls and fences, but the cold Ontario winters prevent the rampant growth that makes this plant troublesome and invasive in warmer climates.

RECOMMENDED

H. helix is a vigorous vine that can grow as high as 30 m (100'), though it is usually pruned to keep it well below its potential size. As a groundcover, it may spread indefinitely but grows about 30 cm (12") high. Many cultivars have been developed. Some, like **'Baltica'** and **'Thorndale,'** are popular for their increased cold hardiness. In a sheltered spot these cultivars are hardy to Zone 4. Others, like **'Gold Heart,'** have interesting foliage but are not exceptionally hardy. This cultivar has yellow variegation in the centre of each leaf. Many varieties of English Ivy are grown as houseplants.

PESTS & PROBLEMS

English Ivy has very few serious problems. Keep an eye open for infestations of spider mites or leaf spot. Plants exposed to winter wind may suffer desiccation of the foliage.

Euonymus

Euonymus

Features: foliage, corky stems (*E. alatus*), habit
Habit: deciduous and evergreen shrubs, small trees, groundcovers, climbers
Height: 0.5–6 m (2–20') **Spread:** 0.5–6 m (2–20')
Planting: B & B, container; spring, fall **Zones:** 4–9

Burning Bush is recommended so often for its fall colour, you'd expect it to become a cliché, but the beautiful deep pinky-red autumn colour is unsurpassed. This plant is far more graceful if allowed to grow into its natural form. Too often it is the victim of severe hacking rather than formative pruning.

Wintercreeper Euonymus is a very useful evergreen groundcover or climber, with leaves that are a restful, glossy green. Beware, though, of turning over large sections of the garden to Wintercreeper. In many areas of Ontario it is under severe attack from scale insects.

The name Euonymus *translates as 'of good name'—rather ironically, given that all parts of these plants are poisonous and violently purgative.*

GROWING

Euonymus species prefer **full sun** and tolerate light or partial shade. Soil of **average to rich fertility** is preferable, but any **moist, well-drained** soil will do.

E. alatus requires very little pruning except to remove dead, damaged or awkward growth but it tolerates severe pruning and can be used to form hedges. *E. fortunei* is a vigorous, spreading plant and can be trimmed as required to keep it within the desired growing area; it too tolerates severe pruning. It is also easy to propagate. Bend a branch to the ground and hold it down with a rock. Cut this branch off once roots have formed and plant it where you wish.

TIPS

E. alatus can be grown in a shrub or mixed border, as a specimen, in a naturalistic garden or as a hedge.

E. alatus (above), *E. fortunei* 'Vegetus' (below)

Dwarf cultivars can be used to create informal hedges. *E. fortunei* can be grown as a shrub in borders or as a hedge. It is an excellent substitute for the more demanding boxwood. The trailing habit also lends it to use as a groundcover or climber.

E. fortunei 'Gold Tip'

E. fortunei 'Vegetus' (above), *E. alatus* (below)

E. alatus (Burning Bush, Winged Euonymus) is an attractive, open, mounding, deciduous shrub. It grows 4.5–6 m (15–20') tall, with an equal or greater spread. The foliage turns a vivid red in fall. The small, red fall berries are somewhat obscured by the bright foliage. Winter interest is provided by the corky ridges, or wings, that grow on the stems and branches. This plant is often pruned to form a neat, rounded shrub, but if left to grow naturally it becomes an attractive, wide-spreading, open shrub. **'Compactus'** (Dwarf Burning Bush) is a popular cultivar. It has more dense, compact growth— up to 3 m (10') tall and wide—and it lacks the corky ridges on the branches. It is commonly used as a hedge plant and in shrub and mixed borders.

E. fortunei (Wintercreeper Euonymus) as a species is rarely grown owing to the wide and attractive variety of cultivars. These can be prostrate, climbing or mounding evergreens, often with attractive, variegated foliage. **'Coloratus'** (Purple Leaf Wintercreeper) is a popular cultivar, usually grown as a groundcover. The foliage turns red or purple over winter. **'Emerald Gaiety'** is a vigorous, shrubby cultivar that grows about 1.5 m (5') tall, with an equal or greater spread. It sends out long shoots that will attempt to scale any nearby wall. This rambling habit can be encouraged or the long shoots can be trimmed back to maintain the plant as a shrub. The foliage is bright green with irregular, creamy margins that turn pink in winter. **'Gold Tip'**

('Gold Prince') is a compact, mounded form that grows to about 60 cm (24") in height and spread. The leaves are deep green and edged with gold. **'Sunspot'** grows about 90 cm (36") tall, with an equal or greater spread. It has dark green leaves, each with a yellow spot in the centre. The habit is fairly upright, making this cultivar a good choice for a hedge. **'Vegetus'** grows up to 1.5 m (5') in height and width. This cultivar has large, dark green leaves, and it can be either trained up a trellis as a climber or trimmed back to form a shrub.

PESTS & PROBLEMS

The two worst problems are crown gall and scale insects, both of which can prove fatal to the infected plant. Other possible problems include leaf spot, aphids, powdery mildew, tent caterpillars and leaf miners.

E. alatus *achieves the best fall colour when grown in full sun.*

E. alatus (this page)

False Arborvitae

Hiba Arborvitae

Thujopsis

Features: foliage, cones, habit **Habit:** pyramidal, evergreen tree
Height: 1–21 m (3–70') **Spread:** 1–9 m (3–30')
Planting: container; any time **Zones:** 5–8

If you are one of the many gardeners who savour the hunt for unusual plants, add False Arborvitae to your list of plants to seek. Seeing one in the garden will confound your friends. Its pyramidal silhouette is similar to that of arborvitae but the foliage is deep emerald green, with silvery markings underneath, and it is composed of much larger scales than those of arborvitae. It makes a shapely specimen, and the dwarf form is at home in the rock garden. This species is not susceptible to the many pests that can plague the more commonly grown arborvitae.

If you have tried growing arborvitae without success as a result of pest problems, try the resistant False Arborvitae instead.

GROWING

False Arborvitae prefers a sheltered site in **full sun.** The soil should be **fertile, humus rich, moist** and **well drained.**

Pruning is unnecessary; simply remove dead or damaged growth. This plant is easy to propagate yourself. Ten-centimetre (4") cuttings taken in late fall can be started in a sand and peat moss mixture. Before planting, dust the cut end with a rooting hormone intended for hardwood cuttings. Keep the sand and peat mix moist until the cuttings have rooted, and keep the container in a bright, cool, but frost-free location. A sheltered porch or greenhouse is ideal. The cuttings should have rooted by the following spring and can be planted in containers or directly into a sheltered spot in the garden.

TIPS

Use this beautiful tree as a specimen plant in a large garden. The smaller cultivars are suitable for mixed and shrub borders as well as rock gardens.

False Arborvitae can be difficult to find at garden centres. You may have to ask somebody who already has a mature tree if you can take a cutting or two.

As with many resinous evergreens, contact with the foliage may cause skin irritation.

RECOMMENDED

T. dolabrata is a beautiful evergreen tree with shiny, green, large-scaled foliage. It grows up to 21 m (70') tall and spreads 6–9 m (20–30'). **'Nana'** is a dwarf cultivar that grows about 90 cm (36") tall, with an equal or slightly lesser spread.

The silvery effect on the underside of the foliage is caused by lines of stomata (pores).

False Cypress

Chamaecyparis

Features: foliage, habit, cones **Habit:** narrow, pyramidal, evergreen trees and shrubs
Height: 0.5–45 m (1–150') **Spread:** 0.5–20 m (1–65')
Planting: B & B, container; spring, fall **Zones:** 4–9

Conifer shoppers are blessed with an inspirational choice of evergreens, including a marvellous selection of false cypresses. In just one nursery catalogue I picked up at random, I found 15 different cultivars among three species. Choose from the very attractive 'Nana Gracilis,' with golf course–green foliage arranged in artistic clusters, or for a living piece of sculpture consider 'Pendula.' This weeping false cypress has a soft airiness uncommon, but much appreciated, in an evergreen.

GROWING

False cypresses prefer **full sun.** The soil should be **fertile, moist, neutral to acidic** and **well drained.** Alkaline soils are tolerated. In shaded areas, growth may be sparse or thin.

No pruning is required on tree specimens. Plants grown as hedges can be trimmed any time during the growing season. Avoid severe pruning because new growth will not sprout from old wood. Dry, brown leaves can be pulled from the base by hand to tidy shrubs.

TIPS

Tree varieties are used as specimen plants and for hedging. The dwarf and slow-growing cultivars are used in borders and rock gardens and as bonsai. False cypress shrubs can be grown near the house or as evergreen specimens in large containers.

As with the related arborvitae and False Arborvitae, oils in the foliage of false cypresses may be irritating to sensitive skin.

C. nootkatensis (below), 'Pendula' (right)

C. *nootkatensis* (above)

C. *pisifera* dwarf cultivar (below)

RECOMMENDED

C. nootkatensis (Yellow-cedar, Nootka False Cypress) grows 9–30 m (30–100') tall, with a spread of about 7.5 m (25'). The scaly foliage of this species is quite pendulous. **'Pendula'** has a very open habit and even more pendulous foliage than the species. (Zones 4–8.)

C. obtusa (Hinoki False Cypress), a native of Japan, has foliage arranged in fan-like sprays. It grows about 21 m (70') tall, with a spread of 6 m (20'). **'Minima'** is a very dwarf, mounding cultivar. It grows about 25 cm (10") tall and spreads 40 cm (16"). **'Nana Aurea'** grows 1–1.8 m (3–6') in height and spread. The foliage is gold-tipped, becoming greener in the shade and bronzy in winter. **'Nana Gracilis'** (Dwarf Hinoki False Cypress) is a slow-growing cultivar that reaches 60–90 cm (24–36") in height, with a slightly greater spread.

C. pisifera (Japanese False Cypress, Swara Cypress) is another Japanese native. It grows 21–45 m (70–150') tall and spreads 4.5–7.5 m (15–25'). The cultivars are more commonly grown than the species. **'Filifera Aurea'** (Golden Thread-Leaf False Cypress) is a slow-growing cultivar with golden yellow, thread-like foliage. It grows about 12 m (40') tall. **'Nana'** (Dwarf False Cypress) is a dwarf cultivar with feathery foliage similar to that of the species. It grows into a mound about 30 cm (12") in height and width. **'Plumosa'** (Plume False Cypress) has very feathery foliage. It grows about 6–7.5 m (20–25') tall, with an equal or greater spread. **'Squarrosa'** (Moss False Cypress) has less pendulous foliage than the other cultivars. Young plants grow very densely, looking like fuzzy stuffed animals. The growth becomes more relaxed and open with maturity. This cultivar grows about 20 m (65') tall, with a spread that may be equal or a little narrower.

PESTS & PROBLEMS

False cypresses are not prone to problems but can occasionally be affected by spruce mites, root rot, gall or blight.

In the wild, C. nootkatensis *trees can grow as tall as 50 m (165') and as old as 1800 years.*

C. nootkatensis (above)

C. obtusa 'Nana Gracilis' (below)

Fir

Abies

Features: foliage, cones
Habit: narrow, pyramidal or columnar, evergreen trees and shrubs
Height: 0.5–25 m (2–80') **Spread:** 0.5–7.5 m (2–25')
Planting: B & B, container; spring **Zones:** 3–8

Fir trees are stately conifers, and they are more friendly to the touch than the prickly spruce. But they are also among the least used needled evergreens for landscaping because many can't tolerate a wide range of soil and climate conditions. Balsam Fir, for instance, is a beautiful tree that can withstand shade and very cold temperatures, but it doesn't like summer dry spells and heavy clay. White Fir is the most adaptable to stressful conditions. Try your luck at one of the dwarf cultivars if you have a small garden.

GROWING

Firs usually prefer **full sun** but tolerate partial shade. The soil should be **rich, moist, neutral to acidic** and **well drained.** These trees prefer a **sheltered** site, out of the wind, and are generally not tolerant of extreme heat or of polluted, urban conditions. No pruning is required. Dead or damaged growth can be removed as needed.

TIPS

Firs make impressive specimen trees in large areas. The species tend to be too large for the average home garden. Several compact or dwarf cultivars can be included in shrub borders or used as specimens, depending on their size.

A. concolor is far more tolerant of pollution, heat and drought than other *Abies* species, thus is better adapted for city conditions.

RECOMMENDED

A. balsamea (Balsam Fir) is quite pyramidal when young but narrows as it ages. This slow-growing tree can reach 14–23 m (45–75') in height, with a spread of 4.5–7.5 m (15–25'). Though Balsam Fir prefers a well-drained soil, it will tolerate wet soil. This species is native to northcentral and northeastern North America and does better in the northern and central regions of Ontario than the southern regions. **'Hudsonia'** ('Nana') grows to only 60 cm (24") in height, with a spread of 60–90 cm (24–36"). It is a natural form of the species, but it is usually sold as a cultivar. **'Nana'** is sometimes sold as a different plant. The two are

A. balsamea

Firs make attractive Christmas trees, but the needles drop quickly in a warm, dry home.

A. *balsamea* 'Hudsonia' (above)

Firs and spruces resemble each other, but fir needles are flat and spruce needles are sharply pointed. Also, fir cones sit on top of the branches, while spruce cones hang downwards.

very similar in size and habit. These dwarf cultivars are more suitable to a small garden than the much larger parent species. (Zones 3–6.)

A. concolor (White Fir) is an impressive specimen. The needles have a whitish coating, which gives the tree a hazy blue appearance. It grows 12–21 m (40–70') tall in garden conditions, but can grow up to 40 m (130') in unrestricted natural conditions. It spreads 4.5–7.5 m (15–25'). **'Compacta'** is a dwarf cultivar. It has whiter needles than the species and grows to 3 m (10') in height and spread. This cultivar makes an attractive specimen tree. **'Violacea'** has silvery blue needles and is very attractive; it grows as large as the species. (Zones 4–8.)

A. koreana (Korean Fir) is slow growing and small, by evergreen standards. It grows 4.5–9 m (15–30') tall and spreads 3–6 m (10–20'). The unusual, attractive purple-blue cones are produced while the tree is still young. **'Horstmann's Silberlocke'** ('Silberlocke') has unusual, twisted needles that show off the silvery stripes on their undersides. **'Prostrata'** is a low-growing cultivar with bright green needles. (Zones 4–8.)

The mounding habit of *A. balsamea* 'Hudsonia' (background) complements the upright, textured foliage of *Erica carnea* (foreground).

PESTS & PROBLEMS

Firs are susceptible to quite a few problems, including aphids, bark beetles, spruce budworm, bagworm, rust, root rot and needle blight.

Chickadees, squirrels and porcupines enjoy the oil-rich seeds of the native Balsam Fir, and moose and deer browse the foliage.

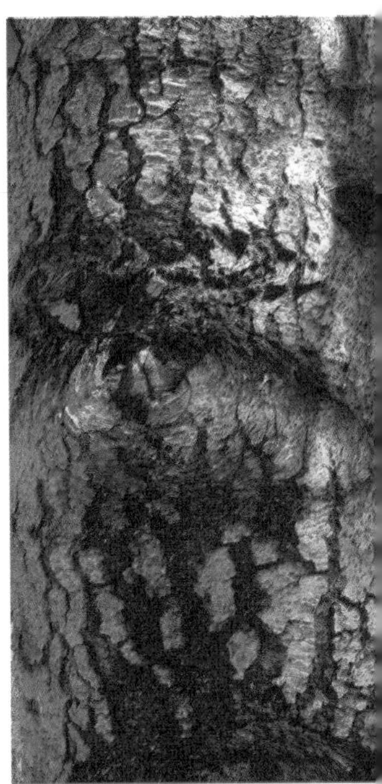

A. balsamea 'Hudsonia' (above), *A. concolor* (below & right)

Firethorn

Pyracantha

Features: foliage, early-summer flowers, late-summer and fall fruit
Habit: dense, thorny, evergreen or semi-evergreen shrub
Height: 1.8–5.5 m (6–18') **Spread:** equal to or greater than height
Planting: container; spring **Zones:** 5–9

I was most impressed with the Firethorn I saw during a visit to Charleston, South Carolina. In tiny courtyard gardens I saw it climbing the walls of Georgian-style houses, with the branches bending under the weight of hundreds of orange berries. Inspired, I planted it against our Victorian brick house. While it did not look as thick and tidy as I'd seen it in Charleston, Firethorn in my garden did look dramatic. It has grown without any special attention in the dry, lean soil at the base of our house. Because there is a certain spastic quality to the growth pattern of Firethorn—branches tend to splay in all directions—I think it looks best espalied against the side of a house. The thorns of Firethorn are sharp and painful, so it makes an effective barrier plant.

GROWING

Firethorn prefers **full sun** and tolerates partial shade, but does not fruit as heavily in partial shade. The soil should be **rich, moist** and **well drained**. Well-established plants will tolerate dry soil. Shelter plants from strong winds. Firethorn resents being moved once established, and you will resent having to move this prickly plant.

Some pruning is required in order to keep this plant looking neat and attractive. In a naturalized setting, this shrub can be left much to its own devices. Remove any damaged growth or wayward branches, and trim back new growth to better show off the fruit.

If you are using Firethorn in a shrub or mixed border, you will have to prune more severely to prevent it from overgrowing its neighbours. Hedges can be trimmed in early summer to mid-summer. Espalier

Firethorn obeys the version of Murphy's Law that states that the more prickly a plant is, the more pruning it will need.

and other wall-trained specimens can be trimmed in mid-summer. Growth to be used to extend the framework of the specimen can be tied in place as needed.

TIPS

Despite its potential for rampant growth, Firethorn has a wide variety of uses. It is often used for formal or informal hedges and barriers because the prickles make this plant unappealing to walk through. It can be grown as a large informal shrub in naturalized gardens and borders. It can also be used as a climber if tied to a trellis or other supportive framework. Firethorn's responsiveness to pruning and its dense growth habit make it an ideal espalier specimen.

RECOMMENDED

P. coccinea is a large, spiny shrub that grows 1.8–5.5 m (6–18') tall and wide. White flowers

The showy fruits of Firethorn resemble tiny apples and are attractive to birds.

cover the plant in early summer, followed by bright scarlet fruit in fall and winter. **'Aurea'** is remarkable for its distinctive yellow fruit. It is hardy in Zones 6–9. **'Chadwick'** is a compact, spreading plant. It bears a prolific amount of red-orange fruit. This is one of the most hardy cultivars, to Zone 5. **'Fiery Cascade'** is an upright cultivar hardy in Zones 6–9. It grows about 3 m (10') tall and spreads 2.5 m (8'), making it ideal for use in a border or as a hedge. The fruit ripens from orange to bright red.

PESTS & PROBLEMS

Unfortunately, Firethorn is susceptible to a few problems, the worst of which are fire blight and scab. Fire blight can kill the plant, and scab disfigures the fruit, turning it a sooty brown. A few less serious or less frequent problems are root rot, aphids, spider mites, scale insects and lace bugs.

Fiveleaf Akebia

Akebia

Features: foliage, habit, flowers, fruit
Habit: twining, deciduous climber
Height: 6–12 m (20–40') **Spread:** 6–12 m (20–40')
Planting: container; any time **Zones:** 4–8

Vigorous vines make gardeners uneasy, and Fiveleaf Akebia ranks right up there with Silver Lace Vine *(Polygonum aubertii)* for quick growth. It is highly ornamental but will twine, wrap and snake around anything in its way. It needs a watchful eye and firm restraint. Properly harnessed, it offers many landscape uses, from covering ugly fences to shading a dining area. The palmate leaves give the vine an unusual but handsome effect. This species is not widely used, so it still seems like a fresh discovery when it is encountered in a garden.

GROWING

Fiveleaf Akebia grows equally well in **full sun, light shade** or **partial shade**. The soil should be of **average to high fertility** and **well drained**. This vine tolerates dry or moist soils and full shade.

Pruning is essential with this vigorous vine. Cut it back as much and as often as needed to keep it under control.

The 5–10 cm (2–4") fruits of Fiveleaf Akebia are edible but not tasty.

TIPS

Though the flowers and fruit are interesting, this vine is worth growing for the foliage alone. Fiveleaf Akebia will twine up anything that gets in its way. A sturdy structure such as a porch railing, trellis, pergola, arbour or fence will quickly be covered by this vine. It can become invasive, so keep the pruning shears handy.

RECOMMENDED

A. quinata is a fast-growing vine. The new foliage is tinged purple in spring and matures to an attractive blue-green. Deep purple flowers are borne in spring, followed by sausage-like fruit pods. **'Alba'** bears white flowers and fruit.

Flowering Quince

Chaenomeles

Features: spring flowers, fruit, spines
Habit: spreading, deciduous shrubs with spiny branches
Height: 0.6–3 m (2–10') **Spread:** 0.6–4.5 m (2–15')
Planting: B & B, container; spring, fall **Zones:** 4–9

Flowering quinces are much overlooked plants in the garden and are often left to grow into a chaotic, impenetrable tangle. However, for gardeners developing artistic pruning techniques, these prickly plants provide a challenge and are worth the effort. Espalier and bonsai specimens reveal a side of flowering quinces that few ever try to find. Their unusual forms and clusters of attractive, delicate flowers will amply reward the artistic gardener.

GROWING

Flowering quinces grow equally well in **full sun** or **partial shade** but bear fewer flowers and fruit in shaded locations. The soil should be of **average fertility, moist** and **well drained**, and **slightly acidic** soil is preferred. These shrubs tolerate urban pollution.

Prune back about one-third of the old growth on established plants to the ground each year. Tidy plants by cutting back flowering shoots to a strong branch after flowering is finished.

The fruits of flowering quinces are edible when cooked.

TIPS

Flowering quinces can be included in a shrub or mixed border. They are very attractive grown against a wall. The spiny habit also makes them useful for barriers. Use them along the edge of a woodland or in a naturalistic garden. The dark bark stands out well in winter until the plants are buried under snow.

Leaf drop in mid- to late summer is usually caused by leaf spot. Try hiding the plant with later-flowering perennials.

RECOMMENDED

C. japonica (Japanese Flowering Quince) is a spreading shrub that grows 60–90 cm (24–36") tall and spreads up to 1.8 m (6'). Orange or red flowers appear in early to mid-spring, followed by small, fragrant, greenish-yellow fruit. This species is not as common as *C. speciosa* and its cultivars.

C. speciosa (Common Flowering Quince) is a large, tangled, spreading shrub. It grows 1.8–3 m (6–10') tall and spreads 1.8–4.5 m (6–15'). Red flowers emerge in spring and are followed by fragrant, greenish-yellow fruit. Many cultivars are available. **'Cameo'** has large, peach-pink double flowers. **'Texas Scarlet'** bears red flowers over a long period on plants about half the size of the species. **'Toyo-Nishiki'** is more upright than the species, and a mixture of white, pink and red flowers all appear on the same plant. (Zones 5–8.)

PESTS & PROBLEMS

In addition to leaf spot (see above), possible but not often serious problems include aphids, canker, fire blight, mites, rust and viruses.

C. speciosa 'Texas Scarlet' (this page)

Forsythia

Forsythia

Features: early- to mid-spring flowers
Habit: spreading, deciduous shrubs with upright or arching branches
Height: 1–3 m (3–10') **Spread:** 1.5–3.5 m (5–12')
Planting: B & B, container in spring or fall; bare-root in spring
Zones: 3–9

Forsythias may not deliver interest all year in the garden, but it is hard to shake our sentimental attachment to these shrubs. Perhaps our enduring fondness for forsythias is connected to childhood, when their blooming signalled the time to take off the winter boots, drag out the bikes and enjoy the promise of more warm days to come. As adults we may lament the forsythias' selfish claim to space in the garden, but those saturated yellow flowers still stir the soul.

GROWING

Forsythias grow best in **full sun** but tolerate light shade. The soil should be of **average fertility, moist** and **well drained.**

Correct pruning is essential to keep forsythias attractive. Flowers are produced on growth that is at least two years old. Prune after flowering is finished. On mature plants, one-third of the oldest growth can be cut right back to the ground.

Some gardeners trim these shrubs into a formal hedge, but this practice often results in uneven flowering. An informal hedge allows the plants to grow more naturally. Size can be restricted by cutting shoots back to a strong junction.

TIPS

These shrubs are gorgeous while in flower, but they aren't very exciting the rest of the year. Include one in a shrub or mixed border where other flowering plants will take over once the forsythia's early-season glory has passed.

The cold-hardiness designation for forsythias can be somewhat misleading. The plants themselves are very cold hardy, surviving in Zone 3 quite happily. The flowers, however, are not as tolerant because the buds form in summer and are then vulnerable to winter cold.

Gardeners in the warmest areas of Ontario will have no trouble getting this plant to flower consistently. In colder areas snowcover is often the deciding factor in flower bud survival. A tall shrub may flower only on the lower half—the part that was buried in, and protected by, snow. Don't despair, therefore, if your garden is outside the recommended region. If you have a good snowfall every year and choose a hardy cultivar,

F. x intermedia

Forsythias can be used as hedging plants, but they look most attractive when grown informally.

F. ovata 'Northern Gold'

pile some salt-free snow over the plant and you should be able to enjoy forsythia flowers each spring.

RECOMMENDED

***F.* 'Arnold Dwarf'** is an attractive, low, mounding shrub with long, trailing branches. It is sometimes listed as a cultivar of *F.* x *intermedia.* It generally grows about 90 cm (36") tall but can reach 1.8 m (6') tall, and it spreads up to 2 m (7'). The flowers are a slightly greenish yellow and are rather sparse on young plants, becoming more abundant on plants over six years old. This cultivar makes an interesting groundcover and can be used to prevent erosion on steep banks. (Zones 5–8.)

F.* x *intermedia is a large shrub with upright stems that arch as they mature. It grows 1.5–3 m (5–10') tall and spreads 1.5–3.5 m (5–12'). Yellow flowers emerge in early to mid-spring before the leaves. Many cultivars have been developed from this hybrid. **'Lynwood'** ('Lynwood Gold') reaches 3 m (10') in both height and width. The light yellow flowers open widely and are distributed evenly along the branches. **'Spectabilis'** grows to 3 m (10') in height and width. It bears bright yellow flowers that are more cold tolerant than those of the hybrid. (Zones 6–9.)

For an early touch of spring indoors, cut forsythia for forcing. Simply cut the dormant branches, smash the stem ends with a hammer and place in warm water. Change the water daily and you should have flowers in about a week.

Early-flowering forsythia brightens up the most drab landscapes, as in this community garden waiting for spring clean-up.

F. ovata (Early Forsythia) is an upright, spreading shrub that grows up to 1.8 m (6') tall. This species has the hardiest buds, and its flowers open in early spring. It has been crossed with other species to create more attractive, floriferous, hardy hybrids. **'Northern Gold'** is a hardy, upright shrub that develops a more arching habit as it matures. It grows 1.5–2.5 m (5–8') tall and spreads up to 3 m (10'). The bright yellow flowers are very cold hardy. **'Ottawa'** is another hardy cultivar, this one introduced by Agriculture Canada. It has a more compact, tidy growth habit. It grows to 1.5 m (5') tall.

Allow a clematis to twine through your forsythia for an ongoing display of flowers and colour.

PESTS & PROBLEMS

Most problems are not serious but may include root-knot nematodes, stem gall and leaf spot.

Forsythia was named after Scotsman William Forsyth (1737–1804), who served as superintendent of the Royal Gardens at Kensington Palace.

F. x intermedia

Fothergilla

Fothergilla

Features: spring flowers, scent, fall foliage
Habit: dense, rounded or bushy, deciduous shrubs
Height: 0.6–3 m (2–10') **Spread:** 0.6–3 m (2–10')
Planting: B & B, container; spring, fall **Zones:** 4–9

Fothergillas aren't available at every garden centre, but it is worth the extra effort to locate one of these charming shrubs. The spring flowers look like airy, white bottle brushes. Often fothergillas give a winning display of fall colour similar to that of witch-hazels, to which fothergillas are related. Fothergillas look lovely mixed in with rhododendrons and prefer the same conditions. I cannot achieve moist, acidic conditions in my garden, but I do have a Dwarf Fothergilla growing on my slope. It sulked for a few years but now looks perfectly healthy.

The name honours British physician John Fothergill (1712–80), who studied the cultivation of American plants.

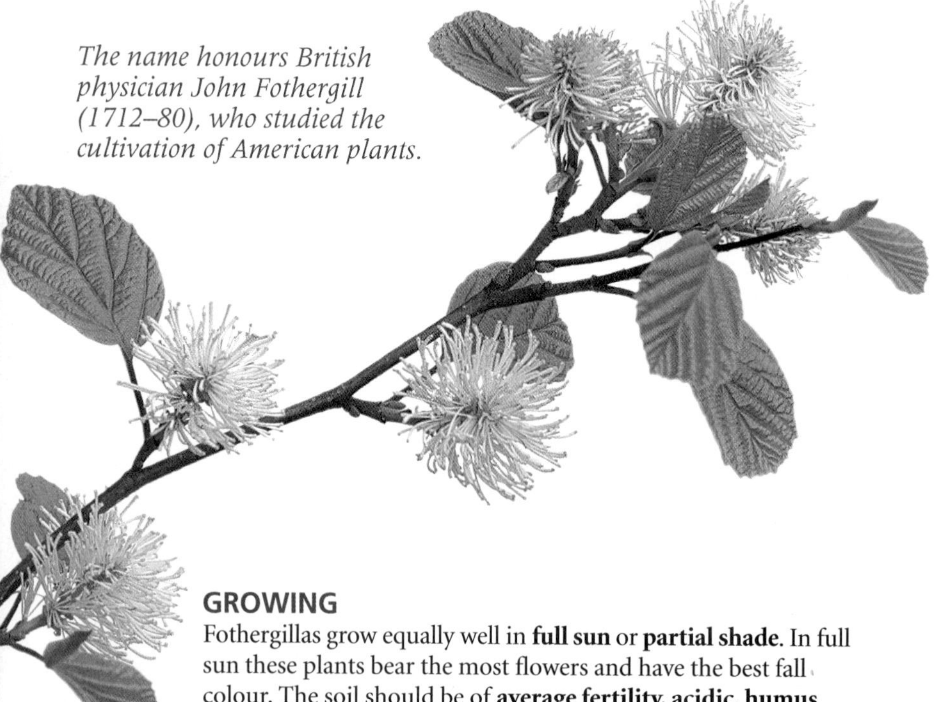

GROWING

Fothergillas grow equally well in **full sun** or **partial shade**. In full sun these plants bear the most flowers and have the best fall colour. The soil should be of **average fertility, acidic, humus rich, moist** and **well drained.**

These plants require little pruning. Remove wayward and dead branches as needed.

TIPS

Fothergillas are attractive and useful in shrub or mixed borders, in woodland gardens and when combined with evergreen groundcovers.

The bottle brush–shaped flowers of fothergillas have a delicate honey scent. Use these plants with rhododendrons and azaleas.

RECOMMENDED

F. gardenii (Dwarf Fothergilla) is a bushy shrub that grows 60–90 cm (24–36") tall, with an equal spread. In mid- to late spring it bears fragrant white flowers. The foliage turns yellow, orange and red in fall. **'Blue Mist'** is similar to the species, but the summer foliage is blue-green rather than dark green.

F. major (Large Fothergilla) is a rounded shrub that grows 1.8–3 m (6–10') tall, with an equal spread. The fall colours are yellow, orange and scarlet. **'Mount Airy'** is a more compact cultivar, growing 1.5–1.8 m (5–6') in height and width. It bears lots of flowers and has more consistent fall colour than the species.

F. major (this page)

Fringe Tree

Chionanthus

Features: early-summer flowers, bark, habit
Habit: rounded or spreading, deciduous large shrubs or small trees
Height: 3–7.5 m (10–25') **Spread:** 3–7.5 m (10–25')
Planting: B & B, container; spring **Zones:** 4–9

Tree aficionados do not have a single criticism of fringe trees. Over a long period in spring, they are densely covered in silk white, honey-scented flowers that shimmer in the wind. Though they like moisture, they adapt to a wide range of growing conditions, and they are cold hardy. Fringe trees can be grown as large shrubs or small trees and add sophistication and elegance to any garden. Because they take so long to propagate, they are not found in many garden centres. I have seen them at specialist nurseries and at sales put on by botanical gardens and by universities with arboretums. If you do get the chance to buy one, be sure to take it.

These small, pollution-tolerant trees are good choices for city gardens.

GROWING

Fringe trees prefer **full sun.** They do best in soil that is **fertile, acidic, moist** and **well drained** but will adapt to most soil conditions. In the wild they are often found growing alongside stream banks. Little pruning is required on mature plants. The stems can be thinned out when the plant is young to encourage an attractive habit. Prune after flowering.

TIPS

Fringe trees work well as specimen plants, as part of a border or beside a water feature. Plants begin flowering at a very early age.

These trees may not produce fruit because not all trees of a given species bear both female and male flowers. When fruit is produced it attracts birds.

Fringe trees can be very difficult to find in nurseries. Home gardeners who have seen how beautiful this tree can be may want to propagate them at home. Seeds planted outdoors in early or mid-summer will germinate after about two years. Semi-ripe cuttings or layerings can be started from Chinese Fringe Tree in mid- or late summer.

RECOMMENDED

C. retusus (Chinese Fringe Tree) is a rounded, spreading shrub or small tree. It grows 4.5–7.5 m (15–25') tall, with an equal spread. In early summer it bears erect, fragrant white flowers followed in late summer by dark blue fruit. The bark is deeply furrowed and peeling. (Zones 5–9.)

C. virginicus (White Fringe Tree) is a spreading small tree or large shrub. It grows 3–6 m (10–20') tall and has an equal or greater spread. In early summer it bears drooping, fragrant white flowers, followed only occasionally by dark blue fruit.

C. virginicus (this page)

PESTS & PROBLEMS

Fringe trees rarely have any serious problems but can be affected by borers, leaf spot, powdery mildew or canker.

Ginkgo

Ginko, Maidenhair Tree

Ginkgo

Features: summer and fall foliage, habit, fruit, bark
Habit: conical in youth, variable with age; deciduous tree
Height: 12–30 m (40–100') **Spread:** 3–30 m (10–100')
Planting: spring, fall **Zones:** 3–9

The leaves of ginkgo, with their shiny, leathery thickness and simple pleasing shape, leave a lasting impression, like those of the Tulip Tree and Sassafras. Unlike those trees, which prefer to grow in their native habitats, the Ginkgo is adaptable. It can be found growing happily next to bus routes or marooned in a sidewalk planting. In the home garden it starts out looking lean and hungry but develops into a tree of majestic proportions.

GROWING

Ginkgo prefers **full sun**. The soil should be **fertile, sandy** and **well drained**, but this tree adapts to most conditions. It is also tolerant of urban conditions and cold weather. Little or no pruning is necessary.

TIPS

Though its growth is very slow, Ginkgo eventually becomes a large tree that is best suited as a specimen tree in parks and large gardens. It can be used as a street tree. If you buy an unnamed plant, be sure it has been propagated from cuttings. Seed-grown trees may prove to be female, and the stinky fruit is not something you want dropping all over your lawn, driveway or sidewalk.

RECOMMENDED

G. biloba is variable in habit. It grows 15–30 m (50–100') tall, with an equal or greater spread. The leaves can turn an attractive shade of yellow in fall, after a few cool nights. Female plants are generally avoided because the fruits have a very unpleasant odour. Several cultivars are available. **'Autumn Gold'** is a broadly conical male cultivar. It grows 15 m (50') tall and 9 m (30') wide. Fall colour is bright yellow-gold. **'Princeton Sentry'** is a narrow, upright male cultivar. It grows 12–25 m (40–80') tall and spreads 3–7.5 m (10–25').

Ginkgo appears to have been saved from extinction by its long-time use in Asian temple gardens. Today this 'living fossil' grows almost entirely in horticultural settings.

PESTS & PROBLEMS

This tree seems to have outlived most of the pests that might have afflicted it. A leaf spot may affect Ginkgo, but it doesn't cause any real trouble.

The unique and beautiful leaves of Ginkgo are shaped like those of the Maidenhair Fern (inset).

Goldenchain Tree

Laburnum

Features: late-spring to early-summer flowers
Habit: spreading, deciduous tree
Height: 4.5–7.5 m (15–25')
Spread: 4.5–7.5 m (15–25')
Planting: B & B, container; spring
Zones: 5–7

When conditions are favourable, the Goldenchain Tree puts on an unforgettable spring show, with its many dangling clusters of sulphur yellow, wisteria-like flowers. In Ontario the conditions are rarely perfect for this display, because the Goldenchain Tree prefers a cooler, more even climate and can be short-lived when exposed to temperature extremes. Still, this tree is worth a try and some impressive specimens can be found in our province.

GROWING

Goldenchain Tree prefers **full sun** or **light shade**. The soil should be of **average fertility** and **well drained.** This tree tolerates alkaline soils. Plant it in light or afternoon shade in hot areas, because Goldenchain Tree is not heat tolerant.

This tree needs very little pruning, but it responds well to training and can be encouraged to grow over arbours, pergolas and other such structures.

TIPS

Goldenchain Tree can be used as a specimen tree in small gardens. This plant is not very attractive when not in flower. Plant an annual or perennial vine like a morning glory or clematis at the foot of your Goldenchain Tree, and let the vines climb up to provide summer flowers once the golden chains have faded.

All parts of this tree, but especially the seeds, contain a **poisonous** alkaloid. Children can be poisoned by eating the seeds, which resemble beans or peas.

RECOMMENDED

L.* x *watereri bears bright yellow flowers in pendulous clusters up to 25 cm (10") long. This plant lives longest in cool-summer climates. **'Vossii'** has a denser growth habit and bears flower clusters up to 60 cm (24") long. This cultivar can be trained to form an espalier.

PESTS & PROBLEMS

Goldenchain Tree may have occasional difficulties with aphids, canker, laburnum vein mosaic, leaf spot, mealybugs and twig blight.

Grape

Vitis

Features: summer and fall foliage, late-summer to fall fruit, habit
Habit: woody, climbing, deciduous vines
Height: 7–15 m (22–50') **Spread:** 7–15 m (22–50')
Planting: bare-root, container; spring **Zones:** 5–8

We usually think of grape vines for their wine-producing fruit and their winding habit that overruns trees and bushes in the wild, but they also work as ornamental plants for the garden and, in fact, are popular ornamental vines in Europe. It is possible to find grapes that offer handsome leaf colour and texture. Their fast-growing nature, dense habit and attractive foliage make them ideal for quickly creating privacy barriers and providing shade for porches.

GROWING

Grapes prefer **full sun** or **partial shade**. The soil should be **moist, acidic** and **well drained**. These plants tolerate most well-drained soils.

Trim grape plants to fit the space you have, in mid-winter and again in mid-summer. If you wish to train a grape more formally, cut the side shoots back to within two or three buds of the main stems. Such pruning encourages flowering and fruiting.

TIPS

Grape vines can be trained to grow up and over almost any sturdy structure. They may need to be tied in place until the basic structure is established.

The ripe fruit can attract wasps. Avoid planting this vine near the house if any family members are allergic to bee or wasp stings.

RECOMMENDED

V. cognetiae (Crimson Glory Vine) is a woody climber that can grow up to 15 m (50') tall. It has attractive scarlet fall colour and bears inedible, small, dark purple fruit. This species can be difficult to find.

V. rotundifolia (Muscadine Grape) can climb up to 9 m (30'). The purple or greenish-purple fruits are edible but quite bitter. Fall colour is yellow.

V. vinifera (Wine Grape) is a woody climber, best known for the wine grapes it produces. It also makes an attractive addition to the garden. It grows up to 7 m (22') tall and bears edible fruit. **'Purpurea'** (Purple-leaf Grape) is an attractive cultivar. It has inedible fruit. The leaves are the main attraction; greenish purple in summer, they turn dark purple in fall. (Zones 6–8.)

PESTS & PROBLEMS

Downy mildew, powdery mildew, canker, dieback, grey mould, black rot, root rot, leaf spot, grape leaf skeletonizer, scale insects and mealybugs are possible problems but they are not likely to be as serious in a garden with only one or two plants as they are in a vineyard.

V. vinifera (this page)

Though the fruits of garden grapes are edible, they can be quite bitter. They can be used to make jelly, juice or wine.

Hawthorn

Crataegus

Features: late-spring or early-summer flowers, fruit, foliage, thorny branches
Habit: rounded, deciduous trees, often with a zig-zag, layered branch pattern
Height: 4.5–9 m (15–30')
Spread: 3.5–9 m (12–30')
Planting: B & B, container; early spring
Zones: 3–8

The hawthorns are uncommonly beautiful trees, but their beauty comes with a price. Hawthorns are susceptible to blight and rust diseases. The trouble shows up in late summer, long after the hawthorns have put on their generous spring show of beautiful, apple-like blossoms. In addition to their welcome spring fling, hawthorns also produce glossy red fruit which persists into winter. The fruit, along with the tree's rough-hewn beauty, gives the hawthorn a strong winter presence.

Hawthorn fruits are edible but dry and seedy. Some people use them to make jelly or ferment them and mix them with brandy.

GROWING

Hawthorns grow equally well in **full sun** or **partial shade**. They adapt to any well-drained soil and tolerate urban conditions.

When grown as trees, hawthorns need little pruning. Those grown as hedges can be pruned after flowering or in fall. Remove any dead or diseased growth immediately, to prevent the spread of diseases such as fire blight and rust.

Hawthorns can become weedy, with seedlings and suckers popping up unexpectedly. Remove any that you find while they are young, because they become quite tenacious once they get bigger.

C. laevigata 'Paul's Scarlet' (this page)

TIPS

Hawthorns can be grown as specimen plants or hedges in urban sites, lakeside gardens and exposed locations. They are popular in areas where vandalism is a problem because very few people wish to grapple with plants bearing stiff 5 cm (2") long thorns. As a hedge, hawthorns create an almost impenetrable barrier.

These trees are small enough to include in most gardens. With the long, sharp thorns, however, a hawthorn might not be a good selection if there are children about.

RECOMMENDED

C. laevigata *(C. oxycantha)* (English Hawthorn) is a low-branching, rounded tree with zig-zag layers of thorny branches. It grows 4.5–7.5 m (15–25') tall and spreads 3.5–7.5 m (12–25'). White or pink late-spring flowers are followed by red fruit in late summer. Many cultivars are available. **'Paul's Scarlet'**('Paulii,' 'Coccinea Plena') has many showy, deep pink double flowers. (Zones 4–8.)

C. phaenopyrum *(C. cordata)* (Washington Hawthorn) is an oval to rounded, thorny tree. It grows 7.5–9 m (25–30') tall and spreads 6–9 m (20–30'). It bears white flowers from early to mid-summer and has persistent shiny red fruit in fall. The glossy green foliage turns red and orange in fall. This species is least susceptible to fire blight.

The hawthorns are members of the rose family, and their fragrant flowers call to mind the scent of apple blossoms.

PESTS & PROBLEMS

Borers, caterpillars, leaf miners, skeletonizers, scale insects, fire blight, canker, rust, powdery mildew, scab and fungal leaf spot are all possible problems. Healthy, stress-free plants will be less susceptible.

The genus name Crataegus *comes from the Greek* kratos, *'strength,' in reference to the hard, fine-grained wood.*

C. laevigata (all photos)

Hazel
Filbert, Corylus
Corylus

Features: early-spring catkins, nuts, foliage, habit
Habit: large, dense, deciduous shrubs or small trees
Height: 2.5–6 m (8–20') **Spread:** 3–4.5 m (10–15')
Planting: B & B, container; spring, fall **Zones:** 3–9

Plant connoisseurs love the exotic-looking Corkscrew Hazel, also known by the wonderfully quirky name of Harry Lauder's Walking Stick. This hazel is at its best in winter, when the bare branches look like electrocuted spaghetti, and cut branches are magical in flower arrangements. I have grown the charming Golden European Filbert. The catkins dominate the shrub in late winter and add a delicate, wispy air. The bright yellow foliage that emerges in spring is a welcome sight after the grey of winter, and this shrub seems to grow effortlessly even in dry soil.

C. avellana *is grown for commercial nut production, both for the delicious nuts themselves and for the extracted oil.*

GROWING

Hazel plants grow equally well in **full sun** or **partial shade**. The soil should be **fertile** and **well drained**. These plants require very little pruning but tolerate it well. Entire plants can be cut back to within 15 cm (6") of the ground to encourage new growth in spring. On grafted specimens of Corkscrew Hazel, suckers that come up from the roots can be cut out and will be easy to spot because they will not have the twisted habit.

TIPS

These plants can be used as specimens or in shrub or mixed borders.

RECOMMENDED

C. avellana (European Hazel, European Filbert) grows as a large shrub or small tree. It reaches 3.5–6 m (12–20') in height and spreads up to 4.5 m (15'). Male plants bear long, dangling catkins in late winter and early spring, and female plants develop edible nuts. Cultivars are more

C. avellana 'Contorta' (below & above right)

commonly grown than the species. **'Aurea'** (Golden European Filbert, Yellow-leaved European Filbert) has bright yellow foliage that matures to light green in summer. **'Contorta'** (Corkscrew Hazel, Harry Lauder's Walking Stick) is perhaps the best known cultivar. It grows 2.5–3 m (8–10') tall. The stems and leaves are twisted and contorted. This is a particularly interesting feature in winter, when the bare stems are most visible. Cut out any growth that is not twisted.

Forked hazel branches have been used as divining rods to find underground water or precious metals.

Another name for Corkscrew Hazel is Harry Lauder's Walking Stick, named after the gnarled, twisted cane the famous vaudeville comedian used.

C. maxima (Giant Filbert) is a large shrub or small tree that is rarely seen in cultivation. More common is **var. *purpurea***, the Purple Giant Filbert. It adds deep purple colour to the spring garden. The rich colour usually fades in the heat of summer to dark green. The best leaf colour develops in full sun. This variety grows 3–3.5 m (10–12') tall, with an equal spread. It is a fine addition to the garden and adapts to many soils.

PESTS & PROBLEMS

Powdery mildew, blight, Japanese beetles, canker, fungal leaf spot, rust, bud mites, tent caterpillars and webworm may cause occasional problems.

C. avellana 'Contorta' (this page)

Heather

Spring Heath, Winter Heath

Erica

Features: late-winter to mid-spring flowers, foliage, habit
Habit: low, spreading, evergreen shrubs
Height: 15–30 cm (6–12") **Spread:** 20–60 cm (8–24")
Planting: container; spring **Zones:** 5–7

Heather looks so alluring at those indoor spring garden shows. Gardeners full of faith and hope take the plants home to their still frozen landscapes. Before plunking one of these plants in the ground, give it a decent chance at survival. Provide moist, well-drained conditions and acidic soil if you can swing it, then hope for the best. If you've gone to the effort to establish good rhododendron beds, then plant your Heather there.

GROWING

Heather prefers **full sun** but tolerates partial shade. The soil should be of **average fertility, acidic, moist** and **well drained**. Though it prefers acidic conditions and enjoys having peat moss mixed in to the soil, this plant will tolerate alkaline soil. Do not overfertilize.

To keep the plants compact and tidy, shear new growth to within 2.5 cm (1") of the previous year's growth once flowering is finished.

The centre of each clump tends to mat down and dry out. Use a claw tool to fluff the soil in the middle of the mound in early spring.

TIPS

Heather plants make excellent groundcovers or rock garden plants. They can be combined with other acid-loving plants in a shrub or mixed border. If you aren't having a lot of luck with them, try a small planting where the soil and conditions can be more easily adjusted to suit Heather's needs.

E. carnea (this page)

RECOMMENDED

E. carnea bears pinkish-purple flowers in late winter. The species and its many cultivars, which are more commonly available, grow to 30 cm (12") high and 60 cm (24") wide. **'Ghost Hill'** has red flowers, **'Springwood Pink'** has light pink flowers and **'Springwood White'** has white flowers.

PESTS & PROBLEMS

Rare problems with rust, verticillium wilt, root rot or powdery mildew are possible.

Hemlock

Tsuga

Features: foliage, habit, cones
Habit: pyramidal or columnar, evergreen tree or shrub
Height: 1.5–25 m (5–80') **Spread:** 1.8–10 m (6–35')
Planting: B & B, container; spring, fall **Zones:** 3–8

Many people are biased against evergreens. Their stiffness, density and blocky shapes can be difficult to blend into gardens. But evergreen indifference can be cured with an introduction to the Canadian Hemlock. The movement, softness and agility of this tree makes it easy to place in the landscape. At any age its pyramidal shape is pleasing, soft and open.

One nursery grower I know believes that if you can nurse Hemlock through a few seasons, it becomes more tolerant of drought and winter wind. I hope so.

GROWING

Hemlock generally grows well in any light from **full sun to full shade**. The soil should be **humus rich, moist** and **well drained**. It is drought sensitive and grows best in cool, moist conditions. It is also sensitive to air pollution and suffers salt damage, so keep Hemlock away from roadways.

Hemlock trees need little pruning. The cultivars can be pruned to control their growth as required. Trim hemlock hedges in summer.

TIPS

This elegant tree, with its delicate needles, is one of the most beautiful evergreens to use as a specimen tree. Hemlock can also be trimmed to form a hedge. The smaller cultivars may be included in a shrub or mixed border.

With the continued popularity of water gardening, Hemlock is in demand for the naturalizing effect it has on pondscapes.

Hemlock can be pruned to keep it within bounds or shaped to form a hedge. The many dwarf forms are useful in smaller gardens.

This Hemlock is not poisonous, bearing no relation to the herb that killed Socrates.

Don't cut the evergreen boughs for use as holiday decorations. The needles drop quickly once the branches are cut.

'Jeddeloh' (below)

RECOMMENDED

T. canadensis (Eastern Hemlock, Canadian Hemlock) is a graceful, narrowly pyramidal tree that grows 12–25 m (40–80') tall and spreads 7.5–10 m (25–35'). It is a native tree in Ontario's woodlands. Many cultivars are available, including groundcovers and dwarf forms. **'Jeddeloh'** is a rounded, mound-forming, slow-growing cultivar. It grows 1.5 m (5') tall and spreads 1.8 m (6').

'Sargentii' ('Pendula') is a spreading, mounding form with long, pendulous branches. It grows 3–4.5 m (10–15') tall and spreads 6–9 m (20–30'). It can be trimmed back to restrict its growth.

The name Tsuga *is derived from a Japanese word meaning 'tree-mother.'*

PESTS & PROBLEMS

Healthy, stress-free trees have few problems. Possible problems may be caused by grey mould, rust, needle blight, snow blight, weevils, mites, aphids, woolly adelgids or scale insects.

'Jeddeloh' (below)

Holly

Ilex

Features: spiny foliage, fruit, habit
Habit: erect or spreading, evergreen or deciduous shrubs or trees
Height: 1.8–15 m (6–50') **Spread:** 1.8–12 m (6–40')
Planting: B & B, container; spring, fall **Zones:** 3–9

Until the introduction of the Blue Series cultivars, the only holly most northerners could get was wrapped in plastic at a florist's shop. Now cold-hardy hollies such as 'Blue Boy,' 'Blue Girl' and 'Blue Stallion' offer lustrous blue-green leaves and excellent red berries on the females. The beautiful American Holly, which can grow in warmer areas of the Niagara Peninsula, grows to the size of a large Christmas tree, with dark green shiny leaves and abundant fruit. The deciduous holly Winterberry has bright red fruit that persists into January, adding winter interest. To come across a sunny patch of it is like stumbling into a red fog. It likes moisture, I know. I planted two of these plants in my desert-like garden, and the dead stems are there to remind me of my foolishness.

GROWING

These plants prefer **full sun** but tolerate partial shade. The soil should be of **average to rich fertility, humus rich, moist** and **well drained**. Shelter from winter wind helps prevent the leaves from drying out. Apply a summer mulch to keep the roots cool and moist. Grown as shrubs, hollies require little pruning. Damaged growth can be removed in spring. Trim plants grown as hedges in summer. Dispose of all trimmings carefully to prevent the spiny leaves from puncturing bare feet and paws.

TIPS

Hollies can be used in groups, in woodland gardens and in shrub and mixed borders. They can also be used as hedge plants.

Male and female flowers occur on separate plants and both must be present for the females to set fruit. One male will adequately pollinate two to three females.

The showy, scarlet berries look tempting, especially to children, but are not edible.

RECOMMENDED

I.* x *meserveae (Blue Holly) is an erect or spreading, dense shrub. It grows 3–4.5 m (10–15') tall, with an equal spread, and bears glossy red fruits that persist into winter. Tolerant of pruning, it makes a formidable hedge or barrier. Many cultivars have been developed, often available in male and female pairs. The males and females can be mixed and matched. **'Blue Boy'** and **'Blue Girl'** grow about 3 m (10') tall, with an equal spread. 'Blue Girl' bears abundant red berries. Both are quite cold hardy. **'Blue Prince'** and **'Blue Princess'** have larger leaves, and 'Blue Princess' bears even more fruit than 'Blue Girl.' These cultivars grow 3–3.5 m (10–12') tall, with an equal spread. (Zones 5–8.)

I. meserveae 'Blue Princess' (above)

I. opaca (below)

I. opaca (American Holly) is an excellent tree holly that grows 12–15 m (40–50') tall and spreads 6–12 m (20–40'). The form is often neatly pyramidal when young, becoming more open at maturity. Leaves and fruits vary among the many cultivars; ask at your local garden centre for the types that grow best in your area. (Zones 5–9.)

I. verticillata (Winterberry, Winterberry Holly) is deciduous and grown for its explosion of red fruit that persists into winter. It is good for naturalizing in moist sites in the garden. It grows 1.8–2.5 m (6–8') tall, sometimes taller, with an equal spread.

PESTS & PROBLEMS

Aphids may attack young shoots. Scale insects and leaf miners can present problems, as can root rot in poorly drained soils.

Honeysuckle

Lonicera

Features: flowers, habit, fruit
Habit: rounded, upright shrub or twining climber; deciduous or semi-evergreen
Height: 1.8–6 m (6–20') **Spread:** 1.8–6 m (6–20')
Planting: container, bare-root; spring **Zones:** 3–8

Honeysuckles can be immense shrubs or rampant twining vines. They require careful consideration and placement so that they do not overrun your garden. Maybe my neighbour had the right idea: she planted a climbing honeysuckle in a half barrel, let it frolic up her front stair railing and always kept shears nearby.

GROWING

Honeysuckles grow well in **full sun** and **partial shade**. The soil should be **average to fertile** and **well drained**. Climbing honeysuckles prefer a **moist**, **humus-rich** soil.

One-third of old growth can be removed each year from shrubby honeysuckles once flowering is complete. Trim back climbing honeysuckles in spring as needed to keep them where you want them. Trim hedges twice a year to keep them neat.

L. x *heckrottii* (above)

TIPS

Shrubby honeysuckles can be used in mixed borders, in naturalized gardens and as hedges. Most are large and take up a lot of space when mature. Climbing honeysuckles can be trained to grow up a trellis, fence, arbour or other structure.

RECOMMENDED

L. fragrantissima (Winter Honeysuckle) is a large, bushy, deciduous or semi-evergreen shrub. It grows 2–3 m (6–10') high, with an equal spread. Over a long period in early or mid-spring it bears small, fragrant, creamy flowers. (Zones 4–8.)

L. x *brownii* 'Dropmore Scarlet' (below & right)

L. sempervirens (Trumpet Honeysuckle, Coral Honeysuckle) is a twining, deciduous climber. It grows 3–6 m (10–20') tall and can spread equally to fill the space provided. It bears orange or red flowers in late spring and early summer. There are many cultivars available with flowers in yellow, red or scarlet. **'Sulphurea'** bears yellow flowers. *L. sempervirens* is also a parent of many hybrids, including ***L.* x *brownii*** (Scarlet Trumpet Honeysuckle, Brown's Honeysuckle), which bears red or orange flowers in summer. **'Dropmore Scarlet'** is a cultivar of this hybrid. It is one of the hardiest of the climbing honeysuckles, cold hardy to Zone 4. It bears bright red flowers for most of the summer. ***L.* x *heckrottii*** (Goldflame Honeysuckle) bears fragrant, pink and yellow flowers profusely in spring and sporadically into fall. (Zones 5–8.)

L. tatarica (above)
L. sempervirens (below)

L. x *brownii* 'Dropmore Scarlet' (below)

L. tatarica (Tatarian Honeysuckle) is a large, bushy, suckering, deciduous shrub that grows 3–3.5 m (10–12') tall, with an equal spread. It bears pink, white or red flowers in late spring and early summer.

PESTS & PROBLEMS

Occasional problems with aphids, leaf miners, leaf rollers, scale insects, powdery mildew and blight can occur.

Honeysuckle flowers are often scented and attract hummingbirds as well as bees and other pollinating insects.

L. x *heckrottii* (above)

Hornbeam

Carpinus

Features: habit, fall colour **Habit:** pyramidal, deciduous tree
Height: 3–20 m (30–70') **Spread:** 3–15 m (10–50')
Planting: B & B; spring **Zones:** 3–9

The native American Hornbeam is also called Ironwood or Bluebeech. The trunks look like bulging muscles, and the very strong wood was used by early settlers to make wedges for splitting other logs. The European Hornbeam shares many qualities with the American Hornbeam. Both are slow growing and therefore useful for small yards. In the wild they are understorey trees, very tolerant of shade. In the home garden this means they can be planted underneath mammoth older trees to create a pleasing visual balance. Their leaves remain a bright, fresh green through the oppressive humidity of summer. The hornbeams may not be spectacular, but they do look good 12 months of the year.

GROWING

Hornbeams prefer **full sun** and tolerate partial shade. The soil should be **average to fertile** and **well drained**.

Pruning is rarely required, though it is tolerated. Remove damaged, diseased and awkward branches as needed; hedges can be trimmed in late summer.

TIPS

These small- to medium-sized trees can be used as specimens or shade trees in smaller gardens or can be pruned to form hedges. The narrow, upright cultivars are often used to create barriers and windbreaks.

RECOMMENDED

C. betulus (European Hornbeam) is a pyramidal to rounded tree. It grows 12–20 m (40–70') tall and spreads 9–15 m (30–50'). The foliage turns bright yellow or orange in fall. **'Columnaris'** is a narrow, slow-growing cultivar. It grows 9 m (30') tall and spreads 6 m (20'). **'Fastigiata'** is an upright cultivar that is narrow when young but broadens as it matures. It grows 15 m (50') tall and spreads 12 m (40'). **'Pendula'** is a mound-forming, prostrate cultivar that is usually grafted to a standard to create a weeping tree. (Zones 4–8.)

C. caroliniana (American Hornbeam, Ironwood, Musclewood, Bluebeech) is a small, slow-growing tree, tolerant of shade and city conditions. It grows 3–9 m (10–30') tall, with an equal spread. This species prefers moist soil conditions and grows well near ponds and streams. The foliage turns yellow to red or purple in fall.

PESTS & PROBLEMS

Rare problems with powdery mildew, canker, dieback and rot can occur.

Propagation of these plants can be quite complicated; it is easier to purchase plants that someone else has had to fuss over.

C. betulus (this page)

Horsechestnut

Buckeye

Aesculus

Features: early-summer flowers, foliage, spiny fruit
Habit: rounded or spreading, deciduous trees
Height: 2.5–25 m (8–80') **Spread:** 2.5–20 m (8–70')
Planting: B & B, container; spring, fall **Zones:** 3–9

Horsechestnuts range from trees with immense regal bearing to small but impressive shrubs. The Common Horsechestnut deserves its status as the kingly tree of parks and large gardens. Red Horsechestnut bears spectacular red flowers in spring. In a smaller yard, two shrubby horsechestnuts are worth considering—Bottlebrush Buckeye is a multi-stemmed shrub that produces big, white wands of flowers in June. It is tolerant of shade and looks lovely with a backdrop of evergreens, or perhaps a dark clapboard wall. Red Buckeye is another low-growing shrubby type that develops remarkable cherry red flowers. It loves moisture and tolerates light shade, and its leaves are very handsome as they begin to unfurl in spring.

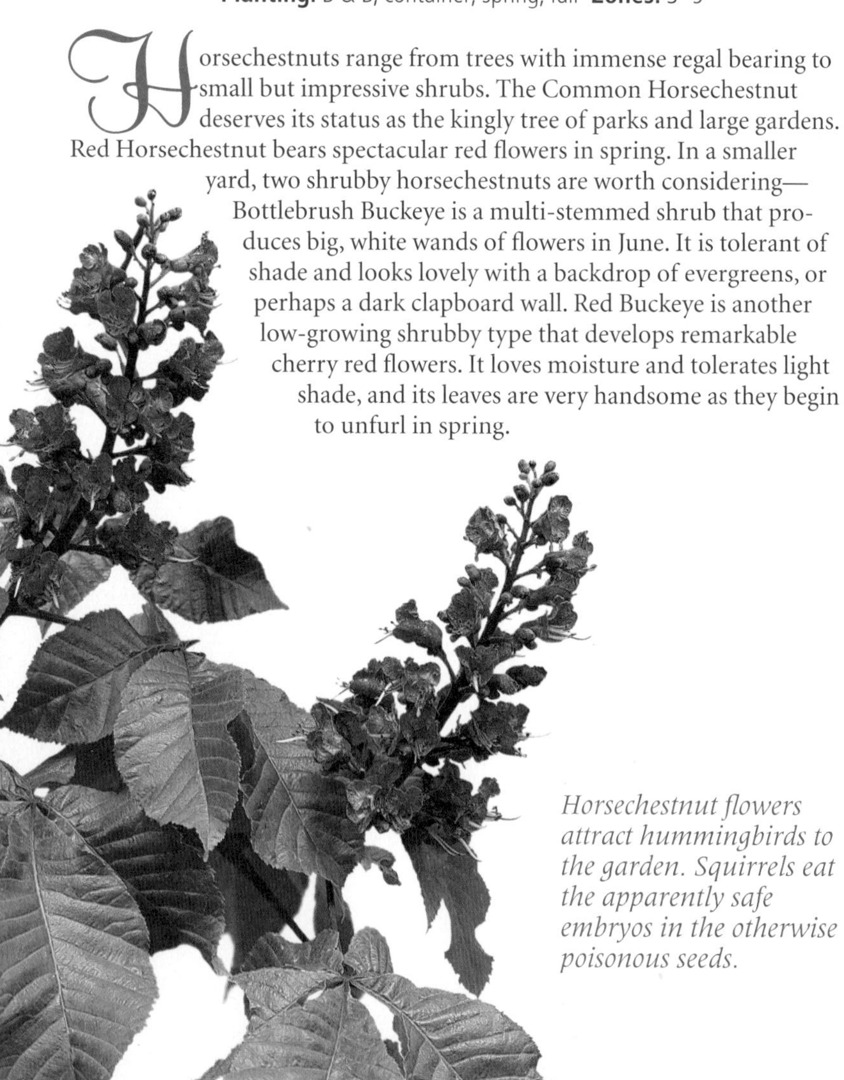

Horsechestnut flowers attract hummingbirds to the garden. Squirrels eat the apparently safe embryos in the otherwise poisonous seeds.

GROWING

Horsechestnuts grow well in **full sun** or **partial shade**. The soil should be **fertile, moist** and **well drained**. These trees dislike excessive drought. Little pruning is required. Remove wayward branches in winter or early spring.

A. hippocastanum (this page)

TIPS

Horsechestnuts are used as specimen and shade trees. The roots of horsechestnuts can break up sidewalks and patios if planted too close.

The smaller, shrubby horsechestnuts grow well near pond plantings and also make interesting specimens. Give them plenty of space as they can form large colonies.

These trees give heavy shade, which is excellent for cooling buildings but makes it difficult to grow grass beneath the trees.

The entire tree and especially the **seeds** contain a **poisonous** compound that breaks down blood proteins. People have been poisoned when they confused the nuts with edible sweet chestnuts (*Castanea* species).

RECOMMENDED

A.* x *carnea (Red Horsechestnut) is a dense, rounded to spreading tree. It grows 9–20 m (30–70') tall, with a spread of 9–15 m (30–50'). It is smaller than the Common Horsechestnut, but needs more regular water in summer. Spikes of dark pink flowers are borne in late spring and early summer. **'Briotii'** has large, lobed leaves and stunning red flowers in spring. It grows 6–10 m (25–40') with an equal spread. Not

A. glabra

as hardy as the species, this cultivar is hardy in Zones 5–9. **'O'Neill'** grows slowly to 10 m (35') in height and bears bright red flowers. (Zones 4–8.)

A. glabra (Ohio Buckeye) is native to central and eastern North America. It is a rounded tree with a dense canopy and grows 6–12 m (20–40') tall, with an equal spread. The flowers are not very showy and the fruit is not as spiny as that of other horsechestnuts. This species is very susceptible to scorch and will look best when grown in damp naturalized conditions such as next to a stream or pond. (Zones 3–7.)

A. hippocastanum (Common Horsechestnut) is a large rounded tree that will branch right to the ground if grown in an open setting. It grows 15–25 m (50–80') tall and spreads 12–20 m (40–70'). The flowers, borne in spikes up to 30 cm (12") long, appear in late spring; they are white with yellow or pink marks. (Zones 3–7.)

A. x carnea

A. parviflora (Bottlebrush Buckeye) is a spreading, mound-forming, suckering shrub. It grows 2.5–3.5 m (8–12') tall and spreads 2.5–4.5 m (8–15'). The plant is covered with spikes of creamy white flowers in mid-summer. It is well worth considering for gardens because it is small and not susceptible to the problems that plague its larger cousins. (Zones 4–9.)

A. pavia (Red Buckeye) is a low-growing to rounded shrubby tree, growing 4.5–6 m (15–20') tall, with an equal spread. The flowers are cherry red, and the leaves are among the most handsome of the horsechestnuts'. It needs consistent moisture. (Zones 4–8.)

A. glabra (above)
A. hippocastanum (below)

PESTS & PROBLEMS

Horsechestnuts are most susceptible to disease when under stress. Canker, leaf scorch, leaf spot, scale insects, anthracnose, rust and powdery mildew can all cause problems.

Hydrangea

Hydrangea

Features: flowers, habit
Habit: deciduous; mounding shrubs, woody climbers, spreading shrubs or trees
Height: 1–25 m (3–80') **Spread:** 1–6 m (3–20')
Planting: container; spring, fall **Zones:** 3–9

Hydrangeas have many attractive qualities. My favourite is the Oakleaf Hydrangea. In fall you could take dozens of pictures and still not capture every nuance of the ever-changing colour. The oak-shaped leaves range from burgundy and maroon to cherry and bronze. The long, showy, white flowers open in spring and persist for weeks. This hydrangea does best in moist, organically rich soil, but even in the impoverished conditions of my garden it remains impeccable and exciting.

GROWING

Hydrangeas grow well in **full sun** or **partial shade**, and some species tolerate full shade. Shade or partial shade will reduce leaf and flower scorch in the hotter regions. The soil should be of **average to high fertility, humus rich, moist** and **well drained**. These plants perform best in cool, moist conditions. Pruning requirements vary from species to species. See the Recommended section for specific suggestions.

TIPS

Hydrangeas come in many forms and have many uses in the landscape. They can be included in shrub or mixed borders, used as specimens or informal barriers and planted in groups or containers. Climbing varieties can be trained up walls, pergolas and arbours.

Hydrangea flowerheads consist of inconspicuous fertile flowers and showy sterile flowers. Hortensia-type flowerheads consist almost entirely of showy sterile flowers clustered together to form a globe shape. Lacecap-type flowerheads consist of a combination of sterile and fertile flowers. The showy flowers form a loose ring around the fertile ones, giving the flowerhead a delicate, lacy appearance.

The leaves and buds of some hydrangeas, but apparently not those of *H. paniculata* 'Grandiflora,' can cause **cyanide poisoning** if eaten or if the smoke is inhaled. Avoid burning hydrangea clippings.

RECOMMENDED

H. anomala* subsp. *petiolaris *(H. petiolaris)* (Climbing Hydrangea) is considered by some gardeners to be the most elegant climbing plant

H. arborescens 'Annabelle' with lupins and pansies.

Hortensia flowerheads can be used in dried or fresh flower arrangements. For the longest-lasting fresh flowers, water the soil around the plant deeply the evening before to help keep the petals from wilting when the flowers are cut.

H. paniculata

available. It clings to any rough surface by means of little rootlets that sprout from the stems. It grows 15–25 m (50–80') tall. Though this plant is shade tolerant, it will produce the best flowers when exposed to some direct sun each day. The leaves are a dark, glossy green and sometimes show yellow fall colour. For more than a month in summer the vine is covered with white lacecap flowers, and the entire plant appears to be veiled in a lacy mist. This hydrangea can be pruned after flowering, if required, to restrict its growth. It can be trained to grow up walls, trees and fences. It will also grow over rocks and can be used as a groundcover. With careful pruning and some support when young, it can be trained to form a small tree or shrub. (Zones 4–9.)

H. arborescens (Smooth Hydrangea) forms a rounded shrub 1–1.5 m (3–5') tall, with an equal width. This plant tolerates shady conditions. It is grown as a perennial in most of Ontario with new growth forming from the base each year. The plants flower on new growth each year and will look most attractive if cut right back to the ground in fall. The flowers of the species are not very showy, but the cultivars have large, showy blossoms. **'Annabelle'** bears large, ball-like clusters of white hortensia flowers. A single flowerhead may be up to 30 cm (12") in diameter. This cultivar is more compact than the species and is useful for brightening up a shady wall or corner of the garden.

H. paniculata (Panicle Hydrangea) is a spreading to upright large shrub or small tree. It grows 3–7 m (10–22') tall and spreads to 2.5 m (8'). It bears white flowers from late summer to early fall. This plant requires little pruning. When young it can be pruned to encourage a shrub-like or tree-like habit. The entire shrub can be cut to within 30 cm (12") of the ground each fall to encourage vigorous new growth the next summer. **'Grandiflora'** (Pee Gee Hydrangea) is a spreading large shrub or small tree 4.5–7.5 m (15–25') tall and 3–6 m (10–20') in spread. The mostly sterile flowers are borne in hortensia clusters up to 45 cm (18") long. (Zones 4–8.)

H. quercifolia (Oak-leaf Hydrangea) is a mound-forming shrub with attractive, cinnamon brown, exfoliating bark. It grows 1.2–2.5 m (4–8') tall, with an equal spread. The large leaves are lobed like an oak's and often turn bronze or bright red in fall. Conical clusters of sterile and fertile flowers last from mid-summer to fall. Pruning can be done after flowering. Remove spent flowers and cut out some of the older growth to encourage young replacement growth.
'Snowflake' bears clusters of double flowers 30–45 cm (12–15") long that open white and fade to pink as they age. The flowers are so heavy that they cause the stems to arch towards the ground. This cultivar prefers partial shade. (Zones 4–8.)

PESTS & PROBLEMS

Occasional problems for hydrangeas include grey mould, slugs, powdery mildew, rust, ringspot virus and leaf spot. Hot sun and excessive wind will dry out the petals and turn them brown.

H. anomala subsp. *petiolaris* (above)
H. paniculata 'Grandiflora' (below)

Japanese Pagoda-Tree

Sophora

Features: fall foliage, fragrant summer flowers, habit
Habit: dense, rounded, wide-spreading, deciduous tree
Height: 3–15 m (10–50') **Spread:** 3–15 m (10–50')
Planting: B & B, container; spring, fall **Zones:** 4–7

If you have the space and are looking for an undemanding, stately tree for the garden, consider the Japanese Pagoda-tree. It will reach a grand size but has the valuable quality of casting a light shade, so turf grass and other groundcovers can grow beneath it. It flowers at a useful time, in July and August, when the creamy flowers take the edge off the scorching summer heat. This refined tree adapts to urban conditions and brings serenity to the garden.

GROWING

Japanese Pagoda-tree grows best in **full sun**. The soil should be of **average fertility** and **well drained**. Once established, this species tolerates most conditions, even polluted urban settings. Pruning is rarely required.

TIPS

Use Japanese Pagoda-tree as a specimen tree or a shade tree. The cultivar 'Pendula' can be used in borders.

Plant in a sheltered location and provide some protection to young trees, which can be quite tender until they are established.

The **seeds** are **poisonous** and can even be fatal if eaten.

RECOMMENDED

S. japonica may reach heights of 30 m (100') in the wild, but usually grows to about 15 m (50') in garden settings. It grows quickly to about 6 m (20'), then growth is much slower. It bears fragrant white flowers in summer, and the foliage may turn yellow in fall. **'Pendula'** has long, drooping branches that are usually grafted to a standard, creating a small but dramatic weeping tree. The size depends on the height of the standard, usually 3–7.5 m (10–25'), with an equal or greater spread. This cultivar rarely flowers.

PESTS & PROBLEMS

Possible problems can be caused by twig blight, verticillium wilt, canker, rust, powdery mildew and leafhoppers.

This tree might be considered messy when the flowers drop, but the blanket of delicate petals beneath the tree is really quite attractive.

Juniper

Juniperus

Features: foliage, variety of colour, size and habit
Habit: evergreen; conical or columnar trees, rounded or spreading shrubs, prostrate groundcovers
Height: 0.2–21 m (0.5–70') **Spread:** 1–7.5 m (3–25')
Planting: B & B, container; spring, fall **Zones:** 3–9

I think there may a juniper in every gardener's future, with all the choices available. The handsome Creeping Juniper will hug the ground tenaciously. Shore Juniper is content in dry, sandy soil and tolerates salt. I am fond of my Eastern Redcedar. It's tough, resilient, aromatic and artistic. Many of its cultivars start off with a pyramidal shape but become more open and intriguing as they age. Junipers are good space-saving evergreens for small gardens.

GROWING

Junipers prefer **full sun** but tolerate light shade. Ideally the soil should be of **average fertility** and **well drained**, but these plants tolerate most conditions.

Very overgrown junipers can be pruned back hard but often lose their attractive form. It may be better to remove an overgrown specimen and start over with a plant that will not get as big.

Though these evergreens rarely need pruning, they tolerate it well. They can be used for topiary and can be trimmed in summer as required to maintain their shape or limit their size.

TIPS

With the wide variety of junipers available, there are endless uses for them in the garden. They make prickly barriers and hedges, and they can be used in borders, as specimens or in groups. The larger species can be used to form windbreaks, while the low-growing species can be used in rock gardens and as groundcovers.

The prickly foliage gives some gardeners a rash. It is a good idea to wear long sleeves and gloves when handling junipers. Juniper 'berries' are **poisonous** if eaten in large quantities.

RECOMMENDED

J. chinensis (Chinese Juniper) is a conical tree or spreading shrub. It grows 15–21 m (50–70') tall and spreads 4.5–6 m (15–20'). Many cultivars have been developed from

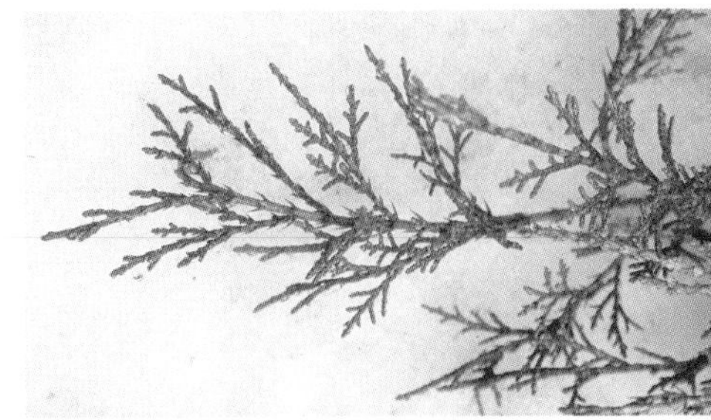

J. chinensis 'Pfitzeriana' (above)

J. horizontalis (centre)

J. squamata

this species. **'Hetzii'** is a large, upright, spreading shrub that may reach 1.5–4.5 m (5–15') in height, with an equal spread. **'Pfitzeriana'** is a wide-spreading shrub that grows 1.5–3 m (5–10') tall, with an equal spread. 'Hetzii' and 'Pfitzeriana' still appear in many gardens, but they are beginning to be passed over in favour of the new, attractive, more reasonably sized cultivars derived from them. **'Hetzii Columnaris'** forms an attractive, narrow pyramid about 6 m (20') tall. **'Pfitzeriana Compacta'** is a dwarf form cultivar that grows about 1.2 m (4') tall, with an equal or greater spread. **Var. *sargentii*** (Sargent Juniper) is a low-growing, spreading variety. It grows only 30–60 cm (12–24") tall, but can spread to 3 m (10'). (Zones 3–9.)

J. conferta (Shore Juniper) is a stellar groundcover for dry, sandy soils. It grows 0.3–0.5 m (1–1.5') tall and spreads 1.8–2.7 m (6–9'). **'Blue Pacific'** has excellent blue-green foliage and compact growth, rarely growing higher than 30 cm (12"). **'Emerald Sea'** is the hardiest cultivar, to Zone 5.

Juniper was used traditionally to purify homes affected by sickness and death.

J. horizontalis 'Wiltonii'

It is similar to 'Blue Pacific' but has a looser habit and grows taller. (Zones 6–9.)

J. horizontalis (this page)

J. horizontalis (Creeping Juniper) is a prostrate, creeping groundcover that is native to boreal regions across North America. It grows 30–60 cm (12–24") tall and spreads up to 2.5 m (8'). This juniper is attractive when grown on top of rock walls, where it can cascade down. The foliage is blue-green and takes on a purple hue in winter. **'Bar Harbor'** grows 30 cm (12") tall and spreads 1.8–3 m (6–10'). The foliage turns a distinct purple in winter. **'Wiltonii'** ('Blue Rug') is very low growing, with trailing branches and silvery blue foliage. It grows 10–15 cm (4–6") tall and spreads 1.8–2.5 m (6–8'). (Zones 3–9.)

J. procumbens (Japanese Garden Juniper) is a wide-spreading, stiff-branched, low shrub. It grows 30–90 cm (12–36") tall and 1.8–4.5 m (6–15') wide. **'Nana'** is a dwarf, compact, mat-forming shrub. It grows 30–60 cm (12–24") tall and spreads 1.8–3.5 m (6–12'). (Zones 4–9.)

The blue 'berries' (actually fleshy cones) are used to flavour meat dishes and to give gin its distinctive character. They also make a nice addition to potpourri.

J. virginiana

Junipers come in all shapes and sizes and can suit almost any garden. Grow them in the sun to avoid open, straggly growth.

J. sabina (Savin Juniper) is a variable, spreading to erect shrub. It grows 1.2–4.5 m (4–15') tall and 1.5–6 m (5–20') wide. The cultivar **'Broadmoor'** is a low spreader with erect branchlets. It grows 60–90 cm (24–36") tall and spreads up to 3 m (10'). (Zones 3–7.)

J. scopulorum (Rocky Mountain Juniper) is rounded or spreading. It grows 9–15 m (30–50') tall and spreads 1–6 m (3–20'). **'Skyrocket'** is a very narrow, columnar tree with grey-green needles. It grows up to 6 m (20') tall, but spreads only 30–60 cm (12–24"). **'Tolleson's Weeping'** has arching branches and pendulous, silvery blue, string-like foliage. It grows about 6 m (20') tall and spreads 3 m (10'). It is sometimes grafted to create a small, weeping standard tree. This cultivar can be used in a large planter. (Zones 3–7.)

J. squamata (Singleseed Juniper) forms a prostrate or low, spreading shrub or a small, upright tree. It grows up to 9 m (30') tall and spreads 1–7.5 m (3–25'). It is rarely grown in favour of the cultivars. **'Blue Carpet'** forms a low groundcover with blue-grey needles. It grows 20–30 cm (8–12")

J. sabina

high and spreads 1.2–1.5 m (4–5'). **'Blue Star'** is a compact, rounded shrub with silvery blue needles. It grows 30–90 cm (12–36") tall and spreads about 1 m (3–4'). (Zones 4–7.)

J. virginiana (Eastern Redcedar) is a durable tree of variable habit native to most of eastern and central North America. It can be upright or wide spreading. It usually grows 12–15 m (40–50') tall, but can grow taller, and spreads 2.5–6 m (8–20'). **'Glauca'** is a narrow, upright cultivar with silvery blue new foliage that matures to silvery green in summer. It grows up to 7.5 m (25') tall. **'Silver Spreader'** is a low, wide-spreading cultivar with silvery foliage. It grows up to 90 cm (36") tall and spreads 1.2–2.5 m (4–8').

PESTS & PROBLEMS

Although junipers are tough plants, occasional problems may be caused by aphids, bagworm, bark beetles, canker, caterpillars, cedar-apple rust, leaf miners, mites, scale insects and twig blight.

J. chinensis 'Columnaris'

J. chinensis

J. chinensis 'Pfitzeriana'

J. virginiana (below)

Kalmia
Mountain Laurel
Kalmia

Features: foliage, late-spring to mid-summer flowers
Habit: large, dense, bushy, evergreen shrub
Height: 1–4.5 m (3–15') **Spread:** 1–4.5 m (3–15')
Planting: spring, fall **Zones:** 4–9

Meet the exacting standards demanded by Kalmia, and you will have one of the most exquisite of the broad-leaved evergreens. Kalmia, or Mountain Laurel, belongs with the rhododendrons in terms of growing needs and must have excellent drainage, winter shelter and acidic soil. If the cultural challenge is met, Kalmia will produce beautifully complex flowers in May or June, along with lustrous green leaves.

GROWING

Kalmia prefers **light or partial shade**, but it tolerates full sun if the soil is consistently moist. The soil should be of **average to high fertility, moist, acidic** and **well drained**. A mulch of leaf mould or pine needles will protect the roots of this drought-sensitive plant, keeping them from drying out.

Little pruning is required, but spent flowerheads can be removed in summer and awkward shoots removed as needed.

TIPS

Use Kalmia in a shaded part of a shrub or mixed border, in a woodland garden or combined with other acid- and shade-loving plants such as rhododendrons.

Do not make a tea with or otherwise ingest Kalmia flowers or foliage, which are extremely **poisonous**.

RECOMMENDED

K. latifolia grows 2–4.5 m (7–15') tall, with an equal spread. It has glossy green leaves and pink or white flowers. Cultivars are more commonly grown. **'Alpine Pink'** has a very dense habit and dark pink buds that open to light pink flowers. **'Elf'** is a dwarf cultivar that grows to 90 cm (36") in height and width. It has pink buds, white flowers and quite small leaves. **'Ostbo Red'** has bright red buds and light pink flowers. **'Silver Dollar'** has large white flowers.

PESTS & PROBLEMS

Kalmia suffers from no serious problems, but it can be affected by borers, lace bugs, leaf blight, leaf gall, leaf spot, powdery mildew, scale insects and weevils.

Kalmia was named after Pehr Kalm (1715–79), who was a student of the famous botanist Carolus Linnaeus.

'Ostbo Red' (above)

Katsuratree

Cercidiphyllum

Features: summer and fall foliage, habit
Habit: rounded or spreading, often multi-stemmed, deciduous tree
Height: 3–21 m (10–70') **Spread:** 3–21 m (10–70')
Planting: B & B, container; spring **Zones:** 4–8

The Katsuratree is a classic tree that will add distinction and grace to the garden. Even as a young plant, the Katsuratree is poised and elegant. It is easy to imagine what a bewitching specimen this tree will become. The heart-shaped leaves are delicate and distinctive, starting out wine coloured in spring, changing to blue-green in summer and turning a delicious apricot in autumn. When young, the Katsuratree is arching and pyramidal, later developing a spreading crown. As the trunk ages, it develops character. Furrows and ridges and occasionally peeling bark contribute to winter interest.

GROWING

Katsuratree grows equally well in **full sun** or **partial shade**. The soil should be **fertile, humus rich, neutral to acidic, moist** and **well drained**. This tree will become established more quickly if watered regularly during dry spells for the first year or two.

Pruning is unnecessary. Damaged branches can be removed as needed.

TIPS

Katsuratree is useful as a specimen or shade tree. The species is quite large and is best used in large gardens. The cultivar 'Pendula' is quite wide spreading but can be used in a smaller garden than the species.

This tree is native to eastern Asia, and the delicate foliage blends well into Japanese-style gardens.

RECOMMENDED

C. japonicum grows 12–21 m (40–70') tall, with an equal or sometimes greater spread. It is a slow-growing tree that takes a long time to exceed 12 m (40'). The heart-shaped, blue-green foliage turns yellow and orange in fall and develops a spicy scent. **'Pendula'** is one of the most elegant weeping trees available. It is usually grafted to a standard and grows 3–7.5 m (10–25') tall, with an equal or greater spread. Mounding, cascading branches sweep the ground, giving the entire tree the appearance of a waterfall tumbling over rocks. Ungrafted specimens of 'Pendula' may grow as tall as the species; they vary in the degree to which the branches droop and sweep the ground. They are attractive, but not always as dramatic as the grafted specimens.

When changing to their fall colour, the leaves of Katsuratree emit a spicy aroma.

Kerria
Japanese Kerria
Kerria

Features: mid- to late-spring flowers, habit
Habit: suckering, mounding or arching, deciduous shrub
Height: 1–3 m (3–10') **Spread:** 1–3 m (3–10')
Planting: B & B, container; spring, fall **Zones:** 4–9

I think Kerria is at its best in a mass planting. In winter the straight and bare stems are an eye-catching apple green—such a good green, in fact, that they look like fresh growth. At a time when the landscape is grey and brown, the green of Kerria brightens the garden. In spring, small yellow flowers follow the outline of the arching branches, like buttons up the back of a bride's dress. This shrub is fine in the shade, and if it begins to look unkempt over the years, shear it back to the ground for a new start.

GROWING

Kerria prefers **light shade, partial shade** or **full shade**. The soil should be of **average fertility** and **well drained**. Fewer flowers will appear on a plant grown in soil that is too fertile.

Prune after flowering. Cut the flowering shoots back to young side shoots, strong buds or right to the ground. The entire plant can be cut back to the ground after flowering if it becomes overgrown and needs rejuvenating.

TIPS

Kerria is useful in group plantings, woodland gardens and shrub or mixed borders.

Most flowers emerge in spring, but some may appear sporadically in summer.

RECOMMENDED

K. japonica grows about 1–1.8 m (3–6') tall and spreads 1–2.5 m (3–8'). It bears single yellow flowers. **'Aurea-variegata'** has yellow leaf margins. **'Pleniflora'** has double flowers; it grows 3 m (10') tall, with an equal spread. Its habit is more upright than that of the species.

PESTS & PROBLEMS

Leaf spot, leaf blight, twig blight, canker and root rot may occur but are not serious.

The distinct yellow-green to bright green, arching stems of Japanese Kerria add interest to the winter landscape.

Kiwi

Actinidia

Features: early-summer flowers, edible fruit, habit
Habit: woody, climbing, deciduous vines
Height: 4.5–9 m (15–30') **Spread:** indefinite
Planting: spring, fall **Zones:** 3–8

The Hardy Kiwi is handsome in its simplicity. Its lush green leaves, vigour and adaptability make it very useful, especially on difficult sites. When blotches of pink and white are added, the attractive Variegated Kiwi is created. Nursery catalogues make a convincing case for planting Variegated Kiwi—there is nothing else quite like it in the twining world. But it really doesn't perform like the pictures when it comes right out of the pot. A few years' maturity helps to produce variegation, and very hot weather and shade will reduce it. This species does not grow as rampantly as the Hardy Kiwi.

GROWING

Kiwi vines grow best in **full sun**. The soil should be **fertile** and **well drained**. These plants require shelter from strong winds.

Prune in late winter. Plants can be trimmed to fit the area they've been given, or, if greater fruit production is desired, side shoots can be cut back to two or three buds from the main stems.

TIPS

These vines need a sturdy structure to twine around. Pergolas, arbours and sufficiently large and sturdy fences provide good support. Given a trellis against a wall, a tree or some other upright structure, kiwis will twine upwards all summer. They can also be grown in containers.

Kiwi vines can grow uncontrollably. Don't be afraid to prune them back if they are getting out of hand.

RECOMMENDED

A. arguta (Hardy Kiwi, Bower Actinidia) grows 6–9 m (20–30') high, but can be trained to grow lower through the judicious use of pruning shears. The leaves are dark green and heart shaped. White flowers are followed by smooth-skinned, greenish-yellow, edible fruit.

A. kolomikta (Variegated Kiwi Vine, Kolomikta Actinidia) grows 4.5–6 m (15–20') high. The green leaves are strongly variegated with pink and white, and some of the leaves may be entirely white. White flowers are followed by smooth-skinned, greenish-yellow, edible fruit. (Zones 4–8.)

PESTS & PROBLEMS

Kiwis are occasionally afflicted with fungal diseases, but these are not a serious concern.

To produce fruit, male and female kiwi plants must be grown together. Containers are often sold with plants of both sexes in the same pot.

A. arguta

Larch

Larix

Features: summer and fall foliage, cones, habit
Habit: pyramidal, deciduous conifers
Height: 9–30 m (30–100') **Spread:** 3.5–12 m (12–40')
Planting: B & B, container; early spring **Zones:** 1–7

The native larch, Tamarack, turns a rich burnished gold in fall before losing its needles. This deciduous evergreen likes cool, wet sites. In the boreal forest of Ontario it grows in wetlands along with arborvitae. With slender trunks and drooping branches, larches look surprisingly lithe for forest evergreens. They detest heat and drought, so careful placement is a must. Larches take up a lot of room in the garden and need space to grow.

GROWING

Larches grow best in **full sun**. The soil should be of **average fertility, acidic, moist** and **well drained.** Though tolerant of most conditions, these trees don't like dry or chalky soils. Pruning is rarely required.

TIPS

Larches make interesting specimen trees. They are among the few needled trees that lose their foliage each year. In fall the needles turn golden yellow before dropping, and in winter the cones stand out on the bare branches.

RECOMMENDED

L. decidua (European Larch) is a large, narrow, pyramidal tree. It grows 21–30 m (70–100') tall and spreads 3.5–9 m (12–30'). **'Pendula'** has a weeping habit and is usually grafted to a standard. Specimens vary greatly from the bizarre to the elegant. (Zones 3–6.)

Larches are good trees for attracting birds to the garden.

L. kaempferi (Japanese Larch) grows 15–30 m (50–100') tall and spreads 4.5–12 m (15–40'). It has pendulous branchlets. The summer colour of the needles is bluer than that of the European Larch. Fall colour is excellent. (Zones 4–7.)

L. laricina (Tamarack, Eastern Larch) is an open, pyramidal tree with drooping branchlets. It is very tolerant of moist soils because it naturally grows in bogs. It grows 9–25 m (30–80') tall and spreads 4.5–9 m (15–30'). It is native to Ontario and most of the northern regions of North America. (Zones 1–6.)

PESTS & PROBLEMS

Problems may be caused by aphids, case bearers, caterpillars, needle blight, rust and sawflies.

Be prepared to reassure your neighbours that your larch is not dying when it loses its needles in fall.

L. laricina (above & centre)

L. decidua 'Pendula' (below & left)

Leucothoe
Rainbow Bush
Leucothoe

Features: spring flowers, summer foliage
Habit: upright, bushy, evergreen shrubs
Height: 1–1.8 m (3–6') **Spread:** 1–3 m (3–10')
Planting: container; spring **Zones:** 5–8

When healthy and thriving, Leucothoe is a broad-leaved evergreen with graceful, arching branches and pendulous white flowers. Gardeners hoping for success with this plant will have to be prepared to pamper it a bit. It loves the same conditions required by other garden stars such as rhododendrons and Kalmia—moist, acidic, well-drained soil and shade. You'll have to block those drying winds too. If this shrub's natural habitat isn't recreated, expect stress-related problems such as leaf spot. When provided with the right conditions, Leucothoe will reward you with beauty and elegance in your shade garden.

Be sure to give Leucothoe moist, well-drained soil and shelter from the direct sun to ensure optimum performance.

GROWING

Leucothoe grows well in **light shade, partial shade** or **full shade**. The soil should be **fertile, acidic, humus rich** and **moist**.

Pruning is rarely needed. Old plants can be rejuvenated by cutting them back to within 15 cm (6") of the ground once flowering is finished, in early summer.

TIPS

Leucothoe makes an excellent foliage plant. Include it in a woodland garden or shaded border.

RECOMMENDED

L. fontanesiana (Drooping Leucothoe) is an upright, evergreen shrub with arching branches. It grows 1–1.8 m (3–6') tall and spreads 1–3 m (3–10'). White flowers hang in drooping clusters. **'Rainbow'** (Rainbow Bush) is a commonly used cultivar. It grows 1.5 m (5') tall and spreads 1.8 m (6'). The green leaves are mottled with cream and pink. The foliage colour may fade on plants grown in full sun.

PESTS & PROBLEMS

Possible problems include leaf spot, powdery mildew, leaf gall, lace bugs and scale insects. Root rot may occur in very wet soil. Tip growth may turn black and die in harsh or windy locations.

Cut the colourful foliage and use it in indoor arrangements.

L. fontanesiana (this page)

Lilac

Syringa

Features: late-spring to early-summer flowers, habit
Habit: rounded or suckering, deciduous shrubs or small trees
Height: 1.2–9 m (4–30') **Spread:** 1.2–7.5 m (4–25')
Planting: B & B, container; late winter, early spring **Zones:** 2–8

The hardest thing about growing lilacs is choosing from the many species and hundreds of cultivars available. Almost any garden with a spot of sun can support lilacs, and should. Detractors will carp about the plant's lack of charm once it finishes blooming. But what shrub can rival the fragrance and romance of the lilac? There are lilacs available with variegated leaves and flowers, such as *S. patula* 'Miss Kim' with small, attractive, oval leaves; or *S. vulgaris* 'Wonderblue,' which promises sky blue flowers and a dwarf habit. When choosing lilacs, a good place to start is a visit to the inspiring Lilac Festival in May at the Royal Botanical Gardens in Hamilton.

GROWING

Lilacs grow best in **full sun**. The soil should be **fertile, humus rich** and **well drained**. These plants tolerate open, windy locations, and the improved air circulation helps keep powdery mildew at bay. Clear up leaves in fall to help discourage overwintering pests.

Most lilacs need little pruning. Deadhead as much as possible to keep plants neat. On established French Lilac plants, one-third to one-half of the growth can be cut right back each year after flowering. This treatment will make way for vigorous young growth and prevent the plants from becoming leggy, overgrown and unattractive.

S. vulgaris (this page)

TIPS

Include lilacs in a shrub or mixed border or use them to create an informal hedge. Japanese Tree Lilac can be used as a specimen tree.

RECOMMENDED

S. meyeri (Meyer Lilac) is a compact, rounded shrub that grows 1.2–2.5 m (4–8') tall and spreads 1.2–3.5 m (4–12'). This lilac bears fragrant pink or lavender flowers in late spring and early summer. (Zones 3–7.)

S. microphylla (Littleleaf Lilac) is an upright, broad-spreading shrub. It grows 1.8 m (6') tall and spreads 3–3.5 m (9–12'). It bears fragrant, lilac-pink flowers in early summer and sometimes again in fall. This is a very neat shrub with small, tidy leaves and attractive, airy clusters of flowers. (Zones 4–8.)

The wonderfully fragrant flowers have inspired the development of eight or nine hundred cultivars of S. vulgaris.

S. patula (Manchurian Lilac) is a hardy lilac from Northern China and Korea. It grows 1.5–3 m (5–10') tall and spreads 1.2–2.5 m (4–8'). It bears small clusters of fragrant lilac-coloured flowers. **'Miss Kim'** is similar to the species in shape and size but is denser in habit. The dark green leaves turn burgundy red in fall.

S. reticulata (Japanese Tree Lilac) is a rounded large shrub or small tree that grows 6–9 m (20–30') tall and spreads 4.5–7.5 m (15–25'). It bears white flowers in early summer. This species and its cultivars are resistant to the troublesome powdery mildew, scale insects and borers. **'Ivory Silk'** has a more compact habit and produces more flowers than the species. It grows 3–3.5 m (10–12') tall and spreads 1.8 m (6'). (Zones 3–7.)

S. vulgaris (French Lilac, Common Lilac) is the plant most people think of when they think of lilacs. It grows 2.5–7 m (8–22') tall, spreads 1.8–7 m (6–22') and bears fragrant, lilac-coloured flowers in late spring and early summer. This suckering, spreading shrub has an irregular habit, but consistent maintenance pruning will keep it neat and in good condition. Many cultivars are available, of

S. reticulata 'Ivory Silk' (below & right)

which the following are but a few examples. **'Alba'** has white single flowers. **'Belle de Nancy'** has pink double flowers. **'Charles Joly'** has magenta double flowers. **'Mme. Lemoine'** has large, white double flowers. **'President Lincoln'** has very fragrant, blue single flowers. **'Wonderblue'** is a dwarf cultivar with sky blue flowers and dark green leaves. (Zones 3–8.)

PESTS & PROBLEMS

Powdery mildew, leaf spot, borers, caterpillars, scale insects and root-knot nematodes are all possible troublemakers for lilacs.

Lilacs are frost-loving plants that don't flower at all in the warm southern U.S.

S. vulgaris 'Alba'

S. vulgaris (above & below)

Linden

Tilia

Features: habit, foliage
Habit: dense, pyramidal to rounded, deciduous tree
Height: 15–21 m (50–70') **Spread:** 6–14 m (20–45')
Planting: spring, fall **Zones:** 2–8

The Littleleaf Linden is famous for its tolerance of urban conditions. It is used widely in street plantings and in parks. In addition to being tough, it is shapely, straight growing and fragrant. The sweet smell of the lindens' small, white flowers captures the essence of summer. But with those flowers comes a dripping honeydew that will coat anything underneath, so don't plant lindens near a driveway. The Basswood can also be used as a landscape specimen. It is a hardy, fast-growing tree with a pyramidal shape. Basswood is one of the lightest in weight of Canadian hardwoods and is prized for use by carvers.

Given enough space, lindens will naturally branch all the way to the ground.

GROWING

Lindens grow best in **full sun.** The soil should be **average** to **fertile, moist** and **well drained.** These trees adapt to most pH levels but prefer an **alkaline** soil. They tolerate pollution and urban conditions.

Little pruning is required. Remove dead, damaged, diseased or awkward growth as needed. On multi-stemmed specimens, all but the strongest stems should be pruned out.

TIPS

Lindens are useful and attractive street trees, shade trees and specimen trees. Their tolerance of pollution and their moderate size make lindens ideal for city gardens.

RECOMMENDED

T. americana (Basswood, American Linden) is rarely used in gardens. It grows 18–24 m (60–80') tall and spreads about half this wide. This tree is very cold hardy and is native to most of eastern North America. The smaller **'Redmond'** is more commonly grown than the species. It becomes a pyramidal tree, more densely branched than the species, and grows about 6–9 m (20–30') tall.

T. cordata (Littleleaf Linden) is a dense, pyramidal tree that may become rounded with age. It grows 18–21 m (60–70') tall, spreads 9–14 m (30–45') and bears small flowers with narrow yellow-green bracts in summer. **'Greenspire'** is a compact cultivar. It grows 12–15 m (40–50') tall and spreads 6–8 m (20–25'). (Zones 3–7.)

T. tomentosa (Silver Linden) has a broad pyramidal or rounded habit. It can be grown as a multi-stemmed tree. It grows 15–21 m (50–70') tall and spreads 8–14 m (25–45'). This species bears small, fragrant flowers in summer; the glossy green leaves have fuzzy, silvery undersides. (Zones 4–7.)

PESTS & PROBLEMS

Anthracnose, aphids, mites, Japanese beetles, canker, powdery mildew, caterpillars, leaf spot, leaf miners and borers can afflict lindens.

London Planetree

Planetree, London Plane

Platanus

Features: bark, fall foliage
Habit: broad, rounded or pyramidal, deciduous tree
Height: 21–30 m (70–100') **Spread:** 20–25 m (65–80')
Planting: B & B, container in spring, fall; bare-root in spring **Zones:** 4–8

The London Planetree has a bold and regal presence, making anything near it look better. It grows up to 30 m (100') tall, and almost as wide. There is a grove of London Planetrees outside Hamilton City Hall, and it is enchanting to walk beneath them on a summer day. In addition to its bold, artistic bulk, the London Planetree features bark in a gorgeous patchwork of cream, olive and sage. Its size makes the London Planetree good in large spaces, but I have also seen this tree planted in tiny gardens. Hard pruning (pollarding) every other year keeps the canopy in harmony with a small yard, while allowing the trunk to dominate like a piece of sculpture with its multi-toned bark.

'Plane' is derived from the Greek word for 'broad,' referring to the beautiful, wide, maple-like leaves.

GROWING

London Planetree grows well in **full sun**. Any soil conditions are tolerated. This tree even thrives in compacted soil with poor air circulation.

Pruning is rarely required. London Planetree can, however, withstand heavy pruning and can be used as a very large hedge.

TIPS

This tree is best suited to parks, streetsides and spacious gardens. Severe pruning every year or two can make this tree suitable for a smaller yard.

RECOMMENDED

P.* x *acerifolia is a large tree with wide, spreading branches. It is grown for its ability to tolerate adverse conditions and for its attractive exfoliating bark. The flaking patches leave the smooth bark mottled with different colours. In fall the leaves turn golden brown. **'Bloodgood'** is a popular, quick-growing, drought-tolerant cultivar that has some resistance to anthracnose.

PESTS & PROBLEMS

Originally this tree had few, if any, serious problems. Its overuse as a street tree, however, has made it more vulnerable to some diseases. Anthracnose blight and canker stain are the two most serious problems. Other possible problems include borers, branch canker, caterpillars, mites, powdery mildew and scale insects.

London Planetree is the dominant street and park tree in London, England, a use which gave rise to its common name.

This young tree will broaden, becoming rounder as it matures.

Magnolia

Magnolia

Features: flowers, fruit, foliage, habit, bark
Habit: upright to spreading, deciduous shrubs or trees
Height: 2.5–9 m (8–30') **Spread:** 2.5–9 m (8–30')
Planting: B & B, container; winter, early spring **Zones:** 3–9

One of the breathtaking spectacles of spring is a Saucer Magnolia in full bloom. Its pink, cup-shaped flowers are enormous, up to 25 cm (10") in diameter, and the dropping petals carpet the ground in lovely layers of pink. A mature Saucer Magnolia is wide and low branched and commands a lot of space in the garden. It is a remarkably adaptable tree, tolerant of a wide range of soil conditions, but the flowers can be marred by late-spring cold snaps. The Star Magnolia is better suited to small gardens than the Saucer Magnolia. The long, narrow white flowers emerge before the leaves and open randomly over 10 to 20 days. Star Magnolia is heat and cold tolerant. Excellent cultivars offer white or pink flowers.

GROWING

Magnolias grow well in **full sun** or **partial shade**. The soil should be **fertile, humus rich, acidic, moist** and **well drained**. A summer mulch will help keep the roots cool and the soil moist.

Very little pruning is needed. When plants are young, thin out a few branches to encourage an attractive habit. Avoid transplanting; if necessary, transplant in early spring.

TIPS

Magnolias are used as specimen trees, and the smaller species can be used in borders.

Avoid planting magnolias where the morning sun will encourage the blooms to open too early in the season. The blossoms can be damaged by cold, wind and rain.

M. liliiflora (right), *M.* x *soulangiana* (below)

M. stellata

Despite their often fuzzy coats, magnolia flower buds are frost sensitive.

RECOMMENDED

M. liliiflora *(M. quinquepeta)* (Lily Magnolia) forms a large, rounded shrub. It grows 2.5–3.5 m (8–12') tall, with an equal spread. The outsides of the petals are purple and they open to reveal white insides. Flowers are borne in mid- to late spring. The species is hardy in Zones 5–9. It can look scruffy by the end of the season and is more famous as one of the parent plants of *M.* x *soulangiana.* Several hybrids hardy to Zone 3 have been developed from crosses with *M. stellata.* **'Betty'** bears white flowers with many petals that are dark purple on the outsides. **'Susan'** bears large, purple-red flowers.

M.* x *soulangiana (Saucer Magnolia) is a rounded, spreading, deciduous shrub or tree. It grows 6–9 m (20–30') tall, with an equal spread. Pink, purple or white flowers emerge in mid- to late spring. **'Alexandrina'** is an upright tree. Its flower petals are pink on the outside and white on the inside. **'Brozzonii'** has white

M. x soulangiana

flowers with a pinkish-purple tinge on the base of the petals. (Zones 5–9.)

M. stellata (Star Magnolia) is a compact, bushy or spreading, deciduous shrub or small tree. It grows 3–6 m (10–20') tall and spreads 3–4.5 m (10–15'). Many-petalled, fragrant white flowers appear in early to mid-spring. The species is hardy in Zones 4–9. **'Centennial'** is a vigorous, upright cultivar that is cold hardy to Zone 3. Its white flowers have 28 to 32 petals each.

PESTS & PROBLEMS

Possible problems affecting magnolias include leaf spot, canker, dieback, treehoppers, powdery mildew, scale insects, snails, thrips and weevils.

M. x *soulangiana* (left & below)

Maple

Acer

Features: foliage, bark, fruit, fall colour, form, flowers
Habit: small, multi-stemmed, deciduous trees or large shrubs
Height: 1.8–24 m (6–80') **Spread:** 1.8–21 m (6–70')
Planting: B & B, container; preferably spring **Zones:** 2–9

Maples are attractive all year, with delicate flowers in spring, attractive foliage and hanging samaras in summer, vibrant leaf colour in fall and interesting bark and branch structures in winter. There is a wonderful selection of maples available for the garden. The Paperbark Maple has papery, peeling bark in shades of orange, cinnamon and copper that look captivating against a fresh snowfall. In fall its brilliant leaf colour varies from yellow to orange and red. Japanese Maple casts a similar spell. Choose wisely from the over 1000 selections of Japanese Maple; many of them are wide spreading and need space to show their graceful outline. The Amur Maple is a perfect choice for cold-climate gardens.

GROWING

Generally maples do well in **full sun** or **light shade**, though this varies from species to species. The soil should be **fertile, moist,** high in **organic** matter and **well drained**. Pruning is largely up to you. Maples can be allowed to grow naturally, with dead, damaged or diseased branches removed at any time. These trees respond well to pruning, however, and can even be used to create bonsai specimens. The amount of pruning depends on what purpose the tree will serve in the garden. Informal and naturalistic gardens will require less pruning, while a formal garden may demand more effort. In general, pruning should take place in mid-summer to late fall because the heavy sap flow in spring makes pruning at that time unwise.

A. ginnala (above)

A. saccharum (centre & below)

TIPS

Maples can be used as specimen trees, as large elements in shrub or mixed borders or as hedges. Some are useful as understorey plants bordering wooded areas; others can be grown in containers on patios or terraces. Few Japanese gardens are without the attractive smaller maples. Almost all maples can be used to create bonsai specimens.

RECOMMENDED

A. campestre (Hedge Maple) forms a dense, rounded tree. The low-branching habit and tolerance of heavy pruning make this species popular as a hedge plant. It grows 7.5–10.5 m (25–35') tall, with an equal spread. The foliage is often killed by frost before it turns, but in a warm fall it may turn an attractive yellow. (Zones 4–8.)

The sap of A. saccharum *is used to make the famous, and delicious, maple syrup, but other maples can also be tapped for the sweet sap.*

A. saccharum in flower (right)
A. griseum (below)

A. ginnala (Amur Maple) is both attractive and extremely hardy; it can withstand winter temperatures as low as –46° C (–50° F). It also adapts to many soil types and a wide pH range. This species grows 4.5–7.5 m (15–25') tall, with an equal or greater spread. It can also be grown as a large, multi-stemmed shrub or can be pruned to form a small tree. Amur Maple responds well to pruning and in cold climates is often used in place of the tender Japanese Maple in Japanese-style gardens. This tree has attractive dark green leaves, bright red samaras and smooth bark with distinctive vertical striping. The fall foliage is often a brilliant crimson. The colour develops best in full sun, but the tree will also grow well in light shade. This is a popular tree for patios and terraces because it can be grown in a large planter. (Zones 2–8.)

A. griseum (Paperbark Maple) is attractive and adaptable to many conditions. It grows slowly to 6–10.5 m (20–35') tall, with a width half or equal the height. Paperbark Maple is popular because of its orange-brown bark that peels and curls away from the trunk in papery strips. Unfortunately, this species is difficult to propagate, so it can be expensive and sometimes hard to find. (Zones 4–8.)

A. palmatum (Japanese Maple) is considered by many gardeners to be one of the most beautiful and versatile trees available. Though many cultivars and varieties are quite small, the species itself generally grows 4.5–7.5 m (15–25') tall, with an equal or greater spread. With enough space this tree may even reach 15 m (50'). Because it leafs out early in spring, this tree can be badly damaged or killed by a late-spring frost.

Two distinct groups of cultivars have been developed from *A. palmatum* varieties. Types without dissected leaves, derived from ***A. p.* var. *atropurpureum***, are grown for their purple foliage, though many lose their purple colouring as summer progresses. Two that keep their colour are **'Bloodgood'** and **'Moonfire,'** both of which grow to about 4.5 m (15') tall. Types with dissected leaves, derived from ***A. p.* var. *dissectum***, have foliage so deeply lobed and divided that it appears fern-like or even thread-like. The leaves can be green, as in the cultivar **'Waterfall,'** or red, as in **'Red Filigree Lace.'** These trees are generally small, growing to 1.8–3 m (6–10') tall. (Zones 5–8.)

A. palmatum

A. rubrum (above)

A. campestre (centre)
A. saccharinum (below)

A. saccharum (above)

Maple wood is hard and dense and is used for fine furniture construction and for some musical instruments.

The wings of maple samaras act like miniature helicopter rotors and help in dispersal.

A. platanoides

A. platanoides (Norway Maple) is a dense, rounded or oval tree; grass may not grow well beneath it. It grows 12–15 m (40–50') tall or taller, with an equal or slightly lesser spread. Its fall colour can be good unless an early frost hits before the colour develops. **'Crimson King'** has dark purple foliage and casts a heavy shade. **'Drummondii'** (Harlequin Maple) has light green foliage with wide creamy margins. Any growth that doesn't develop the variegated foliage should be pruned out. (Zones 4–8.)

A. rubrum (Red Maple) is pyramidal in habit when young and becomes more rounded as it matures. Single- and multi-stemmed specimens are available. It grows 12–21 m (40–70') tall and has a variable spread of 6–21 m (20–70'). The cold tolerance of Red Maple varies depending on where the plant has been grown. Locally grown trees will adapt best to the local climate. Fall colour varies from tree to tree, some developing no fall colour and others developing bright yellow, orange or red fall foliage. Choose named cultivars for the best fall colour. **'Morgan'** is fast growing with an open habit; its fall colour is bright orange to red. **'Red Sunset'** ('Franksred')

has deep orange to red fall colour and good cold tolerance. (Zones 4–8.)

A. saccharinum (Silver Maple) is a fast-growing, large, rounded tree with drooping branches. It grows 15–24 m (50–80') tall and spreads 9–15 m (30–50'). This native species is a poor choice close to buildings and on small properties because the weak wood is prone to breaking in high winds and the tree tends to drop a lot of messy debris. On a rural or large property, this fast-growing tree can be quite impressive, particularly when a light breeze stirs the leaves and reveals the silvery undersides. (Zones 3–9.)

A. saccharum (Sugar Maple) is considered by many to be the most impressive and majestic of all the maples. It has a rounded pyramidal outline, grows 18–24 m (60–80') tall and spreads 12–15 m (40–50'). Its brilliant fall colour ranges from yellow to red. This large tree does not tolerate restricted, polluted urban conditions but makes a spectacular addition to parks, golf courses and large properties. (Zones 3–8.)

PROBLEMS & PESTS

Anthracnose, verticillium wilt, aphids, caterpillars, leaf cutters, leafhoppers, borers, leaf spot, scale insects, and canker can occur. Iron deficiency (chlorosis) can occur in alkaline soils. Leaf scorch can be prevented by watering young trees during hot, dry spells.

A. palmatum var. *dissectum* (below)

A. palmatum (below)

A. palmatum var. *atropurpureum* (below)

Mock-Orange

Philadelphus

Features: early-summer flowers
Habit: rounded, deciduous shrubs with arching branches
Height: 0.5–3.5 m (1.5–12') **Spread:** 0.5–3.5 m (1.5–12')
Planting: spring, fall **Zones:** 3–8

The smell of orange blossoms is one of my strongest memories of the time I lived in California. The closest I get to that here is an encounter with a mock-orange. This is the kind of shrub you wish your neighbour would grow. Once the fragrant flowering is finished, there isn't much to recommend it, although the hybrids offer some useful variety in form. If you are shopping for a mock-orange, try to sample a smell before you buy to be sure you are getting a really scented one.

GROWING

Mock-oranges grow well in **full sun, partial shade** or **light shade**. The soil should be of **average fertility, humus rich, moist** and **well drained**.

On established plants, remove one-third of the old wood each year, after flowering. Overgrown shrubs can be rejuvenated by cutting them right back to within 15 cm (6") of the ground. Established mock-oranges transplant readily, although they have a huge mass of woody roots in relation to the amount of top growth.

TIPS

Include mock-oranges in shrub or mixed borders or in woodland gardens. Use them in groups to create barriers and screens.

RECOMMENDED

P. coronarius (Sweet Mock-orange) is an upright, broadly rounded shrub with fragrant white flowers. It grows 2.5–3.5 m (8–12') tall, with an equal width. **'Aureus'** has bright yellow young foliage that matures to yellow-green. It grows 2.5 m (8') tall and spreads 1.5 m (5'). **'Variegatus'** has leaves with creamy white margins. It grows 2.5 m (8') tall and spreads 1.8 m (6'). (Zones 4–8.)

***P.* 'Natchez'** grows 2.5–3 m (8–10') tall and 1.2–2.5 m (4–8') wide. It bears slightly fragrant white flowers in late spring.

***P.* 'Snowdwarf'** is a compact shrub with arching branches. It grows 45–90 cm (18–36") tall and spreads 45 cm (18"). The fragrant white flowers appear in summer.

P. coronarius (above)
P. x *virginalis* 'Minnesota Snowflake' (below)

***P.* x *virginalis* 'Minnesota Snowflake'** is a hardy, dense, upright shrub. It grows 2.5 m (8') tall and spreads 2.5–3 m (8–10'). It bears fragrant, white double flowers in mid-summer. (Zones 3–7.)

PESTS & PROBLEMS

Mock-oranges may be affected by fungal spots, grey mould, powdery mildew, rust and scale insects, but these problems are rarely serious.

Oak

Quercus

Features: summer and fall foliage, bark, habit, acorns
Habit: large, rounded, spreading, deciduous trees
Height: 12–37 m (40–120') **Spread:** 7.5–24 m (25–80')
Planting: B & B, container; spring, fall **Zones:** 3–9

I felt I had 'arrived' in horticulture when I finally established an oak in my garden. Many of my other trees and shrubs were the type described as 'good for waste sites,' and it was a little embarrassing. Now, thanks to the University of Guelph Arboretum plant sale, I have a Dwarf Chinquapin Oak (*Q. prinoides*). This slow-growing, native species is found on dry, rocky ridges. I love it even though the Canadian Forestry Service calls it the least important of the Canadian oaks. The really impressive oaks include the White Oak, Scarlet Oak and Red Oak. The oaks' classic shape, outstanding fall colour, deep roots and long life are some of their many assets. It is a selfless act to plant an oak today to enrich the landscape for generations to come.

GROWING

Oaks grow well in **full sun** or **partial shade**. The soil should be **fertile, moist** and **well drained**. No pruning is needed. These trees can be difficult to establish. Transplant them only while they are young.

Acorns (above)

TIPS

Oaks are large trees best suited as specimens or groves in parks and large gardens. Do not disturb the ground around the base of an oak; these trees are very sensitive to changes in grade.

The acorns are generally not edible. Acorns of certain oak species are edible but usually must be processed first to leach out the bitter tannins.

RECOMMENDED

Q. alba (White Oak) is a rounded, spreading tree with peeling bark. It grows 15–30 m (50–100') tall, with an equal spread. The leaves turn purple-red in fall. This tree is native to southern Ontario.

Q. coccinea (Scarlet Oak) is noted for having the most brilliant red fall colour of all the oaks. It grows 12 m (40') tall and spreads 12–15 m (40–50'). (Zones 4–8.)

Q. rubra (centre & below)

Bark of *Q. alba*

Q. palustris (Pin Oak) is a fast-growing, pyramidal to columnar tree. It grows 18–21 m (60–70') tall and spreads 7.5–12 m (25–40'). Fall foliage is red to reddish-brown. (Zones 4–8.)

Q. prinoides (Dwarf Chinquapin Oak) is hard to find but worth seeking out. This oak thrives in dry soil and alkaline conditions. It is a close cousin to *Q. muehlenbergii*, the Chinquapin Oak, and in nature the two often hybridize. Dwarf Chinquapin grows 1–3 m (3–10') tall and often forms a multistemmed, shrubby colony, while Chinquapin grows 12–15 m (40–50') tall and generally has a single trunk. (Zones 4–7.)

Q. robur (English Oak) is a rounded, spreading tree, growing 12–37 m (40–120') tall and spreading 12–24 m (40–80'). The fall colour is golden yellow. Narrow, columnar cultivars that will grow in a smaller garden than the species are also available. Most of these grow 18 m (60') tall but spread only 3–4.5 m (10–15'). (Zones 3–8.)

Oak is an important commercial species. It is used for furniture, flooring, veneers, boat building and wine and whisky casks.

Q. robur

Bark of *Q. robur*

Q. rubra (Red Oak) is a rounded, spreading tree native to southern Ontario. It grows 18–23 m (60–75') tall, with an equal spread. The fall colour ranges from yellow to red-brown. This species prefers a moist, acidic soil. The roots are shallow, so be careful not to damage them if you cultivate the ground around the tree. (Zones 4–9.)

PESTS & PROBLEMS

The many possible problems are rarely serious: borers, canker, caterpillars, leaf gall, leaf miners, leaf rollers, leaf skeletonizers, leaf spot, powdery mildew, rust, scale insects, twig blight and wilt.

Oaks are prone to fuzzy oak galls. They are more unsightly than damaging to the tree.

Male flowers (catkins) on *Q. rubra* (bottom right)

Q. rubra (centre)

Oregon Grapeholly

Oregon-Grape

Mahonia

Features: spring flowers, summer fruit, late-fall and winter foliage
Habit: upright, suckering, evergreen shrub
Height: 0.5–1.8 m (2–6') **Spread:** 0.5–1.8 m (2–6')
Planting: B & B, container; spring, fall **Zones:** 5–9

Oregon Grapeholly's name describes it well. This broad-leaved evergreen produces lustrous leaves similar to those of holly, the yellow spring flowers are very showy and the grape-like fruit contrasts beautifully with the glossy foliage. This shrub benefits from careful placement and annual maintenance. Keep it out of exposed, windy sites or the leaves will become brown, dry and crunchy. The growth can be irregular with a tendency to sucker, so an annual, artful pruning will lend Oregon Grapeholly a more pleasing shape.

The juicy berries are edible but very tart. They can be eaten fresh or used to make jellies, juices or wine.

GROWING

Oregon Grapeholly prefers **light to partial shade** but tolerates full sun if the soil is moist. The soil should be of **average fertility, humus rich, moist** and **well drained**. Provide **shelter** from winter winds to prevent the foliage from drying out. Awkward shoots can be removed in early summer. Deadheading will keep the plant looking neat but will prevent the attractive, edible (though sour) fruit from forming.

TIPS

Use in shrub or mixed borders and in woodland gardens. Low-growing specimens can be used as groundcovers.

RECOMMENDED

M. aquifolium grows 1–1.8 m (3–6') tall, with an equal spread. Bright yellow flowers appear in spring and are followed by clusters of purple or blue berries. The foliage turns a bronze-purple colour in late fall and winter. **'Compactum'** is a low, mounding shrub with bronze foliage. It grows 60–90 cm (24–36") tall, with an equal spread.

PESTS & PROBLEMS

Rust, leaf spot, gall and scale insects may cause occasional problems. Plants in exposed locations may develop leaf scorch in winter.

Try this attractive plant as a hedge.

Peashrub

Caragana

Features: late-spring flowers, foliage, habit
Habit: prickly, grafted weeping or upright rounded shrub
Height: 1–6 m (3–20') **Spread:** 2.5–5.5 m (8–18')
Planting: spring or fall **Zones:** 2–7

Here is a plant that is hardy to Zone 2, holds its own on dry, exposed sites, and has the ability to fix nitrogen in the soil. The Peashrub is native to Siberia and Mongolia. When all other shrubs have succumbed to wicked conditions, Peashrub keeps thriving. It is not highly ornamental with its wispy leaves and hard-to-find yellow flowers, but its airiness allows it to work hard as a background plant.

GROWING

Peashrub prefers **full sun**, but will tolerate partial or light shade. Soil of **average to high fertility** is preferred. This plant will adapt to just about any growing conditions and tolerates dry, exposed locations.

Prune out awkward or damaged shoots as needed to maintain a neat shape. Rejuvenate unruly or overgrown plants by pruning them to within 15 cm (6") of the ground.

Grafted weeping specimens cannot be pruned to the ground but can be pruned back to within a few buds of the graft or trimmed back lightly to control spread. Growth that sprouts from the ground or along the trunk of weeping standards should be removed as it will not show the weeping habit.

TIPS

Peashrub plants are grown as windbreaks and formal or informal hedges. Peashrub can be included in borders, and weeping forms are often used as specimen plants.

C. arborescens 'Walker' (below)

RECOMMENDED

C. arborescens is a large, twiggy, thorny shrub that grows up to 6 m (20') tall, with a lesser spread. Branches may be upright or arching. Yellow, pea-like flowers are borne in late spring followed by seed pods that ripen to brown in summer and rattle when blown by the wind. **'Pendula'** has long, weeping branches and is generally grafted to a standard that ranges from 1 to 2 m (3 to 6') in height. **'Walker'** is a similar weeping form with fine, feathery foliage.

PESTS & PROBLEMS

Aphids and leafhoppers may disfigure young foliage but are generally not a problem.

In late summer the seeds can be heard rattling inside the pods before they burst.

Pieris
Lily-of-the-Valley Shrub
Pieris

Features: colourful new growth, late-winter to spring flowers
Habit: compact, rounded, evergreen shrub
Height: 1–3.5 m (3–12') **Spread:** 1–3 m (3–10')
Planting: B & B, container; spring, fall **Zones:** 5–8

In the proper setting, Pieris is a great plant. Its new growth is a mixture of rich red, bronze and mint green. The leaves appear to have been buffed to a fine sheen. The flowers are like bracelets, festooned with blossoms like those of lily-of-the-valley. The creamy, bell-shaped flowers are fragrant and sturdy. This broad-leaved evergreen is often grown in the company of rhododendrons, but experts say its growing needs are not as exacting. Pieris wants partial shade and moist, organically rich soil, but an acidic soil is not as essential as it is for rhododendrons.

GROWING

Pieris grows equally well in **full sun** and **partial shade**. The soil should be of **average fertility, acidic, humus rich, moist** and **well drained**. Provide a **sheltered** location with protection from the hot sun and drying winds.

Remove spent flowers once flowering is complete. Prune out awkward shoots at the same time.

TIPS

Pieris can be used in a shrub or mixed border, in a woodland garden or as a specimen. Try grouping it with rhododendrons and other acid-loving plants. With its year-round good looks, this is a great shrub to use in a protected entryway.

All parts of Pieris plants, and even honey made from the nectar, are extremely **poisonous**. Children have died from eating the leaves.

RECOMMENDED

P. japonica grows 2.5–3.5 m (8–12') tall and spreads 1.8–3 m (6–10'). It bears white flowers in long, pendulous clusters at the ends of the branches. **'Mountain Fire'** has bright red new growth that matures to chestnut brown. The flowers are white. **'Variegata'** also has white flowers but its green leaves have creamy white margins. **'Valley Rose'** has dark green foliage and pink flowers. There are several dwarf cultivars that grow about 90 cm (36") tall and wide.

PESTS & PROBLEMS

Canker, lace bugs, nematodes and root rot can cause occasional problems. Plants may suffer dieback if exposed to too much wind.

The flower buds of Pieris form in late summer in the year before flowering and provide an attractive show all winter.

'Mountain Fire' (above)

Pine

Pinus

Features: foliage, bark, cones, habit
Habit: upright, columnar or spreading, evergreen trees
Height: 2.5–36 m (8–120') **Spread:** 1.8–15 m (6–50')
Planting: B & B, container; spring, fall **Zones:** 2–8

Pines offer exciting possibilities for any garden, and there is a fascinating world beyond the commonly grown Austrian Pine. Gardeners can explore the species from *a* to *w*. That would take you from *Pinus aristata* to *Pinus wallichiana*. Exotic-looking pines are available with soft or stiff needles, needles with yellow bands, trunks with patterned or mother-of-pearl-like bark and varied forms. The readily available Eastern White Pine remains one of the most beautiful choices. Even as a huge, mature tree, this pine has a flexible grace as the soft needles respond to the wind with a gentle sway and soft sound. *P. cembra* is a shapely specimen that holds its columnar shape throughout its life.

GROWING

Pines grow best in **full sun**. These trees adapt to most **well-drained** soils but do not tolerate polluted urban conditions. Generally, little or no pruning is required. Hedges can be trimmed in mid-summer. Pinch up to one-half the length of the 'candles,' the fully extended but still soft new growth, to shape the plant or to regulate growth.

TIPS

Pines can be used as specimen trees, as hedges or to create windbreaks. Smaller cultivars can be included in shrub or mixed borders. These trees are not heavy feeders. Fertilizing will encourage rapid new growth that is weak and susceptible to pest and disease problems. The Austrian Pine, *P. nigra*, was often recommended as the most urban-tolerant pine, but overplanting has led to severe disease problems, some of which can kill a tree in a single growing season.

RECOMMENDED

P. aristata (Bristlecone Pine) is a fairly small, slow-growing pine with a conical or shrubby habit. It grows 2.5–9 m (8–30') tall and spreads 1.8–6 m (6–20'). It is not pollution tolerant but survives in poor, dry, rocky soil. Its needles may dry out in windy winter locations. (Zones 4–8.)

P. banksiana (Jack Pine) is rounded to conical when young and becomes irregular and sometimes unruly as it matures. It grows 9–15 m (30–50') tall with a variable but lesser spread. It is useful in cold northern Ontario gardens, but is often considered too scruffy where less hardy, more attractive species will thrive.

P. cembra (Swiss Stone Pine) has a dense, columnar habit. It grows 9–21 m (30–70') tall and spreads 4.5–7.5 m (15–25'). This slow-growing pine is resistant to white pine blister rust. (Zones 3–7.)

P. mugo (this page)

P. sylvestris

Pines are more diverse and widely adapted than any other conifers.

Most pines' seeds are edible ('pine nuts'), though many are too small to bother with.

P. mugo (Mugo Pine) is a low, rounded, spreading shrub or tree. It grows 3–6 m (10–20') tall and spreads 4.5–6 m (15–20'). **Var. *pumilio*** (var. *pumilo*) is dense and prostrate, growing to 2.5 m (8') tall. Its slow growth and small size make this variety a good choice for planters and rock gardens. (Zones 2–7.)

P. parviflora (Japanese White Pine) is conical or columnar when young and matures to a spreading crown. It grows 6–21 m (20–70') tall and spreads 6–15 m (20–50'). This species is used to create bonsai. (Zones 4–8.)

P. resinosa (Red Pine) is a conical to rounded tree with long, stiff needles. It grows 15–24 m (50–80') tall and spreads 6–12 m (2–40'). This species is useful for creating windbreaks. (Zones 3–7.)

P. strobus (Eastern White Pine) is a slender, conical tree with soft, plumy needles. It grows 15–36 m (50–120') tall and spreads 6–12 m (20–40'). This beautiful species dominates many Ontario forests. It is sometimes grown as a hedge. Mature specimens are resistant, but young trees can be killed by white pine blister rust. **'Compacta'** is a dense, rounded, slow-growing form. **'Fastigiata'** is an attractive, narrow, columnar form that grows up to 21 m (70') tall. **'Pendula'** has long, ground-sweeping branches. It must be trained to form an

P. cembra (below)
P. resinosa (right)

upright leader when young to give it some height and shape; otherwise, it can be grown as a groundcover or left to spill over the top of a rock wall or slope. It develops an unusual, shaggy, droopy appearance as it matures. (Zones 3–8.)

P. sylvestris (Scots Pine, Scotch Pine) is rounded or conical when young and develops an irregular, flat-topped, spreading habit when mature. There is much variety in this species, with differing needle colour and length as well as tree size and habit depending on where the plant originated. It grows 9–21 m (30–70') tall and spreads 6–12 m (20–40'). Young plants of this species are popular as Christmas trees. (Zones 2–7.)

P. wallichiana (Himalayan Pine) is worth searching for. It has graceful, arching blue-green needles. It needs moist, acidic, well-drained soil and protection from drying winds. It grows 9–15 m (30–50') tall, with an equal spread. (Zones 6–8.)

PESTS & PROBLEMS

Blight, blister rust, borers, caterpillars, cone rust, leaf miners, mealybugs, pitch canker, sawflies, scale insects and tar spot can all cause problems. The European pine-shoot moth attacks pines with needles in clusters of two or three.

P. strobus 'Pendula'

P. strobus (above)
P. resinosa (centre)

P. cembra (below)

Potentilla
Shrubby Cinquefoil
Potentilla

Features: flowers, foliage **Habit:** mounding, deciduous shrub
Height: 30–100 cm (12–40") **Spread:** 90–120 cm (36–48")
Planting: container; spring, fall **Zones:** 2–8

Potentilla is a fuss-free shrub that blooms madly all summer. The cheery, yellow-flowered variety is often seen, but cultivars with flowers in shades of pink, red and tangerine have broadened the use of this reliable shrub. Dwarf varieties can live in the rock garden, and taller forms blend well with perennials. These adaptable shrubs will thrive in almost any conditions—sunny, shady, wet or dry.

GROWING

Potentilla prefers **full sun** but will tolerate partial or light shade. The soil should, preferably, be of **poor to average fertility** and **well drained**. This plant tolerates most conditions, including sandy or clay soil and wet or dry conditions. Established plants are drought tolerant. Too much fertilizer or too rich a soil will encourage weak, floppy, disease-prone growth.

On mature plants, prune up to one-third of the old wood each year to keep the growth neat and vigorous. Though they will tolerate more severe pruning, these plants look best if left to grow as informal mounds and rounded shrubs.

TIPS

Potentilla is useful in a shrub or mixed border. The smaller cultivars can be included in rock gardens and on rock walls. On slopes that are steep or awkward to mow, Potentilla can prevent soil erosion and reduce the time spent maintaining the lawn. Potentilla can even be used to form a low, informal hedge.

Potentilla will tolerate excess lime in the soil and can handle extreme cold very well. Try this small shrub as a low-maintenance alternative to turfgrass.

'Abbotswood' (above), 'Tangerine' (below)

'Tangerine' (above)

'Abbotswood' (below)

If your Potentilla's flowers fade in the bright sun or in hot weather, try moving the plant to a more sheltered location. A cooler location that still gets lots of sun or a spot with some shade from the hot afternoon sun may be all your plant needs to keep its colour. Colours should revive in fall as the weather cools. Yellow-flowered plants are the least likely to be affected by heat and sun.

RECOMMENDED

There are many, many cultivars of *P. fruticosa*. The following are a few popular and interesting ones.

'Abbotswood' is one of the best white-flowered cultivars. It grows 75–90 cm (30–36") tall and spreads up to 120 cm (48").

'Goldfinger' has large yellow flowers. It grows up to 100 cm (39") tall, with an equal spread.

'Princess' ('Pink Princess') has light pink flowers that fade to white in hot weather. It grows about 90 cm (36") tall, with an equal spread.

'Tangerine' has orange flowers that bleach to yellow if the plant is exposed to too much direct sunlight, so plant in partial or light shade. This cultivar grows 45–60 cm (18–24") tall and spreads 90–120 cm (36–48").

'Yellow Gem' has bright yellow flowers. It is a low, mounding, spreading cultivar that grows 30–45 cm (12–18") tall and spreads up to 90 cm (36").

PESTS & PROBLEMS

Though rare, problems with mildew, fungal leaf spot or spider mites are possible.

Potentilla varieties offer a rainbow of possible colours: white, yellow, pink, orange and red.

Redbud

Cercis

Features: spring flowers, fall foliage
Habit: rounded or spreading, multi-stemmed, deciduous tree or shrub
Height: 6–9 m (20–30') **Spread:** 7.5–10 m (25–35')
Planting: B & B, container; spring, fall **Zones:** 4–9

In the warmer parts of southern Ontario, Redbud is an outstanding treasure of spring. Deep magenta flowers bloom before the leaves emerge, and their impact is intense. As the buds open, the flowers turn pink, covering the long, thin branches in pastel clouds. One Redbud is a lovely sight, but a group of them is heavenly. Redbud is not uniformly hardy throughout Ontario, but there are specimens growing in Ottawa, and breeding in the much harsher climate of Minnesota is producing hardier cultivars. Redbud is not long-lived, so it should be used to add a delicate, supplemental beauty to other permanent trees in the garden.

Select a Redbud plant from a locally grown source. Plants from seeds produced in the south are not hardy in the north.

GROWING

Redbud grows well in **full sun, partial shade** or **light shade**. The soil should be a **fertile, deep loam** that is **moist** and **well drained**.

Pruning is rarely required. Thin the growth of young plants to encourage an open habit at maturity and remove awkward branches after flowering. Redbud has tender roots and does not like being transplanted.

TIPS

Redbud can be used as a specimen tree, in shrub or mixed borders and in woodland gardens.

RECOMMENDED

C. canadensis (Eastern Redbud) is a spreading, multi-stemmed tree that grows 6–9 m (20–30') tall and spreads 7.5–10 m (25–35'). It bears red, purple or pink flowers in mid-spring, before the leaves emerge. The young foliage is bronze, fading to green over summer and turning bright yellow in fall. **Var. *alba*** has white flowers. **'Forest Pansy'** has purple or pink flowers and reddish-purple foliage that fades to green over summer. The best foliage colour is produced when this cultivar is cut back hard in early spring, but plants cut back this way will not produce flowers. This cultivar is less hardy than the species, to Zone 7 or a sheltered site in Zone 6. **'Silver Cloud'** bears fewer flowers than than the species; its foliage has creamy white spots.

'Redbud' describes the pointed flower buds, which are slightly deeper in colour than the flowers.

PESTS & PROBLEMS

Blight, canker, caterpillars, dieback, downy mildew, leafhoppers, leaf spot, scale insects, weevils and verticillium wilt are potential problems for Redbud.

Rhododendron Azalea

Rhododendron

Features: late-winter to early-summer flowers, foliage, habit
Habit: upright, mounding, rounded, evergreen or deciduous shrubs
Height: 0.5–3.5 m (2–12') **Spread:** 0.5–3.5 m (2–12')
Planting: B & B, container; spring, fall **Zones:** 3–8

In two Ontario gardens I saw rhododendrons and azaleas that looked great. Both gardens contained mature deciduous and evergreen trees. The rhododendrons were planted in groups in raised beds that had plenty of organic matter worked in, and the soil had been amended to be more acidic. All the beds had a deep layer of pine needle mulch, adequate moisture and excellent drainage. The gardeners did a fine job of mimicking the natural conditions in which rhododendrons grow. They are edge-of-the-woodland plants that thrive when combined with oak trees because oak leaves are acidic and the two root systems do not compete. Edwards Gardens in Toronto has a display of rhododendrons growing in a small sheltered valley, well worth the visit for enthusiasts.

GROWING

Rhododendrons prefer **partial shade** or **light shade**. A location sheltered from strong winds is preferable. The soil should be **fertile, humus rich, acidic, moist** and **well drained**. Rhododendrons are sensitive to high pH, salinity and winter injury.

Shallow planting with a good mulch is essential, as is excellent drainage. In heavy soils, elevate the crown of rhododendrons 2.5 cm (1") above soil level when planting to ensure surface drainage of excess water. Don't dig under rhododendrons; their root system is shallow and resents disturbance.

Dead and damaged growth can be removed in mid-spring. Spent flower clusters should be removed if possible. Grasp the base of the cluster between your thumb and forefinger and twist to remove the entire cluster. Be careful not to damage the new buds that form directly beneath the flowerheads.

TIPS

In Ontario rhododendrons grow better and look better when planted in groups. Use them in shrub or mixed borders, in woodland gardens or in sheltered rock gardens. Be aware of the needs of rhododendrons and take care to give them a suitable home with protection from the wind and from full sun. In an

Rhododendrons and azaleas are generally grouped together botanically. Extensive breeding and hybridizing are making it more and more difficult to apply one label or the other.

'Rhododendron' translates as 'rose tree'—an apt description of these beautiful plants.

PJM Hybrid

exposed location they will not do well. In a protected location they should do well and not need an unsightly burlap covering in winter. The **flowers and foliage** of *Rhododendron* species are **poisonous**, as is honey produced from the nectar.

RECOMMENDED

R. catawbiense (Catawba Rhododendron, Mountain Rosebay) is a large, rounded, evergreen species. It grows 1.8–3 m (6–10') tall, with an equal spread. Clusters of reddish-purple flowers appear in late spring. **'Album'** has light purple buds and white flowers. **'Christmas Cheer'** is an early bloomer with light pink flowers. **'Cilpinense'** has white flowers flushed with pink. (Zones 4–8.)

***R.* Exbury Hybrids** are rounded, upright, deciduous rhododendrons. They grow 2.5–3.5 m (8–12') tall and spread 1.8–3.5 m (6–12'). The flower colour varies from cultivar to cultivar. **'Dawn's Chorus'** has pink buds and white flowers with pink veins. **'Firefly'** has red flowers. **'Gibraltar'** has bright orange flowers. **'Gold Dust'** has fragrant, bright yellow flowers. (Zones 5–7.)

***R.* Knap Hill Hybrids** are rounded, upright, deciduous rhododendrons that grow 2.5–3.5 m (8–12') tall and spread 1.8–3.5 m (6–12'). The flower colour varies with the cultivar. **'Altair'** has fragrant, creamy white flowers. **'Cockatoo'** has fragrant, pink-yellow to orange-yellow flowers. **'Fireball'** is a vigorous plant with bronze new foliage that matures to dark green. The flowers are orange-red. (Zones 5–7.)

R. **Kurume Hybrids** are deciduous, dwarf azaleas, often used for bonsai. They grow 60–90 cm (24–36") tall, with an equal spread. The colour of the late-spring flowers varies with the cultivar. **'Mother's Day'** bears red flowers for a long period in May and June. **'Rosebud'** is a compact, low-growing plant with rose pink flowers. (Zones 5–8.)

R. **Northern Lights Hybrids** are broad, rounded, deciduous azaleas. They grow about 1.5 m (5') tall and spread about 1.2 m (4'). They are very cold hardy. **'Apricot Surprise'** has yellow-orange flowers. **'Golden Lights'** has fragrant, yellow flowers. **'Orchid Lights'** is a bushy, compact plant with light purple flowers. **'Rosy Lights'** has fragrant, dark pink flowers. **'Spicy Lights'** has fragrant, light orange-red flowers. **'White Lights'** has fragrant, white flowers. (Zones 3–7.)

R. **PJM Hybrids** are compact, rounded, dwarf, evergreen rhododendrons. They grow 1–1.8 m (3–6') tall, with an equal spread. These hybrids are weevil resistant. **'Elite'** has pink-purple flowers. **'Regal'** has a more spreading habit and pink flowers. **'Victor'** is compact and slow growing with pink flowers. (Zones 4–8.)

PESTS & PROBLEMS

Rhododendrons planted in good conditions, with well-drained soil, suffer few problems. When plants are stressed, however, aphids, caterpillars, lace bugs, leaf galls, leafhoppers, petal blight, powdery mildew, root rot, root weevils, rust, scale insects, vine weevils, Japanese beetles and whiteflies can cause problems.

Northern Lights Hybrid (above)

PJM Hybrid (above), Kurume Hybrid (below)

Rose-of-Sharon

Hibiscus

Hibiscus

Features: mid-summer to fall flowers
Habit: bushy, upright, deciduous or evergreen shrub
Height: 0.3–4.5 m (1–15') **Spread:** 1.8–3 m (6–10')
Planting: B & B, container; spring, fall **Zones:** 5–9

The Rose-of-Sharon isn't one of those fashion-forward shrubs. It has the air of yesterday about it—it was probably in your grandmother's garden. It sort of sits there for most of the season, shrugging on the fringe of more exciting plants. But in late summer, those big flowers reward gardeners' patience and pop open in pink, purple, white or blue, with single- and double-flowering forms. Sterile hybrids such as 'Diana' and 'Helene' have stifled complaints about Rose-of-Sharon's prolific seed set.

GROWING

Rose-of-Sharon prefers **full sun** and tolerates partial shade. The soil should be **humus rich, moist** and **well drained**.

Pinch young plants to encourage bushy growth. Young plants can be trained to form a tree by selectively pruning out all but the strongest stem. The flowers form on the current year's growth; prune back tip growth in late winter or early spring for larger but fewer flowers.

'Blue Bird' (above)

TIPS

Rose-of-Sharon is best used in shrub or mixed borders.

This plant develops unsightly legs as it matures. Plant low, bushy perennials or shrubs around the base to hide the bare stems. The leaves emerge late in spring and drop early in fall. Planting Rose-of-Sharon with evergreen shrubs will make up for the short period of green.

'Lady Stanley'

Rose-of-Sharon attracts birds and butterflies and repels deer.

'Red Heart' (below)
'Diana' (right)

RECOMMENDED

H. syriacus is an erect, multi-stemmed shrub that bears dark pink flowers from mid-summer to fall. It can be trained to form a small, single-stemmed tree. Many cultivars are available. **'Aphrodite'** bears rose pink flowers with dark red centres. **'Blue Bird'** bears large blue flowers with red centres. **'Diana'** bears large white flowers. **'Helene'** has white flowers with red or pink petal bases. **'Lady Stanley'** bears light pink double flowers with darker pink centres and veins. **'Red Heart'** bears white flowers with red centres. **'Woodbridge'** bears pink flowers with deeper pink centres.

ALTERNATE SPECIES

H. rosa-sinensis (Hibiscus, Chinese Hibiscus, Rose of China) is a rounded shrub with glossy, evergreen foliage. This frost-tender plant is generally sold as a house plant but can be used as a container specimen outdoors in summer, then moved indoors for winter. It generally grows 0.3–1.2 m (1–4') as a container plant but can grow to 4.5 m (15') tall where it is hardy. Bring the plant indoors when the temperature is likely to drop below 10° C (50° F). The species bears attractive, funnel-shaped flowers in shades of red, pink, orange,

yellow or white. **'Hula Girl'** bears large yellow flowers with red at the petal bases.

PESTS & PROBLEMS

Rose-of-Sharon can be afflicted with aphids, bacterial blight, caterpillars, fungal leaf spot, mealybugs, mites, root rot, rust, scale insects, stem rot, verticillium wilt and viruses.

H. rosa-sinensis 'Hula Girl' (above)

'Woodbridge' (above & below)

'Woodbridge' (above)

Russian Olive

Elaeagnus

Features: fragrant summer flowers, summer foliage, fruit
Habit: rounded, spreading, deciduous trees or shrubs
Height: 1.8–6 m (6–20') **Spread:** 1.8–6 m (6–20')
Planting: B & B, container; spring, fall **Zones:** 2–8

Russian olives are survivors. They can tough it out on the edge of highways, bombarded by exhaust and road salt. In a garden setting Russian olives can be planted as transitional trees or used in difficult areas where soil improvements haven't been made. The foliage is a distinctly handsome silver-grey. Annual maintenance such as light pruning may be needed to keep a Russian olive presentable.

GROWING

Russian olives grow best in **full sun**. Preferably, the soil should be a **well-drained, sandy loam** of **average to high fertility**. These plants adapt to poor soil because they can fix nitrogen from the air. They also tolerate salty and dry conditions, making them useful for plantings along highways and other salted roads.

These trees or shrubs tolerate hard pruning. One-third of the old growth can be removed each year from multi-stemmed specimens.

TIPS

Russian olives are used in shrub or mixed borders, as hedges and screens and as specimen plants. The fruits are edible but dry and mealy. The branches on some plants can be quite thorny.

RECOMMENDED

E. angustifolia (Russian Olive) is a rounded, spreading tree. It grows 3.5–6 m (12–20') tall, with an equal spread. The fragrant, yellow summer flowers are often obscured by the foliage, as is the silvery yellow fruit. The main attractions of this species are its tolerance of adverse conditions and its narrow, silver-grey leaves.

E. multiflora (Cherry Eleagnus) is a wide-spreading, rounded shrub with somewhat arching branches. It grows 1.8–3 m (6–10') tall, with an equal spread. The bright red fruits are hidden by the silvery green foliage. (Zones 5–7.)

PESTS & PROBLEMS

In stressful conditions these plants are susceptible to canker, dieback, fungal leaf spot, nematodes, root rot and rust.

E. angustifolia (this page)

Serviceberry

Saskatoon, Juneberry

Amelanchier

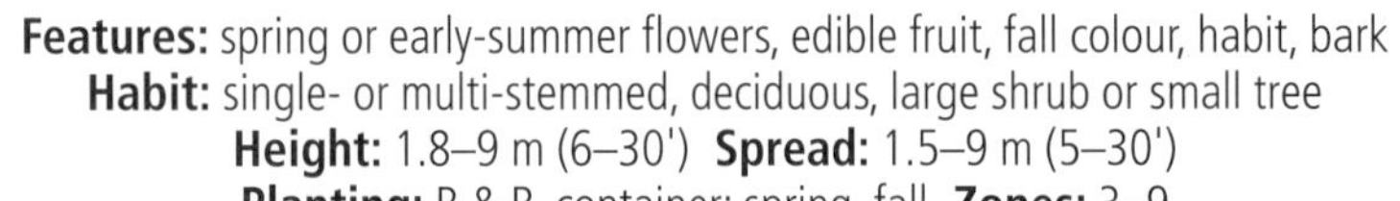

Features: spring or early-summer flowers, edible fruit, fall colour, habit, bark
Habit: single- or multi-stemmed, deciduous, large shrub or small tree
Height: 1.8–9 m (6–30') **Spread:** 1.5–9 m (5–30')
Planting: B & B, container; spring, fall **Zones:** 3–9

The *Amelanchier* species are first-rate North American natives, and breeders have refined the habits to make them more useful in the home landscape. The small trees bear lacy, white flowers in spring, followed by edible berries. In fall the foliage colour ranges from a glowing apricot to deep red. A serviceberry underplanted with a groundcover and bulbs makes a richly textured spring composition. The shrubby, clump forms are especially attractive in a naturalized planting.

GROWING

Serviceberries grow well in **full sun** or **light shade.** They prefer **acidic soil** that is **fertile, humus rich, moist** and **well drained.** They do adjust to drought. Very little pruning is needed. Young plants can be pruned to encourage healthy, attractive growth and form. Dead, damaged, diseased and awkward branches can be removed as needed.

TIPS

With spring flowers, edible fruit, attractive leaves that turn red in fall and often artistic branch growth, serviceberries make beautiful specimen plants or even shade trees in small gardens. The shrubbier forms can be grown along the edges of a woodland or in a border. In the wild these trees are often found growing near water sources, and they make beautiful pond- or stream-side plants.

A. canadensis (below)

RECOMMENDED

A. arborea (Downy Serviceberry, Juneberry) forms a small single- or multi-stemmed tree. It grows 4.5–7.5 m (15–25') tall and spreads 4.5–9 m (15–30'). Clusters of fragrant, white flowers are borne in spring. The edible fruit ripens to reddish purple in summer. The foliage turns in fall to shades ranging from yellow to red. (Zones 4–9.)

A. canadensis (Shadblow Serviceberry) forms a large, upright, suckering shrub. It grows 1.8–6 m (6–20') tall and spreads 1.5–4.5 m (5–15'). White spring flowers are followed by edible dark purple fruit in summer. The foliage turns orange and red in fall. This species tolerates moist, boggy soil conditions. (Zones 3–8.)

A.* x *grandiflora (Apple Serviceberry) is a small, spreading, often multi-stemmed tree. It grows 6–9 m (20–30') tall, with an equal spread. New foliage is often bronze coloured, turning green over summer and bright orange or red in fall. White spring flowers are followed by purple fruit in summer. Plant this hybrid in a sheltered spot to protect it during winter in the coldest regions. **'Ballerina'** has bright red fall colour and is fire blight resistant. (Zones 4–8.)

PESTS & PROBLEMS

Problems with rust, fire blight, powdery mildew, leaf miners, borers and leaf spot can occur but are generally not serious.

The fruit can be used in the place of blueberries in any recipe, having a similar, but generally sweeter, flavour.

Smokebush
Smoketree
Cotinus

Features: early-summer flowers, summer and fall foliage
Habit: bushy, rounded, spreading, deciduous tree or shrub
Height: 3–6 m (10–20') **Spread:** 3–4.5 m (10–15')
Planting: container; spring, fall **Zones:** 4–8

Smoky clusters of flowers against a deep purple background make it easy to see why one cultivar of this large shrub is called Purple Smoketree. It makes a striking specimen near an entryway and can be trained to maintain a shrub or tree form. Bright fall colour, adaptability, flowers of differing colours, and variable sizes and forms make this species and all its cultivars excellent additions to the garden.

GROWING

Smokebush grows well in **full sun** or **partial shade**. It prefers soil of **average fertility** that is **moist** and **well drained**, but it will adapt to all but very wet soils.

Where pruning is concerned, this is an all-or-nothing plant. Long, lanky growth develops from pruning cuts. It can be cut back to the ground each spring to maintain low, shrubby growth, but larger shrubs and tree specimens shouldn't be pruned at all.

TIPS

Smokebush can be used in a shrub or mixed border, as a single specimen or in groups. It is a good choice for a rocky hillside planting.

RECOMMENDED

C. coggygria grows 3–4.5 m (10–15') tall, with an equal spread. It develops large, puffy plumes of flowers that start out green and gradually turn a pinky grey. The green foliage turns red, orange and yellow in fall. **'Daydream'** develops many pink plumes. The habit is more dense than that of the species. **'Flame'** develops into a small, bushy tree or large shrub with purple-pink plumes. It can grow up to 6 m (20') tall. The fall colour is a brilliant red. **'Royal Purple'** (Purple Smoketree) has dark purple foliage and purple-grey flowers.

PESTS & PROBLEMS

Verticillium wilt and powdery mildew are possible problems. Purple-leaved plants are more likely to be affected by powdery mildew.

'Royal Purple' (above)

'Royal Purple' (below)

Spirea

Spiraea

Features: summer flowers, habit
Habit: round, bushy, deciduous shrubs
Height: 0.5–3 m (2–10') **Spread:** 0.5–3.5 m (2–12')
Planting: container; spring, fall **Zones:** 3–9

Spireas, seen in so many gardens and with dozens of cultivars, may be too common for some gardeners, but remain an undeniable favourite for others. With a wide range of forms, sizes and colours of both foliage and flowers, spireas have many possible uses in the landscape. New compact varieties can be massed as an excellent groundcover. Cultivars of Japanese Spirea are short and dainty and fit perfectly in the rock garden. Bridal Wreath Spirea is a sentimental favourite for me—when it was blooming, I would start counting the days until the end of the school year. The introduction of a dwarf species of this big sprawler means it can now be enjoyed in smaller gardens.

Under a magnifying glass the flowers of these shrubs in the rose family indeed resemble tiny roses.

GROWING

Spireas prefer **full sun**. To help prevent foliage burn, provide protection from very hot sun. The soil should be **fertile, acidic, moist** and **well drained.**

Pruning is necessary to keep spireas tidy and graceful. The tight, shrubby types require less pruning than the larger, more open forms, which may require heavy renewal pruning in spring.

Pruning depends on the flowering time for any given species. Those that bloom in spring and early summer usually form their flowers the previous year. These plants should be pruned immediately after flowering is complete. Cut out one-third of the old growth to encourage new, young growth.

Plants that flower later in summer or in fall generally form flowers during the current year. These can be cut back to within 30 cm (12") of the ground in early spring, as the buds begin to swell, to encourage lots of new growth and flowers later in the season.

S. japonica 'Shibori' (this page)

Pruning is necessary to keep spireas tidy and graceful in form.

S. japonica 'Goldmound' (above)

S. japonica (below)

TIPS

Spireas are used in shrub or mixed borders, in rock gardens and as informal screens and hedges.

RECOMMENDED

S.* x *bumalda (*S. japonica* 'Bumalda') is a low, broad, mounded shrub with pink spring or early-summer flowers. It is rarely grown in favour of the many cultivars, which also have pink flowers. **'Anthony Waterer'** grows 1–1.2 m (3–4') tall and spreads 1–1.5 m (3–5'). The new foliage is reddish, turning blue-green over summer and red again in fall. **'Goldflame'** grows 0.5–1 m (2–3') tall and spreads 0.5–1.2 m (2–4'). The new foliage emerges red and matures to yellow-green, with red, orange and yellow fall colour. **'Limemound'** grows about 1 m (3') tall and spreads about 1.8 m (6'). The stems are red and the foliage is yellow with good fall colour. (Zones 3–8.)

S. japonica (Japanese Spirea) forms a clump of erect stems. It grows 1.2–1.8 m (4–6') tall and spreads up to 1.5 m (5'). Pink or white flowers are borne in mid- and late summer. There are many varieties, cultivars and hybrids developed from this species. **Var. *albiflora*** *(S. albiflora)* (Japanese

White Spirea) is a low, dense, mounding shrub. It grows 0.5–1 m (2–3') tall, with an equal spread, and bears white flowers in early summer. **'Goldmound'** has bright yellow foliage and bears pink flowers in late spring and early summer. **'Little Princess'** becomes a dense mound 45 cm (18") tall, and 1–1.8 m (3–6') wide. The flowers are a rose pink. **'Shibori'** ('Shirobana') grows 60 cm (24") tall and wide. Both pink and white flowers appear on the same plant. (Zones 4–9.)

S. nipponica (Nippon Spirea) is an upright shrub with arching branches. It grows 1–2.5 m (3–8') tall, with an equal spread. White flowers appear in mid-summer. **'Snowmound'** (Snowmound Nippon Spirea) is grown more commonly than the species. The spreading, arching branches are covered with flowers in early summer. It grows 1–1.5 m (3–5') tall, with an equal spread. (Zones 4–8.)

S. trilobata (Dwarf Bridal Wreath Spirea, Dwarf Vanhoutte Spirea) is a compact species, similar to S. x *vanhouttei.* The branches are covered in white flowers in late spring and early summer. It grows 1–1.2 m (3–4') tall, with an equal width. (Zones 3–7.)

S. x *vanhouttei* (Bridal Wreath Spirea, Vanhoutte Spirea) is a dense, bushy shrub with arching branches. It grows 1.8–3 m (6–10') tall and spreads 3–3.5 m (10–12'). White flowers are borne in clusters in early summer. (Zones 3–8.)

PESTS & PROBLEMS

Aphids, dieback, fire blight, leaf spot, powdery mildew, scale insects and weevils can cause problems.

S. x *vanhouttei*

Spruce

Picea

Features: foliage, cones, habit
Habit: conical or columnar, evergreen trees or shrubs
Height: 1–25 m (3–80') **Spread:** 1–6 m (3–20')
Planting: B & B, container; spring, fall **Zones:** 2–9

One gem among the many beautiful spruces is the Serbian Spruce. In a space-challenged garden, this evergreen adds grace and charm. It starts as a narrow column and never strays from that profile. Over time the Serbian Spruce can reach forest-tree size, but it is so slow growing that it remains in scale for small yards for many years. The needles are blue-green and the branches look like raised arms. I have the dwarf form 'Nana,' a specimen that demands little and never crowds out other species.

Spruce is the traditional Christmas tree in Europe.

GROWING

Spruce trees grow best in **full sun**. The soil should be **deep, moist, well drained** and **neutral to acidic**. These trees generally don't like hot, dry or polluted conditions. Pruning is rarely needed.

Spruces are best grown from small, young stock as they dislike being transplanted when larger or more mature.

TIPS

Spruces are used as specimen trees. The dwarf and slow-growing cultivars can also be used in shrub or mixed borders.

Oil-based pesticides such as dormant oil can take the blue out of your blue-needled spruces.

RECOMMENDED

P. abies (Norway Spruce) is a fast-growing, pyramidal tree with dark green needles. It grows 21–25 m (70–80') tall and spreads about 6 m (20'). This species is wind resistant. **'Nidiformis'** (Nest Spruce) is a slow-growing, low, compact, mounding form. It grows about 1–1.2 m (3–4') tall and spreads 1–1.5 m (3–5'). (Zones 2–8.)

P. breweriana (Weeping Spruce, Brewer Spruce) is a columnar tree with drooping branchlets up to 90 cm (36") long. It can grow 9–15 m (30–50') tall and spread 3–3.5 m (10–12'). (Zones 4–9.)

P. glauca

P. glauca (White Spruce) is native to Alaska, most of Canada and the northeastern U.S. This conical tree with blue-green needles grows 12–18 m (40–60') tall and spreads 3–6 m (10–20'). It can grow up to 48 m (160') tall in the wild. **'Conica'** (Dwarf White Spruce, Dwarf Alberta Spruce) is a dense, conical, bushy shrub 1.8–6 m (6–20') tall and 1–2.5 m (3–8') wide that works well in planters. (Zones 2–6.)

P. abies 'Nidiformis'

P. omorika (Serbian Spruce) is a slow-growing, narrow, spire-like tree with upward-arching branches and drooping branchlets. Two white stripes run the length of each needle. This tree grows 9–15 m (30–50') tall and spreads 3–4.5 m (10–15'). **'Nana'** is a dwarf cultivar that grows 1–2.5 m (3–8') tall, with a dense, conical or pyramidal habit. (Zones 4–8.)

P. pungens (Colorado Spruce) is a conical or columnar tree with stiff, blue-green needles and dense growth. This hardy, drought-tolerant tree grows 9–18 m (30–60') tall, with a spread of 3–6 m (10–20'). **Var. *glauca*** (Colorado Blue Spruce) is similar to the species, but with blue-grey needles.

Try using a dwarf, slow-growing cultivar such as 'Conica' for plant sculpture and bonsai.

P. abies (above)
P. pungens var. *glauca* cultivars (below)

Some smaller cultivars have been developed from this variety. **'Hoopsii'** grows up to 18 m (60') tall. It has a dense, pyramidal form and even more blue-white foliage than var. *glauca.* **'Mission Blue'** is a broad-based, compact form 1–2.5 m (3–8') tall, with bold blue foliage. (Zones 2–8.)

P. pungens var. *glauca* 'Hoopsii'

PESTS & PROBLEMS

Possible problems include aphids, caterpillars, gall insects, needle cast, nematodes, rust, sawflies, scale insects, spider mites and wood rot.

Stradivarius used spruce to make his renowned violins, and the resonant, lightweight but tough wood is still preferred for violins, guitars, harps and the sounding boards of pianos.

P. pungens var. *glauca* 'Mission Blue'

Sumac

Rhus

Features: summer and fall foliage, summer flowers, late-summer to fall fruit, habit
Habit: bushy, suckering, colony-forming, deciduous shrubs
Height: 0.5–7.5 m (2–25') **Spread:** equal to or greater than height
Planting: container; spring, fall **Zones:** 2–9

If you have poor soil, a windy location and a thrifty nature, try Staghorn Sumac. You can leave the garden centre having spent relatively little on a shrub that is reminiscent of a Japanese Maple in the garden. Its green, finely cut leaves look tropical in summer, and the fall foliage is spellbinding. The shrub's form anchors an underplanting of spring bulbs and wildflowers, while the long, thin branches look like sculpture in the winter garden. It is short-lived, but replacement plants lurk beneath the soil surface.

GROWING

Sumacs develop the best fall colour in **full sun** but tolerate partial shade. The soil should be of **average fertility, moist** and **well drained**.

These plants can become invasive. Remove suckers that come up where you don't want them. Cut out some of the oldest growth each year and allow some suckers to grow in to replace it. You can mow down any young plants that pop up in your lawn.

TIPS

Sumacs can be used to form a specimen group in a shrub or mixed border, in a woodland garden or on a sloping bank. Both male and female plants are needed for fruit to form.

The fruits are edible. For a refreshing beverage, soak the ripe fruits in cold water overnight and then strain and sweeten to taste.

RECOMMENDED

R. aromatica (Fragrant Sumac) forms a low mound of suckering stems. It grows 0.5–1.8 m (2–6') tall and spreads 1.5–3 m (5–10'). This species tolerates hot, dry exposed conditions and is native in Ontario. It can be used to prevent erosion on hills too steep for mowing. The foliage turns red or purple in fall. The cultivar **'Grow-Low'** is a distinctly fragrant groundcover growing about 60 cm (24") tall and spreading up to 2.5 m (8'). (Zones 3–9.)

R. glabra (Smooth Sumac) is a native shrub that forms a bushy, suckering colony. It grows 3–4.5 m (10–15') tall, with an equal or greater spread. Green summer flower spikes are followed, on female plants, by fuzzy, red fruit. The foliage turns brilliant shades of orange, red and purple in fall.

R. typhina (Staghorn Sumac) is a suckering, colony-forming shrub with branches covered by velvety fuzz. It grows 4.5–7.5 m (15–25') tall and spreads 7.5 m (25') or more. Fuzzy, yellow flowers are followed by hairy, red fruit. **'Dissecta'** ('Laciniata') has finely cut leaves that give the plant a lacy, graceful appearance.

This cultivar is more compact than the species, growing 1.8 m (6') high and spreading 3 m (10'). (Zones 3–8.)

PESTS & PROBLEMS

Blister, canker, caterpillars, dieback, leaf spot, powdery mildew, scale insects, wood rot and verticillium wilt can afflict this shrub.

Summersweet Clethra

Sweet Pepperbush

Clethra

Features: fragrant summer flowers, habit, fall foliage
Habit: rounded, suckering deciduous shrub
Height: 1–2.5 m (3–8') **Spread:** 1–2.5 m (3–8')
Planting: B & B, container; spring **Zones:** 3–9

Summersweet Clethra is a delightful shrub that brings late-summer fragrance and flowers to damp areas in the garden. It will withstand heavy shade and contributes fall colour and good winter form to the garden. The attractive flowers range from white to pink and last for a month or so. The wonderful fragrance of Summersweet Clethra is irresistible to bees, so you may wish to keep it away from paths, patios and play areas.

GROWING

Summersweet Clethra grows best in **light** or **partial shade**. The soil should be **fertile, humus rich, acidic, moist** and **well drained**.

Prune up to one-third of the growth back to the ground in early spring. Deadhead if possible to keep the plant looking neat.

TIPS

This shrub tends to sucker, forming a large colony of stems. Use it in a border or in a woodland garden. The light shade along the edge of a woodland is an ideal location.

RECOMMENDED

C. alnifolia forms a large, rounded, suckering colony. It bears attractive spikes of white flowers in late summer. The foliage turns yellow in fall. **'Hummingbird'** is a compact cultivar that grows 60–100 cm (24–40") tall, with a spread similar to that of the species. **'Pink Spires'** bears pink flowers. It grows up to 2.5 m (8') tall and wide.

PESTS & PROBLEMS

This plant is generally trouble free, though some fungal infections such as root rot can occur.

Summersweet Clethra is useful in damp, shaded gardens where the late-season flowers are much appreciated.

Sweetgum

Liquidambar

Features: habit, fall colour, spiny fruit, corky bark
Habit: pyramidal to rounded, deciduous tree
Height: 18–24 m (60–80') **Spread:** 12–15 m (40–50')
Planting: B & B; spring **Zones:** 5–9

The Sweetgum tree has gorgeous star-shaped leaves, rich fall colour and an impressive hardiness range, yet it is often banned from desirable plant lists because its falling fruit has hooked barbs. With careful placement, the Sweetgum adds a pretty silhouette to parks, campuses and naturalized plantings along streams. Plan a low-maintenance shrub and perennial border around the base of Sweetgum, so you can avoid having to deal with the prickly fruit.

GROWING

Sweetgum grows equally well in **full sun** or **partial shade**, but it develops the best colour in full sun. The soil should be of **average fertility, slightly acidic, moist** and **well drained**. This tree requires lots of room for its roots to develop. The foliage may develop late after excessively cold winters.

Little pruning is required. Remove dead, damaged, diseased or awkward branches in spring or early summer.

TIPS

Sweetgum is attractive as a shade tree, street tree, specimen tree or as part of a woodland garden. The falling spiny fruit makes Sweetgum inappropriate near patios or decks or where people may be walking in bare feet.

RECOMMENDED

L. styraciflua is a neat, symmetrical, pyramidal or rounded tree with attractive star-shaped foliage. Spiny, capsular fruits drop off the tree over the winter and often into the following summer. The fall colour of the glossy dark green leaves varies, often from year to year, from yellow to purple or brilliant red. Corky ridges may develop on young bark but disappear as the tree ages.

'Rotundiloba' is not as cold hardy as the species, its leaf lobes have rounded tips, and, more important, it does not bear any fruit. This admirable feature alone makes it worth growing in Zone 6 gardens. Let's hope more fruitless cultivars with better cold hardiness will appear in garden centres in the future.

PESTS & DISEASES

Occasional problems with leaf spot, rot, scale insects, caterpillars and borers can occur. Iron chlorosis can occur in too alkaline a soil.

This beautiful tree would be more popular if not for the messy and potentially dangerous falling fruit.

Thornless Honeylocust

Gleditsia

Features: summer and fall foliage, habit, fall seed pods
Habit: rounded, spreading, deciduous tree
Height: 4.5–30 m (15–100') **Spread:** 4.5–21 m (15–70')
Planting: B & B, container; spring, fall **Zones:** 4–8

Thornless Honeylocust remains a popular tree for lawn and street plantings. Cultivars with vivid yellow spring leaves have been a landscaping mainstay, and the brilliant, deep yellow fall colour is wonderful to behold. The leaves of Thornless Honeylocust are small and the shade cast is filtered, so grass or groundcovers can grow underneath it. There is some concern that overplanting has made this tree vulnerable to pests and diseases. Be wary of planting one if there are already many nearby.

GROWING

Thornless Honeylocust prefers **full sun**. The soil should be **fertile** and **well drained**. This tree adapts to most soil types. No pruning is required. Stake and pinch young plants to establish a good branching pattern.

TIPS

Use Thornless Honeylocust as a specimen tree. Though it is often used as a street tree, this species is a poor choice for that purpose because the vigorous roots can break up pavement and sidewalks. Also, mass plantings (such as along a street) may lead to problems because the roots become entwined and diseases can quickly travel from one tree to another.

The stunning beauty of Thornless Honeylocust in golden fall colour almost makes up for the nuisance the tiny leaflets create. They get into every imaginable place and a broom, rather than a rake, may be needed to clear them up because they slip easily between the tines of a rake. They do, however, disintegrate quickly on soil or lawn.

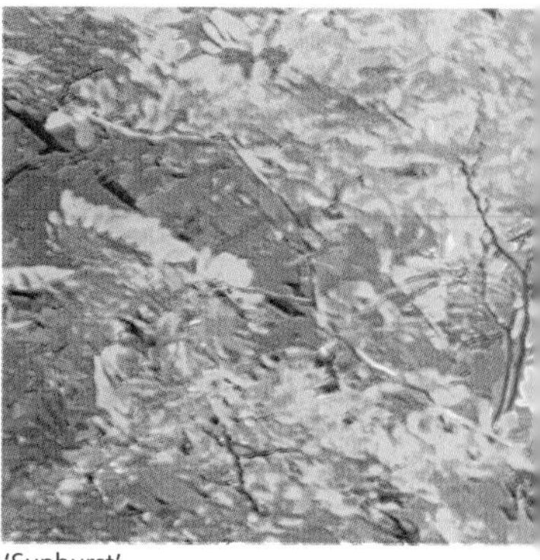

'Sunburst'

The twisted, hanging pods of Thornless Honeylocust contain a sweet, edible pulp. Do not, however, confuse this species with the poisonous Black Locust (Robinia pseudoacacia) *or Kentucky Coffee Tree* (Gymnocladus dioica).

RECOMMENDED

G. triacanthos* var. *inermis is a spreading, rounded tree. It grows up to 30 m (100') tall and spreads up to 21 m (70'). The fall colour is a warm golden yellow. The flowers are inconspicuous, but the long, pea-like pods that develop in late summer persist into fall and sometimes still dangle from the branches after the leaves have fallen. This variety is thornless and many cultivars have been developed from it. **'Elegantissima'** is dense, shrubby, compact and slow growing. It grows 4.5–7.5 m (15–25') tall and spreads up to about 4.5 m (15'). **'Sunburst'** is fast growing and broad spreading. It grows 9–12 m (30–40') tall and spreads 7.5–9 m (25–30'). The foliage emerges a bright yellow in spring and matures to light green over the summer.

PESTS & PROBLEMS

Aphids, borers, canker, caterpillars, heart rot, leaf spot, mites, powdery mildew, tar spot and webworm can cause problems.

This adaptable, quick-growing tree provides very light shade, making it a good choice for lawns.

Trumpetcreeper

Campsis

Features: habit, summer flowers
Habit: clinging, deciduous vine
Height: 9–18 m (30–60') **Spread:** 9–18 m (30–60')
Planting: container; any time **Zones:** 4–9

Trumpetcreepers are vines for people with lots of space to fill and a desire to fill it as quickly as possible. Trumpetcreepers create a privacy screen in a hurry and look beautiful growing on the side of a big, weathered barn or garage with their firm, red trumpets poking out. You may end up wishing your trumpetcreeper was creeping on someone else's building. Keep another plant in mind for the future in case you get tired of frequent pruning. Cultivars with yellow or apricot flowers are available, and they display the same virile growth as the species.

GROWING

These heat-tolerant plants grow well in **full sun, partial shade** or **light shade** but flower best in full sun. Any soil is fine, but the richer the soil the more invasive trumpetcreepers can be.

These vines are perfect for people who love to do a lot of pruning. They are very fast growing and can quickly take over entire gardens if not kept in check. Prune them back hard in spring to encourage lots of new growth, which is where the summer flowers appear.

TIPS

Trumpetcreepers will cling to any surface—a wall, a tree, a fence, a telephone pole. Once you have one you will probably never get rid of it. One of these plants can provide a privacy screen very quickly or can be grown up the wall or over the porch of a house, but it will probably not stay where you put it. They can be used on arbours and trellises but will need frequent pruning to stay attractive.

RECOMMENDED

C. radicans is valued for its fast growth and for the attractive, dark orange, trumpet-shaped flowers it bears for a long period over the summer. **'Crimson Trumpet'** has bright red flowers. **'Flava'** bears yellow flowers.

C.* x *tagliabuana (Tagliabue Trumpetcreeper) is similar to *C. radicans*, but is not as hardy and not as invasive. This species grows up to 9 m (30') tall and bears many bright orange flowers. Ontario gardeners will need to plant this species in a spot sheltered from wind. (Zones 6–9.)

PESTS & PROBLEMS

Problems with powdery mildew, scale insects, leaf spot and whiteflies can occur but are rarely serious.

Hummingbirds are attracted to the long tube-like flowers of trumpetcreepers.

Tulip Tree

Liriodendron

Features: early-summer flowers, foliage, fruit, habit
Habit: large, rounded, oval, deciduous tree
Height: 21–30 m (70–100') **Spread:** 10–15 m (33–50')
Planting: B & B; spring **Zones:** 4–9

The stately Tulip Tree is native in southern Ontario, where many warm-climate species grow. Its impressive range sees the Tulip Tree growing from Florida to Massachusetts and onward to the Lake Ontario shoreline. It is often given a place of honour at grand estates and public parks, including Thomas Jefferson's Monticello. The Tulip Tree reaches up to 30 m (100') at maturity with a remarkably straight trunk, lovely, stylish leaves and tulip-shaped spring flowers. The fall colour is a clear, golden yellow.

GROWING

Tulip Tree grows well in **full sun** or **partial shade**. The soil should be **average to rich, slightly acidic** and **moist**. This tree needs plenty of room for roots to grow. Frequent periods of drought can eventually kill the tree.

Little pruning is required. Remove dead, damaged or diseased growth as needed and awkward growth in winter.

TIPS

This beautiful, massive tree needs lots of room to grow. Parks, golf courses and large gardens can host this tree as a specimen or in a group planting, but its susceptibility to drought and need for root space makes it a poor choice as a specimen, shade or street tree on smaller properties.

RECOMMENDED

L. tulipifera is native to eastern North America. It is known more for its unusually shaped leaves than for its tulip-like flowers because the flowers are often borne high in the tree and go unnoticed until the falling petals litter the ground. The foliage turns golden yellow in fall. The leaves of **'Aureomarginata'** have yellow-green margins.

PESTS & PROBLEMS

Aphids, sooty mould, borers, leaf miners, scale insects, leaf spot and powdery mildew are some of the problems that can afflict Tulip Tree. Drought stress can cause some of the leaves to drop early.

Viburnum

Viburnum

Features: flowers, summer and fall foliage, fruit, habit
Habit: bushy or spreading, evergreen or deciduous shrubs
Height: 0.5–4.5 m (2–15') **Spread:** 0.5–4.5 m (2–15')
Planting: bare-root, B & B, container; spring, fall **Zones:** 2–8

Viburnums bring flowers, form, fruit and fall colour to the garden. Some are understated, and some are aristocratic and regal. The real beauty queen among them has to be the Doublefile Viburnum. It has a graceful, horizontal branching pattern, and in spring white flowers line the tops of the branches, looking like a galaxy of stars. The leaves are large and handsomely patterned with veins and creases. Fall colour tends toward a deep wine colour, and the berries attract birds. It grows wider than tall, but this is an asset. Once it is planted and given adequate moisture, this plant will perform flawlessly, making few demands on the gardener. Good fall colour, attractive form, shade tolerance, scented flowers and attractive fruit put the viburnums in a class by themselves.

GROWING

Viburnums grow well in **full sun, partial shade** or **light shade**. The soil should be of **average fertility, moist** and **well drained**. Viburnums tolerate both alkaline and acidic soils.

These plants will look neatest if deadheaded, but this practice will of course prevent fruits from forming. Fruiting is better when more than one plant of a species is grown.

TIPS

Viburnums can be used in borders and woodland gardens. They are a good choice for plantings near swimming pools.

The edible but very tart fruits of *V. opulus* and *V. trilobum* are popular for making jellies, pies and wine. They can be sweetened somewhat by freezing or by picking them after the first frost or two.

RECOMMENDED

V.* x *burkwoodii (Burkwood Viburnum) is a rounded shrub that is evergreen in warm climates. It grows 1.8–3 m (6–10') tall and spreads 1.5–2.5 m (5–8'). Clusters of pinkish-white flowers appear in mid- to late spring and are followed by red fruits that ripen to black. (Zones 4–8.)

V. carlesii (Korean Spice Viburnum) is a dense, bushy, rounded, deciduous shrub. It grows 1–2.5 m (3–8') tall, with an equal spread. White or pink, spicy-scented flowers appear in mid- to late spring. The fruits are red, ripening to black. The foliage may turn red in fall. **'Aurora'** has dark pink flower buds. (Zones 5–8.)

V. opulus (above), *V. plicatum* (centre)

V. opulus (below)

V. opulus (this page)

V. opulus (European Cranberrybush, Guelder-rose) is a rounded, spreading, deciduous shrub. It grows 2.5–4.5 m (8–15') tall and 2.5–3.5 m (8–12') wide. The flower clusters consist of an outer ring of showy sterile flowers surrounding the inner fertile flowers, giving the plant a lacy look when in bloom. The fall foliage and fruit are red. **'Nanum'** ('Compactum') is dense and slow growing, reaching 0.5–1.5 m (2–5') in height and spread. (Zones 3–8.)

V. plicatum (Japanese Snowball Viburnum) is a bushy, upright, deciduous shrub with arching stems. It grows 3–4.5 m (10–15') tall and spreads 3.5–4.5 m (12–15'). Ball-like clusters of flowers appear in late spring. Fall colour is reddish purple. **Var. *tomentosum*** (Doublefile Viburnum) has graceful, horizontal branching that gives the shrub a layered effect. It grows 2.5–3 m (8–10') tall and spreads 2.5–3.5 m (8–12'). The leaves have fuzzy undersides. Clusters of inconspicuous fertile flowers surrounded by showy sterile flowers blanket the branches. Several cultivars have been developed from this variety. **'Lanarth'** has showier flowerheads with larger sterile flowers. **'Mariesii'** has more distinctly layered branches. (Zones 5–8.)

Many species of birds are attracted to viburnums for edible fruit and the shelter they provide.

V. sargentii (Sargent Viburnum) is a large, bushy, deciduous shrub. It grows 3–4.5 m (10–15') tall,

with an equal spread. The early-spring flowers consist of clusters of inconspicuous fertile flowers surrounded by showy sterile flowers. The fall colour is yellow, orange and red. **'Onondaga'** has purple-stemmed, inconspicuous flowers ringed with showy, sterile, white flowers. The purple-green foliage turns red in fall. (Zones 3–7.)

V. trilobum (American Cranberrybush, Highbush Cranberry) is a dense, rounded shrub that is native to much of central North America. It grows 2.5–4.5 m (8–15') tall, with a spread of 2.5–3.5 m (8–12'). Early-summer clusters of showy sterile and inconspicuous fertile flowers are followed by edible red fruit. The fall colour is red. **'Compactum'** is a smaller, more dense shrub that grows 1.5–1.8 m (5–6') in height and width. Its flowers and fruit resemble those of the species. (Zones 2–7.)

PESTS & PROBLEMS

Aphids, dieback, downy mildew, grey mould, leaf spot, mealybugs, powdery mildew, scale insects, treehoppers, verticillium wilt, weevils and wood rot can affect viburnums.

V. opulus 'Nanum' (below), *V.* x *burkwoodii* (right, centre)

V. opulus (above)

V. plicatum 'Mariesii' (below)

Virginia Creeper

Boston Ivy

Parthenocissus

Features: summer and fall foliage, habit
Habit: clinging, woody, deciduous climbers
Height: 9–21 m (30–70') **Spread:** 9–21 m (30–70')
Planting: container; spring, fall **Zones:** 3–9

Virginia Creeper and Boston Ivy are handsome vines that establish quickly and provide an air of age and permanence, even on new structures. Virginia Creeper develops flaming fall colour and can conquer anything in its path, while growing in clay or sandy soil. Diligent pruning will keep it in shape and in bounds. Boston Ivy has simple, three-lobed leaves that remain glossy through the summer. The fall colour is a bright scarlet. A thick cover of Boston Ivy can transform an ugly wall into a thing of beauty. Keep the pruning shears handy, though—nothing looks more creepy and forlorn than Boston Ivy allowed to smother a house, rambling across windows, filling eaves and invading roof vents.

GROWING

These vines grow well in any light from **full sun to full shade**. The soil should preferably be **fertile** and **well drained**. The plants will adapt to clay or sandy soils.

These vigorous growers may need to be trimmed back frequently to keep them where you want them.

These vines can be used as groundcovers.

TIPS

Virginia creepers can cover an entire building, given enough time. They do not require support because they have clinging rootlets that can adhere to just about any surface—even smooth wood, vinyl or metal.

Give the plants lots of space and let them cover a wall, fence or arbour. Note, though, that when a vine is pulled off, the sticky ends leave little marks that can be hard to remove or even paint over. The **fruits** of Virginia creepers are **poisonous**.

RECOMMENDED

These species are very similar, except for the shape of the leaves.

P. quinquefolia (Virginia Creeper, Woodbine) is a clinging, woody climber that can grow 9–15 m (30–50') tall. The dark green foliage turns flame red in fall. Each leaf is divided into five leaflets.

P. tricuspidata (Boston Ivy, Japanese Creeper) is also a clinging, woody climber. It grows 15–21 m (50–70') tall. The three-lobed leaves turn red in fall. (Zones 4–8.)

PESTS & PROBLEMS

Aphids, bacterial leaf scorch, black rot, canker, dieback, downy mildew, grape leaf beetle, leafhoppers, leaf skeletonizers, leaf spot, powdery mildew, scab and scale insects can cause trouble.

Virginia creepers can cover the sides of buildings and help keep buildings cool in the summer heat. Cut the plants back to keep windows and doors accessible.

P. quinquefolia (this page)

Weigela

Weigela

Features: late-spring to early-summer flowers, foliage, habit
Habit: upright or low, spreading, deciduous shrubs
Height: 0.6–2.7 m (2–9') **Spread:** 1–3.5 m (3–12')
Planting: bare-root, container; spring, fall **Zones:** 3–8

Weigelas have been improved through breeding, and specimens with more compact forms, longer flowering periods and greater cold tolerance are now available. The generous blossoms of rosy pink occur in late spring and early summer on branches that often arch to the ground. Judicious pruning, annually, will prevent this shrub from becoming a huge, rambling mass.

Weigelas are some of the longest-blooming shrubs—the main flush of blooms lasts six weeks and sporadic flowers appear all summer.

GROWING

Weigelas prefer **full sun** but tolerate partial shade. The soil should be **fertile** and **well drained**. These plants will adapt to most well-drained soil conditions.

Once flowering is finished, cut flowering shoots back to strong buds or branch junctions. One-third of the old growth can be cut back to the ground at the same time.

TIPS

Weigelas can be used in shrub or mixed borders, in open woodland gardens and as informal barrier plantings.

RECOMMENDED

W. florida is a spreading shrub with arching branches. It grows 1.8–2.7 m (6–9') tall and spreads 2.5–3.5 m (8–12'). Dark pink flowers in clusters appear in late spring and early summer. **'Variegata'** is a compact plant that grows about 1.5 m (5') tall, with an equal spread. The flowers are pale pink, and the leaves have creamy white margins. (Zones 5–8.)

The following hybrids are sometimes listed as cultivars of *W. florida.*

***W.* 'Minuet'** is a compact, spreading shrub. It grows 60–90 cm (24–36") tall and spreads about 1 m (3–4'). The dark pink flowers have yellow throats. (Zones 3–7.)

***W.* 'Red Prince'** is an upright shrub. It grows 1.5–1.8 m (5–6') tall and spreads about 1.5 m (5'). Bright red flowers appear in early summer, with a second flush in late summer. (Zones 4–7.)

PESTS & PROBLEMS

Scale insects, twig-knot nematodes, twig dieback and verticillium wilt are possible, but usually not serious, problems.

Hummingbirds will be especially attracted to weigelas with long, red flowers.

'Variegata'

This shrub's name honours German botanist Christian Weigel (1748–1831).

Wisteria

Wisteria

Features: late-spring flowers, foliage, habit
Habit: twining, woody, deciduous climbers
Height: 6–15 m (20–50') or more **Spread:** 6–15 m (20–50') or more
Planting: container; spring, fall **Zones:** 4–9

Loose clusters of purple hang like lace from the branches of wisteria. A gardener willing to use the garden shears can create beautiful tree forms and attractive arbour specimens, but let a wisteria get away from you and the vine's grip mangles anything in its path. A flimsy arbour will be consumed by a wisteria, and shoots will weave their way into the garden, twisting around unsuspecting trees and shrubs. If possible, plant wisteria on a stout wooden or metal support and be prepared to prune.

GROWING

Wisterias grow well in **full sun** or **partial shade**. The soil should be of **average fertility, moist** and **well drained**. Vines grown in too fertile a soil will produce lots of vegetative growth but very few flowers. Avoid planting wisteria near a lawn where fertilizer may leach over to your vine.

The first two or three years will be used to establish a main framework of sturdy stems. Once the vine is established, side shoots can be cut back in late winter to within three to six buds of the main stems. Trim the entire plant back in mid-summer if the growth is becoming rampant. Grown on a large, sturdy structure, wisteria can simply be left to its own devices, but be prepared for it to escape once it runs out of room.

TIPS

These vines require something to twine around, such as an arbour or other sturdy structure. You can also train a wisteria to form a small tree. Try to select a permanent site; wisterias don't like being moved.

These vigorous vines may send up suckers and can root wherever branches touch the ground. Regular pruning will prevent your wisteria from getting out of hand.

All parts of wisteria plants, especially the **seeds**, are **poisonous**.

RECOMMENDED

W. floribunda (Japanese Wisteria) grows 7.5–15 m (25–50') tall, or taller. Long, pendulous clusters of fragrant blue, purple, pink or white flowers appear in late spring before the leaves emerge. Long, bean-like pods follow.

W. sinensis (Chinese Wisteria) can grow 6–9 m (20–30') tall, or taller. It bears long, pendant clusters of fragrant blue-purple flowers in late spring. **'Alba'** has white flowers. (Zones 5–8.)

PESTS & PROBLEMS

Aphids, crown gall, dieback, leaf miners, leaf spot, mealybugs and viral diseases may cause problems.

You may need to mistreat your wisteria to get the best blooms. If you have a reluctant bloomer, try pruning the roots and withholding food and water.

W. sinensis (this page)

Witch-Hazel

Hamamelis

Features: flowers, foliage, habit
Habit: spreading, deciduous shrubs or small trees
Height: 1.8–6 m (6–20') **Spread:** 1.8–6 m (6–20')
Planting: B & B, container; spring, fall **Zones:** 3–9

The witch-hazel 'Arnold Promise' is an investment in happiness. In my garden it blooms as early as February, its sulphur yellow flowers clustering like tiny paper streamers on the bare branches. The flowers last for weeks, and their spicy fragrance awakens the senses. Branches can be cut early and forced into bloom indoors. Another outstanding feature is this cultivar's fall colour. Sometimes the handsome leaves have overlapping bands of orange, yellow and red. Though it prefers moist, organic soil, in a dry, exposed location this witch-hazel seems to adapt by growing slowly. Cultivars with red-, orange- or apricot-coloured flowers are also available.

GROWING

Witch-hazels grow best in a **sheltered** spot under **full sun** or **light shade**. The soil should be of **average fertility, neutral to acidic, moist** and **well drained**. Pruning is rarely required. Remove awkward shoots once flowering is complete.

TIPS

Witch-hazels work well individually or in groups. They can be used as specimen plants, in shrub or mixed borders or in woodland gardens. As small trees, they are ideal for space-limited gardens.

The unique flowers have long, narrow, crinkled petals that give the plant a spidery appearance when in bloom. If the weather gets too cold, the petals will roll up, protecting the flowers and extending the flowering season.

H. virginiana (this page)

The branches of these plants have been used as divining rods to find water and gold.

H. virginiana (above)

RECOMMENDED

H.* x *intermedia is a vase-shaped, spreading shrub. It grows 3–6 m (10–20') tall, with an equal spread. Fragrant clusters of yellow, orange or red flowers appear in mid- to late winter. The leaves turn attractive shades of orange, red and bronze in fall. **'Arnold Promise'** has large, fragrant, bright yellow or yellow-orange flowers. **'Diane'** ('Diana') has dark red flowers in late winter and fall foliage of yellow, orange and red. **'Jelena'** has a horizontal, spreading habit. The fragrant flowers are coppery orange and the fall colour is orange-red. **'Pallida'** is a more compact plant, growing 3.5 m (12') tall and wide. Its flowers are bright yellow. **'Ruby Glow'** is a vigorous, upright shrub with deep orange flowers. (Zones 5–9.)

H. vernalis (Vernal Witchhazel) is a rounded, upright, often suckering shrub. It grows 1.8–4.5 m (6–15') tall, with an equal spread. Very fragrant, yellow, orange or red flowers are borne in early spring. The foliage turns bright yellow in fall. (Zones 4–8.)

H. x *intermedia* 'Arnold Promise' (below)

H. virginiana (Common Witch-hazel) is a large, rounded, spreading shrub or small tree that is native to most of eastern North America, including southern and eastern Ontario. It can reach 3.5–6 m (12–20') or more in height, with an equal spread. Yellow fall flowers are often hidden by the foliage that turns yellow at the same time, but this species is attractive nonetheless. (Zones 3–8.)

PESTS & PROBLEMS

Aphids, leaf rollers, leaf spot, powdery mildew, scale insects and wood rot are possible, but rarely serious, problems.

A witch-hazel extract was used traditionally as a general remedy for burns and skin inflammations. Today it is often sold as a mild astringent in facial products.

H. virginiana (this page)

Yew

Taxus

Features: foliage, habit, red seed cups
Habit: evergreen; conical or columnar trees or bushy or spreading shrubs
Height: 0.5–21 m (2–70') **Spread:** 1–9 m (3–30')
Planting: B & B, container; spring, fall **Zones:** 4–8

From sweeping hedges to commanding specimens, yews can serve many purposes in the garden. They accept pruning without complaint and create useful backdrops with their uniform deep green foliage. Some cultivars have golden new growth, so it seems that the plant is always just catching the rising or setting sun. The growth of yews can be spreading, upright or compact, depending on the cultivar. They are often used for topiary, in which their handsome bearing is disguised in cartoon character forms.

GROWING

Yews grow well in any light conditions from **full sun** to **full shade**. The soil should be **fertile, moist** and **well drained**. These trees tolerate windy, dry and polluted conditions, and soils of any acidity. They dislike excessive heat, however, and on the hotter south or southwest side of a building they may suffer needle scorch.

Hedges and topiary can be trimmed back in summer and fall. New growth will sprout from hard prunings. Even old wood can sprout new growth.

TIPS

Yews can be used in borders or as specimens, hedges, topiary and groundcovers.

Male and female flowers are borne on separate plants. Both must be present for the attractive red arils (seed cups) to form.

T. cuspidata

All parts of yews are ***poisonous,*** *except the pleasant-tasting, fleshy red cup that surrounds the inedible hard seed.*

T. baccata

T. baccata (above & right)

*Taxol, a drug for treating ovarian, breast and other cancers, was originally derived from the bark of a Western Yew species (*T. brevifolia*).*

RECOMMENDED

T. baccata (English Yew) is a broad, conical tree with attractive, flaking bark. It grows 9–21 m (30–70') tall and spreads 4.5–9 m (15–30'). The foliage can become discoloured in winter. The species is hardy in Zones 6–8. Among the many cultivars, **'Fastigiata'** (Irish Yew) is a columnar, female cultivar grown for its attractive, upright habit. It grows 4.5–9 m (15–30') tall and spreads 1.5–3 m (5–10'). **'Repandens'** is a wide-spreading, mounding shrub with greater cold hardiness than the species, to Zone 5. It grows 0.5–1.2 m (2–4') tall and spreads 3.5–4.5 m (12–15').

T. cuspidata (Japanese Yew) is a slow-growing, broad, columnar or conical tree. It grows 9–15 m (30–50') tall and spreads 6–9 m (20–30'). **'Nana'** is a compact, spreading cultivar that may grow 1–1.8 m (3–6') tall and 1–3 m (3–10') wide. (Zones 4–7.)

T.* x *media (English Japanese Yew), a cross between the other two species, has the vigour of the English Yew and the cold hardiness of the Japanese Yew. It forms a rounded, upright tree or shrub 0.5–7.5 m (2–25') in height, depending on the cultivar. **'Densiformis'** is a wide, dense, rounded shrub. It grows 1–1.2 m (3–4') tall and spreads 1.8–2.5 m (6–8'). **'Hicksii'** is an open, columnar tree that grows 4.5–7.5 m (15–25') tall and spreads 1.5–3 m (5–10'). This narrow, upright yew is a good choice in colder climates. (Zones 4–7.)

T. cuspidata

The tough wood of T. baccata *was traditionally valued for carving and for making longbows. Robin Hood is said to have made his bow from this wood.*

PESTS & PROBLEMS

Black vine weevils, dieback, mealybugs, mites, needle blight, root rot and scale insects are possible but not serious problems. A wash with soapy water during hot weather can help control mites. Be sure to rinse plants well.

Yucca

Adam's Needle

Yucca

Features: summer flowers, foliage, habit
Habit: rounded rosette of long, stiff, spiky, evergreen leaves
Height: 60–90 cm (24–36"); up to 1.8 m (6') in flower
Spread: 60–90 cm (24–36")
Planting: spring, fall **Zones:** 5–9

Happiest in dry, hot, sandy soil, Yucca is often consigned to spare little plantings that mimic a desert setting. Its big, creamy flowers seem somewhat incongruous, billowing in spherical shapes above those sword-like leaves of green and gold. A grouping of two or three Yucca plants in a mixed border will provide contrast and make a unique impression on visitors wandering through the garden.

GROWING

Yucca grows best in **full sun**. Any **well-drained** soil is suitable. This plant is drought tolerant. Pruning is not needed, but the flower spikes can be removed when flowering is finished, and dead leaves can be removed as needed.

The striking white flowers are edible raw or cooked and are said to taste like Belgian endive. Try adding them to a salad.

TIPS

Yucca is used as a specimen, usually in groups or in planters, to give a garden a southern appearance. In pots, planters and urns this plant also makes a strong architectural statement.

RECOMMENDED

Y. filamentosa has long, stiff, finely serrated, pointed leaves with threads that peel back from the edges. It is the most frost-hardy *Yucca* species available. **'Bright Edge'** has leaves with yellow margins. **'Golden Sword'** has leaves with yellow centres and green margins.

PESTS & PROBLEMS

Cane borers, fungal leaf spot and scale insects can cause problems.

Yucca fruits are rarely seen in cultivation. The Yucca moth, which pollinates the flowers, is uncommon outside the plant's natural range in the southeastern U.S.

'Bright Edge' (this page)

Other Trees & Shrubs to Consider

Black Walnut

Black Walnut

Juglans nigra

Deciduous, rounded tree 15–22 m (50–75') tall with an equal spread. Leaves drop throughout the growing season and develop no appreciable fall colour. Large, hard-shelled, edible nuts fall in late summer and fall; avoid plantings near patios and driveways as people and vehicles can be hit by the falling nuts. A chemical that leaches out of the nuts can inhibit the growth of plants growing nearby. The wood is valued for furniture making.

Black Walnut grows well in **full sun** and **fertile, moist, well-drained** soil. Little pruning is required, but any pruning should take place in late summer to avoid excessive sap bleeding. These trees are too large for the average garden but are grown as specimens and for their wood in larger spaces. Drought stress can cause early leaf drop and make the tree more susceptible to pests and diseases. (Zones 4–9.)

Bald Cypress

Bald Cypress

Taxodium distichum

Deciduous or semi-evergreen, conical coniferous tree 15–40 m (50–130') tall and 6–9 m (20–30') wide. Becomes more open and asymmetrical with age. Bright green foliage turns orangy brown in fall. In or near swampy areas this tree forms gnome-like 'knees' *(pneumatophores)*, knobby roots that poke up out of the water and allow the roots to breathe.

Bald Cypress prefers **full sun** or **partial shade** and **moist, acidic** soil but will adapt to different soil conditions. Alkaline soils can cause the foliage to turn yellow (chlorotic). Bald Cypress has a deep taproot but transplants easily when young. Use as a large specimen tree individually or in groups. (Zones 4–9.)

Blueberry, Lowbush Blueberry

Vaccinium angustifolium

Blueberry

Deciduous, low, spreading shrub 10–60 cm (4–24") tall with an equal spread. These shrubs have tiny pink flowers in late spring, dark to bright blue edible berries and bright red fall colour.

Blueberries grow well in **full sun** or **partial shade** and **acidic, moist, well-drained** soil. These plants grow wild in many areas of Ontario but make interesting, hardy groundcover plants for the garden, particularly for northern gardeners who can more easily meet the cultural requirements. Blueberries are reluctant to self-pollinate, and more fruit will be produced when more than one hybrid is planted. Little pruning is required; remove dead or damaged growth as needed. These plants require acidic soil and most potential problems can be avoided by ensuring this requirement is met. (Zones 2–5.)

Camperdown Elm

Ulmus glabra 'Camperdownii'

Deciduous, shrubby form grafted onto a 2 m (6–7') standard to form a domed, weeping tree with ground-sweeping branches. Reaches 6–7.5 m (20–25') in height, with an equal spread. Attractive bare branches provide winter interest.

Camperdown Elm prefers **full sun** and **moist, well-drained** soil. This cultivar is susceptible to Dutch Elm Disease and the many other problems that afflict elms, but it is more resistant than most species. It makes a striking specimen, more suitable for a small garden than many larger trees. (Zones 4–7.)

Camperdown Elm

Cedar

CEDAR
Cedrus

Evergreen, upright trees with spreading branches and often with pendulous branchlets. Some species can grow up to 40 m (130') tall in more welcoming climates, but there are smaller cultivars. Cedars are hardy only in the warm southern regions of Ontario. *C. libani* (Cedar of Lebanon) and its cultivars are the hardiest and most commonly available of the cedars.

Cedars grow well in **full sun** or **partial shade** with an **average to fertile, moist, loamy, well-drained** soil. Very little pruning is required; remove any damaged, dead or diseased growth. The large species are best reserved for large spaces and warmer climates. The smaller cultivars are a better fit in most gardens and are easier to protect in the winter. The biggest problem is dieback, which can be caused by cold, weevils or canker. Root rot can occur in poorly drained soils. (Zones 5–9.)

Douglas-Fir

DOUGLAS-FIR
Pseudotsuga menziesii

Evergreen, columnar tree; can grow 60 m (200') in native stands in the Pacific Northwest but is unlikely to reach such lofty heights in Ontario. Smaller, dwarf cultivars that grow 1.8–6 m (6–20') are more suitable in a small home garden. Cones have unique three-pronged bracts that protrude from between the cone scales and have been described as looking like the hind feet and tail of a mouse or the tongue of a dragon.

Douglas-fir grows well in **full sun** and **average, moist, acidic, well-drained** soil. Pruning is generally not required. Trees can be grown singly or in groups, and dwarf cultivars can be used in borders. Occasional problems with canker, leaf cast, spruce budworm, scale insects and aphids can occur. (Zones 4–6.)

Dove Tree
Davidia involucrata

Dove Tree flowers

Deciduous, rounded, pyramidal tree 6–15 m (20–50') tall with a 9 m (30') spread. The scaly, exfoliating bark provides winter interest. Pairs of large, white, wing-like bracts curve down around the inconspicuous flowers, inspiring such names as Dove Tree, Ghost Tree and Handkerchief Tree.

Dove Tree grows well in **partial shade** or **full sun** and **rich, moist, well-drained, humus-rich** soil. This tree requires **shelter** from strong winds. Encourage a strong central leader and remove any awkward branches while the tree is young; remove branches that are dead or damaged as required. This tree rarely flowers before it is ten years old. Dove Tree is not susceptible to pest or disease problems but is hardy in only the warmest regions of Ontario. (Zones 6–8.)

Dove Tree in the garden

Dutchman's Pipe
Aristolochia macrophylla (A. durior)

Deciduous, twining vine 6–9 m (20–30') tall with an equal spread. Provides a dense curtain of large, heart-shaped leaves that often hide the unusual, pipe-shaped flowers. Some people find the scent of the flowers unpleasant.

Dutchman's Pipe grows well in **full sun** or **partial shade** and **fertile, well-drained** soil. Provide a sturdy support for the vines to twine up. It can be cut back as needed during the growing season and should be thinned to a strong frame of main branches in late fall or spring. These vines are grown on trellises, arbours and buildings as quick-growing screens. Leaf spot, grey mould and root rot can be troublesome on plants grown in too wet a soil. (Zones 5–8.)

False Spirea

False Spirea
Sorbaria sorbifolia

Deciduous, suckering shrub 1.5–3 m (5–10') tall with an equal or greater spread. With its feathery foliage and fleecy flowers, this shrub gives an exotic air to problem spots in the garden. It flowers in mid- to late summer. Spent flowerheads can be removed if you find them unattractive.

False Spirea grows equally well in **full sun, partial shade** or **light shade** and **average, moist, well-drained** soil with plenty of **organic** matter. It tolerates hot, dry conditions. This tree can be invasive; remove suckers that are growing out of bounds and thin out some of the oldest growth each year or two in spring. To rejuvenate an old stand, cut entire plants back to within a few buds of the ground as the buds begin to swell in spring. Useful in large borders, as barrier plants, in naturalized gardens and in lightly shaded woodland gardens. (Zones 2–8.)

Kentucky Coffee Tree

Kentucky Coffee Tree
Gymnocladus dioica

Deciduous tree 18–22 m (60–75') in height and 12–15 m (40–50') wide. Male and female flowers are borne on separate trees; males bear smaller clusters of flowers but do not bear the many toxic bean-like pods that the female trees do.

Kentucky Coffee Tree grows well in **full sun** and **fertile, moist, well-drained** soil though it adapts to many soil types and tolerates polluted urban conditions and drought. The **fruit** is **poisonous** if ingested. Little pruning is needed. Male trees are preferable and several cultivars are available. This tree is suitable as a specimen or shade tree in areas with lots of space. (Zones 5–8.)

Weeping Willow (p. 327) is one of the first deciduous trees to leaf out, and one of the last to drop its leaves. The golden branches provide winter interest.

Mountain Ash
Sorbus

Mountain Ash

Deciduous, single or multi-stemmed tree 6–12 m (20–40') tall and 6–9 m (20–30') wide. Mountain ashes are grown for their attractive, rounded form, spring display of white flowers and red, orange or yellow fall fruit that persists into winter. *S. aucuparia*, the European Mountain Ash, and *S. decora*, the Showy Mountain Ash, are two attractive species.

Mountain ashes grow well in **full sun, partial shade** or **light shade** in **average to fertile, humus-rich, well-drained** soil. These plants will need very little pruning. Remove damaged, diseased and awkward growth as needed. Commonly grown as specimen trees in small gardens, they are also ideal in woodland and natural gardens where they attract a variety of wildlife to the garden. Many birds enjoy the fruits. Very susceptible to fire blight, which will eventually kill the plant. Be prepared to replace this tree in your garden after 10 or 15 years. (Zones 2–7.)

Ninebark, Common Ninebark
Physocarpus opulifolius

Ninebark

Deciduous, suckering shrub 1.5–3 m (5–10') tall and 1.8–4.5 m (6–15') wide. Ninebark is native to Ontario. It has attractive form and foliage, arching branches, exfoliating bark, light pink flowers in early summer and clusters of reddish-green seed pods. Cultivars with yellow foliage are available; they keep their colour best in partially or lightly shaded locations.

Ninebarks grow well in **full sun** or **partial shade** in **fertile, acidic, moist, well-drained** soil. Little pruning is required; remove one-third of the old growth each year after flowering is finished to encourage vigorous new growth. Ninebarks can be included in borders and woodland gardens. Occasional problems with leaf spot, fire blight and powdery mildew can occur. (Zones 2–7.)

Privet

PRIVET, AMUR PRIVET
Ligustrum amurense

Deciduous or semi-evergreen, upright or arching shrub 3.5–4.5 m (12–15') tall and 2.5–4.5 m (8–15') wide. Privet is commonly used as a hedge because it is fast growing and inexpensive. It also makes an attractive border specimen when left unpruned.

Privet grows equally well in **full sun** or **partial shade** in any **well-drained** soil. It tolerates polluted, urban conditions. Privet hedges can be trimmed twice a summer. Specimen plants need almost no pruning. Damaged or awkward branches can be removed as needed. Occasional problems with aphids, scale insects, leaf miners, Japanese beetles, powdery mildew, root rot, canker and leaf spot can occur. (Zones 3–8.)

Silverbell fruit (above), in the garden (below)

SILVERBELL
Halesia

Deciduous, rounded, spreading, multi-stemmed trees 6–12 m (20–40') tall and 6–10 m (20–35') wide. They bear attractive white flowers in spring or early summer before or as the leaves emerge. The persistent winged fruit capsules that follow provide fall and winter interest. The light green leaves are attractive but don't develop much colour in fall.

Silverbells grow well in **full sun, partial shade** or **light shade** and **fertile, humus-rich, neutral to acidic, moist, well-drained** soil. Pruning is rarely required. Silverbells make attractive specimen trees and can be used in woodland gardens, included in a border or used near a pond or stream. Occasional problems with root rot, wood rot and scale insects are possible. These trees can be difficult to find in garden centres. (Zones 5–8.)

Snowbell, Japanese Snowbell

Styrax japonica

Snowbell

Deciduous, upright multi-stemmed tree with arching, spreading branches; can grow 6–9 m (20–30') tall with an equal spread. Loose clusters of pendant white flowers are borne in late spring or early summer and are best admired from directly below the tree. Snowbell is also admired for its dark green foliage and attractive form.

Snowbell grows well in **full sun, partial shade** or **light shade** and **fertile, humus-rich, neutral to acidic, moist, well-drained** soil. Pruning is rarely required; tree forms can be encouraged in young plants by thinning out some of the stems and by pruning some of the lower side growth back to the trunk. Use near entryways or patios, in borders and in woodland gardens. Branches and flowers can be killed back if winter temperatures drop below –28° C (–20° F). (Zones 5–8.)

Weeping Willow

Weeping Willow

Salix alba 'Tristis'

Deciduous, rounded tree 9–15 m (30–50') tall with an equal spread. Delicate, flexible, weeping branches sweep the ground. Long, narrow leaves emerge early in spring and turn bright yellow before dropping late in fall.

Weeping Willow prefers **full sun** with **well-drained** but **moist soil** and lots of room for roots to spread. It suffers in shallow, alkaline soil. This graceful, elegant tree can be used as a specimen or shade tree. It is displayed to best advantage next to a lake, river or other water source. A beautiful tree, but not without problems; the roots can be destructive, breaking into pipes and through foundations, and twigs and leaves drop constantly. (Zones 4–9.)

Quick Reference Chart

TREE HEIGHT LEGEND: Short: < 7. 5 m (25') • Medium: 7.5–15 m (25–50') • Tall: > 15 m (50')

SPECIES by Common Name	FORM						FOLIAGE							
	Tall Tree	Med. Tree	Short Tree	Shrub	Groundcover	Climber	Evergreen	Deciduous	Variegated	Blue/White	Purple/Red	Yellow/Gold	Dark Green	Light Green
Aralia			*	*				*	*				*	
Arborvitae		*	*	*			*					*	*	
Ash	*	*						*						*
Bearberry					*		*						*	
Beauty Bush				*				*						
Beech	*	*						*	*		*	*	*	
Birch	*	*						*						
Bog Rosemary				*	*		*						*	
Boxwood				*			*							
Butterfly Bush				*				*		*			*	*
Caryopteris				*				*				*		*
Cherry, Plum & Almond	*	*	*	*				*			*		*	*
Clematis					*	*		*					*	
Cotoneaster			*	*	*		*						*	
Crabapple		*	*					*						
Daphne				*			*		*	*		*	*	
Dawn Redwood	*							*					*	
Deutzia				*				*						
Dogwood			*	*				*	*				*	
Elder			*	*				*			*	*	*	
English Ivy					*	*	*	*	*	*		*	*	
Euonymus			*	*	*	*	*	*	*	*		*	*	*
False Arborvitae	*			*			*						*	
False Cypress	*	*	*	*			*		*			*	*	
Fir	*	*	*	*			*			*			*	*
Firethorn				*	*	*	*	*					*	
Fiveleaf Akebia						*		*		*				
Flowering Quince				*				*						

SPECIES
by Common Name

FEATURES									BLOOMING					
Form	Flowers	Foliage	Bark	Fruit/Cones	Scent	Spines	Fall Colour	Winter Interest	Spring	Summer	Fall	Zones	Page Number	
	*	*		*		*				*		4-8	74	Aralia
*		*	*	*	*			*				2-9	76	Arborvitae
							*					3-9	80	Ash
*	*	*		*			*	*	*			2-7	82	Bearberry
	*								*			4-8	84	Beauty Bush
*		*	*	*			*	*				4-9	86	Beech
*	*	*	*				*	*	*			2-9	90	Birch
	*	*							*	*		2-6	94	Bog Rosemary
*		*			*			*				4-9	96	Boxwood
*	*	*			*				*	*	*	4-9	100	Butterfly Bush
	*	*			*					*		5-9	104	Caryopteris
*	*	*	*	*	*		*	*	*		*	2-9	106	Cherry, Plum & Almond
*	*							*		*		3-9	112	Clematis
*	*	*		*			*	*		*		4-9	114	Cotoneaster
*	*		*	*	*		*	*	*			4-8	118	Crabapple
	*	*			*			*	*		*	4-7	122	Daphne
*		*	*	*			*	*				4-8	126	Dawn Redwood
*	*									*		4-9	128	Deutzia
*	*	*	*	*			*	*	*	*		2-9	130	Dogwood
	*	*		*			*			*		3-9	134	Elder
*		*					*	*				5-9	138	English Ivy
*		*	*				*	*				4-9	140	Euonymus
*		*		*				*				5-8	144	False Arborvitae
*		*		*				*				4-9	146	False Cypress
*		*		*	*			*				3-7	150	Fir
*	*	*		*		*				*		5-9	154	Firethorn
*	*	*		*						*		4-8	158	Fiveleaf Akebia
	*			*	*	*			*			4-9	160	Flowering Quince

TREE HEIGHT LEGEND: Short: < 7. 5 m (25') • Medium: 7.5–15 m (25–50') • Tall: > 15 m (50')

SPECIES by Common Name	FORM						FOLIAGE							
	Tall Tree	Med. Tree	Short Tree	Shrub	Groundcover	Climber	Evergreen	Deciduous	Variegated	Blue/White	Purple/Red	Yellow/Gold	Dark Green	Light Green
Forsythia				*				*						*
Fothergilla				*				*		*				*
Fringe Tree			*	*				*						*
Gingko	*	*						*						*
Goldenchain Tree			*			*		*						
Grape						*		*			*		*	
Hawthorn		*	*	*				*					*	
Hazel			*	*				*			*	*	*	*
Heather				*	*		*						*	
Hemlock	*	*	*	*			*						*	*
Holly		*	*	*			*		*				*	
Honeysuckle				*		*	*	*						
Hornbeam	*	*						*						*
Horsechestnut	*	*	*	*				*					*	
Hydrangea			*	*		*		*						
Japanese Pagoda-tree		*	*					*					*	
Juniper	*	*	*	*	*		*			*			*	*
Kalmia				*			*						*	
Katsuratree	*	*	*					*		*	*		*	
Kerria				*				*	*			*		*
Kiwi						*		*	*					
Larch	*	*						*						*
Leucothoe				*			*		*					
Lilac		*	*	*				*					*	
Linden	*	*						*						*
London Planetree	*	*						*					*	*
Magnolia		*	*	*				*					*	
Maple	*	*	*	*				*	*		*	*	*	*

SPECIES
by Common Name

FEATURES									BLOOMING					
Form	Flowers	Foliage	Bark	Fruit/Cones	Scent	Spines	Fall Colour	Winter Interest	Spring	Summer	Fall	Zones	Page Number	
	*								*			3-9	162	Forsythia
	*				*		*		*			4-9	166	Fothergilla
*	*		*		*			*		*		4-9	168	Fringe Tree
*		*	*	*	*		*	*				3-9	170	Gingko
*	*			*					*	*		5-7	172	Goldenchain Tree
*		*		*	*		*		*			5-8	174	Grape
*	*	*	*	*		*	*	*	*			3-8	176	Hawthorn
*	*	*	*	*				*	*			3-9	180	Hazel
*	*	*			*				*			5-7	184	Heather
*		*		*				*				3-8	186	Hemlock
*		*		*		*		*				3-9	190	Holly
	*			*	*				*	*	*	3-8	192	Honeysuckle
*		*	*				*	*				3-9	196	Hornbeam
*	*	*		*			*		*	*		3-9	198	Horsechestnut
*	*		*							*	*	3-9	202	Hydrangea
*	*	*			*		*			*		4-9	206	Japanese Pagoda-tree
*		*		*	*	*		*				2-9	208	Juniper
	*	*						*	*	*		4-9	214	Kalmia
*		*			*		*	*				4-8	216	Katsuratree
*	*								*			4-9	218	Kerria
*	*	*		*						*		3-8	220	Kiwi
*		*		*			*					1-7	222	Larch
	*	*							*			5-8	224	Leucothoe
	*				*				*	*		2-8	226	Lilac
*	*	*			*					*		2-8	230	Linden
*		*	*				*	*				4-8	232	London Planetree
*	*	*	*	*	*			*	*	*		3-9	234	Magnolia
*	*	*	*	*			*	*	*			2-9	238	Maple

TREE HEIGHT LEGEND: Short: < 7. 5 m (25') • Medium: 7.5–15 m (25–50') • Tall: > 15 m (50')

SPECIES by Common Name	FORM						FOLIAGE							
	Tall Tree	Med. Tree	Short Tree	Shrub	Groundcover	Climber	Evergreen	Deciduous	Variegated	Blue/White	Purple/Red	Yellow/Gold	Dark Green	Light Green
Mock-orange				*				*						
Oak	*	*	*	*				*					*	
Oregon Grapeholly				*			*				*		*	
Peashrub				*				*						*
Pieris				*			*		*		*	*	*	
Pine	*	*	*	*			*		*				*	
Potentilla				*				*						
Redbud		*	*	*				*	*	*	*			
Rhododendron				*			*						*	
Rose-of-Sharon			*	*				*						*
Russian Olive			*	*				*		*				*
Serviceberry		*	*	*				*					*	
Smokebush			*	*				*			*			
Spirea				*				*			*	*	*	*
Spruce	*	*	*	*			*			*			*	
Sumac			*	*	*			*					*	
Summersweet Clethra				*				*						
Sweetgum	*	*						*					*	
Thornless Honeylocust	*	*	*					*				*		*
Trumpetcreeper						*		*						
Tulip Tree	*							*	*			*	*	
Viburnum			*	*			*	*					*	
Virginia Creeper					*	*		*					*	
Weigela				*				*						
Wisteria						*		*						
Witch-hazel			*	*				*					*	
Yew	*	*	*	*			*						*	
Yucca				*	*		*		*					*

SPECIES
by Common Name

FEATURES									BLOOMING					
Form	Flowers	Foliage	Bark	Fruit/Cones	Scent	Spines	Fall Colour	Winter Interest	Spring	Summer	Fall	Zones	Page Number	
	*				*					*		3-8	244	Mock-orange
*		*	*	*			*					3-9	246	Oak
*	*	*		*	*	*		*	*			5-9	250	Oregon Grapeholly
*	*	*		*		*			*			2-7	252	Peashrub
*	*	*						*	*			5-8	254	Pieris
*		*	*	*	*			*				2-8	256	Pine
*	*	*								*	*	2-8	260	Potentilla
*	*	*					*		*			4-9	264	Redbud
*	*	*						*	*	*		3-8	266	Rhododendron
	*									*	*	5-9	270	Rose-of-Sharon
*		*										2-8	274	Russian Olive
*	*	*	*	*	*		*	*	*	*		3-9	276	Serviceberry
*	*	*					*			*		4-8	278	Smokebush
*	*						*			*		3-9	280	Spirea
*		*		*	*			*				2-9	284	Spruce
*	*	*	*	*	*		*			*		2-9	288	Sumac
*	*				*		*			*		3-9	290	Summersweet Clethra
*		*		*			*					5-9	292	Sweetgum
*		*					*					4-8	294	Thornless Honeylocust
*	*									*		4-9	296	Trumpetcreeper
*	*	*	*				*			*		4-9	298	Tulip Tree
*	*	*		*			*		*			2-8	300	Viburnum
*		*					*					3-9	304	Virginia Creeper
*	*	*							*	*		3-8	306	Weigela
*	*	*		*	*				*	*		4-9	308	Wisteria
*	*	*			*		*	*	*			3-9	310	Witch-hazel
*		*		*				*				4-8	314	Yew
*	*	*			*			*		*		5-9	318	Yucca

Glossary

B & B: abbreviation for balled-and-burlapped stock, i.e., plants that have been dug out of the ground and have had their rootballs wrapped in burlap

Bonsai: the art of training plants into miniature trees and landscapes

Candles: the new, soft spring growth of needle-leaved evergreens such as pine, spruce and fir

Crown: the part of a plant at or just below the soil where the stems meet the roots; also, the top of a tree, including the branches and leaves

Cultivar: a cultivated plant variety with one or more distinct differences from the species; e.g., *Hedera helix* is a botanical species, of which 'Gold Heart' is a cultivar distinguished by leaf variegation

Deadhead: to remove spent flowers in order to maintain a neat appearance, encourage a longer blooming period and prevent the plant from expending energy on fruit production

Dieback: death of a branch from the tip inwards; usually used to describe winter damage

Dormancy: an inactive stage, often coinciding with the onset of winter

Double flower: a flower with an unusually large number of petals, often caused by mutation of the stamens into petals

Dripline: the area around the bottom of a tree, directly under the tips of the farthest-extending branches

Dwarf: a plant that is small compared to the normal growth of the species; dwarf growth is often cultivated by plant breeders

Espalier: the training of a tree or shrub to grow in two dimensions

Gall: an abnormal outgrowth or swelling produced as a reaction to sucking insects, other pests or diseases

Genus: a category of biological classification between the species and family levels; the first word in a Latin name indicates the genus, e.g., *Pinus* in *Pinus mugo*

Girdling: a restricted flow of water and nutrients in a plant caused by something tied tightly around a trunk or branch, or by an encircling cut

Grafting: a type of propagation in which a stem or bud of one plant is joined onto the rootstock of another plant of a closely related species

Heartwood: the wood in the centre of a stem or branch consisting of old, dense, non-functional conducting tissue

Hybrid: a plant resulting from natural or human-induced cross-breeding between varieties, species, or genera; often sterile, but may be more vigorous than either parent and have attributes of both

Inflorescence: a flower cluster

Leader: the dominant upward growth at the top of a tree; may be erect or drooping

Nodes: the places on the stem from where leaves grow; when cuttings are planted, new roots grow from the nodes under the soil

pH: a measure of acidity or alkalinity (the lower the pH, the higher the acidity); the pH of soil influences availability of nutrients for plants

Pollarding: a severe form of pruning in which all the younger branches of a tree are cut back virtually to the trunk to encourage bushy new growth

Procumbent, prostrate: terms used to describe plants that grow along the ground

Rootball: the root mass and surrounding soil of a container-grown or dug-out plant

Rhizome: a modified stem that grows underground, horizontally

Single flower: a flower with a single ring of typically four or five petals

Species: simply defined as a group of organisms that can interbreed to yield fertile offspring; the fundamental unit of biological classification

Standard: a shrub or small tree grown with an erect main stem; accomplished either through pruning and training or by grafting the plant onto a tall, straight stock

Subspecies (subsp.): a naturally occurring, regional form of a species, often geographically isolated from other subspecies but still potentially interfertile with them

Sucker: a shoot that comes up from a root, often some distance from the plant; it can be separated to form a new plant once it develops its own roots

Topiary: the training of plants into geometric, animal or other unique shapes

Variegated: describes foliage that has more than one colour, often patched or striped or bearing differently coloured leaf margins

Variety (var.): a naturally occurring variant of a species; below the level of subspecies in biological classification

Euonymus is an example of a plant with variegated foliage.

Further Reading

Beck, Alison and Kathy Renwald. 2001. *Annuals for Ontario.* Lone Pine Publishing, Edmonton, Alberta.

Beck, Alison and Kathy Renwald. 2001. *Perennials for Ontario.* Lone Pine Publishing, Edmonton, Alberta.

Cavendish Gardens. 1999. *Handbook of Pruning and Training.* Cavendish Books, Vancouver, British Columbia.

Dirr, Michael A. 1997. *Dirr's Hardy Trees and Shrubs: An Illustrated Encyclopedia.* Timber Press, Portland, Oregon.

Editors of Sunset Books and Sunset Magazine. 1997. *Sunset National Garden Book.* Sunset Books Inc., Menlo Park, California.

Ellis, B. W. and F. M. Bradley, eds. 1996. *The Organic Gardener's Handbook of Natural Insect and Disease Control.* Rodale Press, Emmaus, Pennsylvania.

Thompson, P. 1992. *Creative Propagation: A Grower's Guide.* Timber Press, Portland, Oregon.

Index

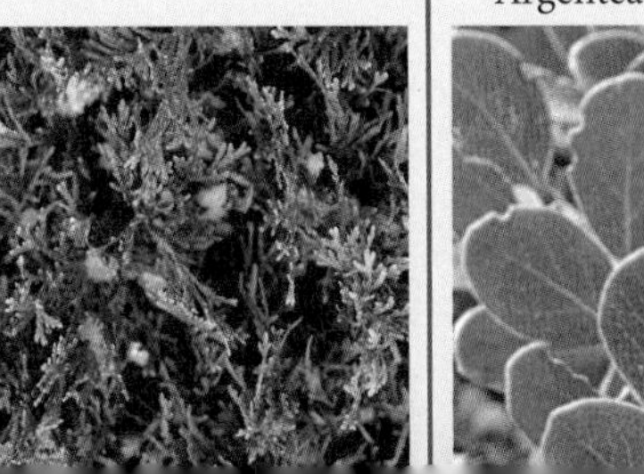

G

H

I

J

Q

R

S